URBAN EDUCATION

WORLD YEARBOOK OF EDUCATION 1992

URBAN EDUCATION

Edited by

DAVID COULBY, CRISPIN JONES and DUNCAN HARRIS

LONDON AND NEW YORK

First published in 1992 by Kogan Page

This edition first published in 2006 by
Routledge
2 Park Square, Milton Park, Abingdon, Oxon, OX14 4RN
711 Third Avenue, New York, NY 10017

Routledge is an imprint of the Taylor & Francis Group, an informa business

First issued in paperback 2012

© 1992 Kogan Page and Named Contributors

All rights reserved. No part of this book may be reprinted or reproduced or utilized in any form or by any electronic, mechanical, or other means, now known or hereafter invented, including photocopying and recording, or in any information storage or retrieval system, without permission in writing from the publishers.

The publishers have made every effort to contact authors and copyright holders of the works reprinted in the *World Yearbook of Education* series. This has not been possible in every case, however, and we would welcome correspondence from those individuals or organisations we have been unable to trace.

These reprints are taken from original copies of each book. In many cases the condition of these originals is not perfect. The publisher has gone to great lengths to ensure the quality of these reprints, but wishes to point out that certain characteristics of the original copies will, of necessity, be apparent in reprints thereof.

British Library Cataloguing in Publication Data
A CIP catalogue record for this book
is available from the British Library

Urban Education

ISBN13: 978-0-415-39307-2 (volume) (hbk)
ISBN13: 978-0-415-50169-9 (volume) (pbk)
ISBN13: 978-0-415-38605-0 (set)

World Yearbook of Education

WORLD YEARBOOK OF EDUCATION 1992

URBAN EDUCATION

Edited by David Coulby, Crispin Jones and Duncan Harris (Series Editor)

First published in 1992 by Kogan Page

Apart from any fair dealing for the purposes of research or private study, or criticism or review, as permitted under the Copyright, Designs and Patents Act, 1988, this publication may only be reproduced, stored or transmitted, in any form or by any means, with the prior permission in writing of the publishers, or in the case of reprographic reproduction in accordance with the terms of licences issued by the Copyright Licensing Agency. Enquiries concerning reproduction outside those terms should be sent to the publishers at the undermentioned address:

© 1992 Kogan Page Limited and contributors

British Library Cataloguing in Publication Data

A CIP record for this book is available from the British Library.

ISBN 0 7494 0479 5

Typeset by DP Photosetting, Aylesbury, Bucks
Printed and bound in Great Britain by
Clays Ltd, St Ives plc

Contents

List of contributors

Asahiro Arai, Nippon Association for Education 2001, Tokyo, Japan *Chapter 18*
Leslie Bash, Anglia Polytechnic, UK *Chapter 2*
Miranda Bell, Polytechnic of North London, UK *Chapter 17*
Cheng Tiying, Beijing University,China *Chapter 11*
David Coulby, Bath College of Higher Education, UK *Chapters 1 & 20*
Dong Jianhong, Chinese National Commission for Unesco *Chapter 11*
Crispin Jones, University of London Institute of Education, UK *Chapters 2, 12 & 19*
Hiroshi Kimura, The National Institute for Educational Research, Tokyo, Japan *Chapter 18*
Mikhail L Levitski, Moscow Pedagogical University, USSR *Chapter 10*
Kevin M Lillis, ODA, London, UK *Chapters 6 & 14*
Tapas Majumdar, Jawaharal Nehru University, New Delhi, India *Chapter 5*
Meng Qingfen, National Centre for Education Development Research, China *Chapter 3*
Kevin J Moran, University of Pittsburgh, PA, USA *Chapter 15*
Nikolai D Nikandrov, Academy of Pedagogical Sciences, Moscow, USSR *Chapter 10*
Ton Peters, Rotterdam City Council, The Netherlands *Chapter 16*
Haruo Sato, Takushoku University, Japan *Chapter 18*
Richard Teese, University of Melbourne, Australia *Chapter 13*
Elwyn Thomas, University of London Institute of Education, UK *Chapter 8*
William B Thomas, University of Pittsburgh, PA, USA *Chapter 15*
Theo Veld, Erasmus University, Rotterdam, The Netherlands *Chapter 7*
Geoff Whitty, Goldsmiths College, University of London, UK *Chapter 4*
Roger R Woock, University of Melbourne, Australia *Chapter 9*
Zhang Li, State Education Commission, Beijing, China *Chapter 3*

Preface

This volume is divided into four parts. In the first part, an attempt is made to locate and contextualize the issues that surround the terms 'urban education' or 'education in cities'. This section is concerned with the major theoretical approaches which have, in the past, been applied to urban education. These approaches are exemplified in various ways in the chapters in Parts 2 and 3. However, this volume does not attempt to establish one particular approach to urban education. Whilst the editors' own views on method are made clear in the first chapter, as is stressed there, a wide variety of approaches can only benefit this field of study. Whilst common issues unite the chapters in this volume there has been no attempt to establish methodological conformity.

In the second part, urban educational issues are explored in a variety of national contexts, revealing the great variety of educational issues and responses that can be found world-wide. The third part concentrates on specific urban areas. In both these sections of the book, the editors have endeavoured to cover a wide range of urban educational systems, in all cases using authors who either work in or who have worked in the systems described. Moreover, the editors have also attempted to achieve some overlap so that a system is studied in Part 2 and a city from that state in Part 3. Thus there are chapters on China and Beijing, on England and Wales and London, on Kenya and Nairobi, on the Netherlands and Rotterdam, on the United States and Pittsburgh. Singapore is an interesting case, being effectively both a city and a state. Where there is no overlap between cities and states, the chapters provide analysis of important examples: India, the USSR, Melbourne, Soweto and Tokyo. Limitations of space and the vagaries of authorial completion mean that, to our regret, Latin America is not represented in these two parts.

The final part contains more general pieces, attempting to synthesize some of the critical issues raised in previous parts and to carry forward the themes and modes of analysis of urban education. It is, then, a development from the previous approaches outlined in Part 1.

What we hope becomes clear in a reading of this book is the immense variety of issues that face schools and other educational institutions in urban areas around the globe. The priorities given to issues and the policies adopted reveal an equally wide variety.

Some issues do seem general, however. The first is that most urban educational systems have serious problems in adequately resourcing their activities. The second is that issues of equity remain intractable in all the states analysed here. Social class and status issues are tackled in most systems as are issues to do with the education of children with disabilities, and issues of race/ ethnicity and gender. Nevertheless, as the chapters make clear, this is a policy area where progress remains less than adequate. Thirdly, and more optimistically, the case studies in this book demonstrate that urban education is a forcing-house for much that is valuable and innovative in education generally, making it an important area for educational policy studies.

The editors would like to thank Jo Edwardes for all the help that she gave in keeping the complex administration of this volume working efficiently. We wish to thank Duncan Harris, the Series Editor, for his help, guidance and support. We would also like to thank the other members of the Urban Education Research Group (UERG), Les Bash, Bob Cowen and Jagdish Gundara for all their help in the making of this book, not least in helping to establish such excellent contacts and contributors in institutions outside the UK. A fourth member of the group who gave us assistance, Keith Kimberley, sadly died as the book was being written and will be sorely missed. A book such as this inevitably places demands on time; we, finally, wish to express our thanks to both of our families for their tolerance and understanding during the period of the editing of this volume.

This volume was the brainchild of Professor John Raynor, one of the founder members of UERG. A pioneer of the study of urban education in Britain, he died unexpectedly as this work was in its early stages. The editors wish to dedicate this volume to his memory, with affection and gratitude.

David Coulby and Crispin Jones
Editors

Part 1: Urban educational issues: international perspectives

1. Theoretical approaches to urban education: an international perspective

David Coulby and Crispin Jones

Introduction

In order to facilitate a better understanding of the issues raised by education in urban areas, this chapter evaluates the major intellectual and conceptual traditions used within this field of enquiry. It considers some of the approaches familiar from the urban education literature, examines some limitations of much that has been written within these approaches, and finally provides some indications of what a revitalized comparative perspective on urban education might offer.

Although there is a wide variety of approaches to the study of urbanization, urbanism and urban life, few of these have education as a specific focus. (Some books that have attempted this task include Bash, 1987; Bash, *et al.*, 1985; Grace, 1984; Miller and Woock, 1970.) Urban politics, finance, housing, industrialization, and de-industrialization, urban social movements, urban/regional relationships, demographic patterns – these are the more familiar themes of this literature (as reviewed in *The International Journal of Urban and Regional Research*, first published in 1977). The study of urban education, however, seldom seems to be aware of this broader urban literature. Where use has been made of such a literature and its sustaining conceptual frameworks, this has commonly been to the early American writings of the Chicago School rather than through the more advanced critiques developed in Europe and North America, much of it following the work of Castells (1977; 1978; 1983) and Harvey (1973). Urban education as a field of study, then, where it has been more than the merely narrative or descriptive, has primarily rested on historical or outdated sociological foundations. These two approaches are considered in turn below and a third section briefly outlines and rejects a traditional comparative approach. This threefold categorization is a matter of convenience and does not imply distinct theoretical areas; indeed the more that historical, sociological and comparative approaches are able to cross-reference and synthesize with one another, the stronger they are likely to be.

A final and, in the context of a *World Yearbook of Education*, important point, is the languages used in the discourses from which the argument of this chapter is derived. For, just as much of the literature referred to relates to urban areas in the mature capitalist states of North America or Europe, much of the literature referred to is in English, although in origination another language may have been used.

Urban education as a field of study first became a significant educational discourse in the USA in the late 1950s. At that stage it was little more than a euphemism for the education of black pupils. Since then the term has gone through several transformations. At present there is a danger that a study is categorized as urban education purely on the grounds that the person who wrote it considers him/herself to be an urban educationist. This chapter makes the apparently uncontentious assumption that urban education is concerned with education in cities. However, it is worth questioning this apparently obvious assumption, in that some approaches to urban education might confuse it with education *per se*, or with education in all regions whether urban, suburban or rural.

In looking at more general urban social theory Saunders (1981) has suggested that 'urban' is used as an adjective not to indicate the geographical location under consideration but to suggest that the work in question fits into some particular theoretical or research orientation.

It is difficult to see how either urban managers or the provision of collective consumption can be separated from the question of space. Both the people and the provision are spatially located. Certainly there are managers and provisions of collective consumption in rural areas too, but their workings are not as visible nor as open to contest and conflict as those in urban areas. This is to say that the difference is one of concentration rather than of kind. But the difference is highly marked, nevertheless, in social and political terms as well as in the fabric of the visible environment.

In a similar sense, urban schools have many common features with schools in other areas but the differences between them can also be qualitatively marked. The levels of linguistic and cultural diversity, the visibility of extreme poverty, the conflicts evident in daily transactions, all make urban educational institutions significantly different from most of those elsewhere. Thus, urban education has, as its subject matter, the workings of educational institutions in cities and the way in which these relate to the wider political areas. This may mean that certain theoretical approaches are preferable, for instance those that give accounts of conflict and those concerned with inequalities between groups. But these approaches, as far as urban education is concerned, cannot be removed from the subject of cities and the educational institutions which operate within them. As a consequence, space should not then be removed from the terms of the approaches to urban education.

Informing this discussion of approaches to urban education are at least three presuppositions. These presuppositions are different in kind but each concentrates on what may be expected of urban educational theory. The first presupposition is that cities are sites of social conflict and inequality which educational institutions play a sometimes crucial role in ameliorating, exacerbating or reproducing. The second presupposition is that analyses centred in one country or culture are of diminishing power as the new international division of labour increasingly leads to both greater inter-urban economic dependence and greater cultural diversification of the populations of the large cities. The third presupposition is that there is an iterative relationship between urban educational theory and urban educational practice. These three rather normative sounding presuppositions are themselves examined and refined in the course of the chapter before the final section attempts to move beyond previous approaches to urban education by consolidating these interrogatory presuppositions into an international approach.

Historical approaches

In the UK and even more in the USA, much of the work done by urban educationists is historical in its orientation. Published works range from broad canvases to much more tightly constrained studies of a particular area or a particular school board/local education authority or school. Interesting and informative accounts can be found of a single school in Sheffield or of school policies in Detroit between 1836 and 1842. Given the amount of data now available from schools, school boards and local education authorities, there appears to be no reason why such studies should not proliferate almost endlessly.

It is possible, however, that some of the resulting studies may seem remote from the exigencies of those working in urban educational institutions. For example, issues confronting urban educational systems in the early 1990s continue to generate intense conflict at both institutional and system level. Many of these conflicts centre on how to deal with inequalities and prejudice against a background of shrinking financial resources. The belief in urban educational institutions as critical vehicles towards the establishment of greater social equality continues to motivate debate and struggle in cities across the world. Against this background, an exclusively historical approach to urban education may be perceived as a retreat from politics, indeed from policy. More, such historical approaches may be seen to permit urban educationists the luxury of distancing themselves from the struggles of the present. There would then be a risk that they would be seen as having nothing to contribute to the current concerns of policy makers and practitioners.

This is not to assert that history has no relevance to the present nor that it is not an important aspect of urban educational studies. It is to contest a too-rigid restriction on what is conceived to be history in relation to urban education. As a discipline, history itself can hardly be said to be tightly constrained; it certainly does not exclude economic, political or social forces; its terms of reference are rarely limited to events in one locality or state. But, for urban educationists adopting an historical approach, these wider issues can all too often be overlooked in the fascination of researching specific topics in specific areas at a specific time.

Of course, urban education cannot be ahistorical but neither can it be exclusively historical. This is a particularly important insistence where the historical approach itself may be narrowly conceived in terms of data collection and description without significant social, political and economic contextualization. In order to have relevance to the intensity of current debates and in order to do full justice to history itself, urban educationists need to adopt approaches which take account of the full context within which urban educational institutions operate.

It is equally difficult to point to instances where specific policy decisions have been made in the light of historical analysis. Perhaps historical approaches cannot aspire to this kind of direct 'relevance'. On the other hand some historical studies have been particularly forceful in framing the wider debate. Grace's work (1978) on social control in the UK is a good example here. It is unlikely that this work has led to the re-organization of pastoral care in many urban schools but it is certain that it has helped many teachers who work in such schools to reflect critically on the wider implications of their role. Such inspiration of critical reflection is a task not without relevance, though its influence on policy decisions may necessarily be difficult to substantiate.

Historical approaches to urban education have been increasingly common in the USA; at their best, the commentaries have played a significant part in contemporary debates and conflicts over urban educational issues. These historical studies have been able to absorb important sociological categories such as social and racial stratification and the role of the state at national, regional and local levels.

However, if an historical approach is to be adopted, it needs to be one which can reveal discontinuity as much as continuity. There have been dramatic changes in the educational history of cities in many states. These cannot be ignored in the stress on continuity in structures and conflicts. Indeed there is a danger of projecting analyses onto the past in order to explain the present. In other words, to stress continuity may lead to the overlooking of important discontinuities.

Historical approaches, it must be reiterated, do have the potential to provide a valuable component towards the understanding of urban education. However, they can lead to analysis and description which is precariously separated from practice. Furthermore, there may be other more critical approaches to the undrstanding of the mutual impact of, on the one hand, social economic and political forces and, on the other, urban educational systems. Of these other approaches, perhaps the most significant is the sociological approach, the concern of the next section.

Sociological approaches

Sociological enquiry with a specifically urban focus has had at least two important manifestations, the first the Chicago School, the second the European writings of the 1970s and 1980s which may best be represented by the earlier work of Castells. In neither instance is education an important research focus. The Chicago School concentrated on demographic movement, social differences and subcultures; the European urban sociologists on the economic and political structures within which capitalist cities operated. As a consquence, in looking to these theoretical areas for an approach to urban education, it is necessary to apply theories to issues which were rarely addressed by their originators.

This, of course, is not to say that sociology has not addressed the issue of schooling in cities. There is a strong literature on this, not least in the UK. However, these studies rarely give more than cursory attention to the concept of the urban context within which the schools are located. In looking for overarching social theories of urban education, then, the two movements suggested earlier are probably the most likely to be helpful.

Park and his colleagues of the Chicago School developed a theory of the social organization and growth of cities based on an analogy with ecological balance (Park, 1952; Park *et al.*, 1925). Burgess, for instance, (in Park *et al.*, 1925) developed a dynamic model of urban growth in terms of population extension, invasion and succession. Cities were seen to have different 'natural' areas within them, where certain types of human activity and social life could thrive. These areas could be transformed as the city, like an organism, grew outwards. The ecological framework prompted an interest in how these 'natural' areas retained or lost their stability and balance. This led to a focus on the norms and institutional arrangements whereby urban social order could be maintained.

Although this theoretical position has not been overtly espoused by educationists or education policy makers, similar types of thinking may be seen to lie behind some initiatives in urban education. Policies such as some compensatory education programmes or the creation of educational priority areas have been based on similar notions that specific areas of the city suffer from social, if not moral decline. Indeed the whole enterprise of urban education, to the extent that it signifies special policies for particular geographical regions, may be seen to be an extension of the ecological approach. It must be insisted, however, that the links between social class, life style and spatial location cannot be assumed to be 'natural' and self-determining. Rather, they are part of larger social processes and need to be studied alongside them. The human ecology approach ignores the importance of elements such as political and economic power in the shaping of urban social and spatial stratification. Indeed this approach may conceal the important economic underpinnings which determine city life. In the UK at least, the concept of isolated areas of cities being subjected, as if by nature, to cultural or educational deprivation, has not proved to be a firm foundation on which to build policy as was demonstrated by the experience of evaluating the Educational Priority Area policy in the years following 1968 (Halsey, 1972).

In a conscious rejection of this part of the work of the Chicago School, Castells uses the concept of contradiction to apply to urban conflicts between the bourgeoisie and the proletariat, or between different factions within each class. He stresses that urban contradictions are a spatial intensification of the consequences of a socio-political structure linked to a capitalist mode of production. For Castells, therefore, the process which underlies the shaping of cities is the reproduction of labour power – the maintenance of a large, mobile, skilled workforce. It is from this position that Castells condemns ecological approaches which reduce social and economic injustice to a limited and natural urban difficulty.

Although Castells makes few specific links to education, his acknowledged debt to Althusser in his earlier work is clear. However, in his more recent work on urban development, Castells is taking a more pragmatic position in relation to the harsh structuralism of Althusser, although he continues to maintain that education has little impact on urban processes (Castells, 1985a; 1985b). His work continues to have value for an understanding of urban education as it provides a vital context in which to understand key educational conflicts about social control or about which groups should determine the nature of school knowledge, particularly within urban environments increasingly structured by new information technologies.

However, if much of the work of the Chicago School and the more recent post-Marxist writers on urbanization and urbanism seems to ignore or dismiss urban education, many of the sociological writers on urban education seem to have ignored the urban element of their concern, save in a somewhat unproblematic manner. Despite the range and power of much of the writing in this tradition, from both North America and Europe, sociological commentary which places urban education firmly within an explanatory rather than a descriptive urban context is still in its infancy. Urban social theorists, nevertheless, offer a potentially dynamic approach to urban education both in terms of their analysis of urban conflicts and in their insistence on the close mutual link between theory and practice.

Comparative approaches

The potential to examine issues, patterns and policies within the setting of different cities in different nation states might make a comparative approach an attractive one for urban educationists (indeed *The World Yearbook of Education* for 1970 (Lauwerys and Scanlon, 1970) was a comparative examination of education in cities). Urbanization is now an international phenomenon and comparative educationists may respond to this phenomenon in at least two ways. The first, traditional method, would be to discuss similar issues or policies in two or more cities. Such comparisons are not without value provided they are focused on contents and policies and not on the technique of the comparison itself. Without such a focus, comparative approaches can be solipsistically obsessed with method or can degenerate into the increasingly esoteric. Cities and policies may be compared without any criterion of selection beyond the satisfaction of academic research. To adopt an approach which insists that New York be compared detail by detail with Cairo or which considers 'black swan' references to Leningrad or Tokyo as sufficient refutation of any theoretical position is to miss the point. In economic, political, social, cultural and demographic terms, the boundaries of the modern state are permeable. Urban educational analysis needs to be able to consider units both larger and smaller than the state. International political and economic groupings must be considered as well as social and economic contrasts within nation states.

A second approach, which could be termed 'international' to distinguish it from certain traditional forms of comparative educational investigation, might consider the international relations of urban education. Such an approach would not be concerned with the activity of comparison *per se*; it would draw on information from various cities and nation states in order to reveal the international forces which are operant in urban educational systems. As a starting point such an approach might consider the importance of various kinds of international movement: the movement of people, capital, produce, knowledge and culture.

Urban education: towards an international approach

It is important to stress three major limitations of the approaches mentioned so far. First, the writing and research on urban phenomena rarely address education, and writing and research on schooling in urban areas seldom address the urban problematic within which urban education takes place. This limitation has been discussed in the section on sociological approaches above. The second limitation is the Western orientation of much of the work so far reviewed. The third is the lack of advanced comparative analysis, noticeably in the fact that most studies are nation – if not city – specific.

However, it is not the intention of this chapter to indulge in pleas for methodological restrictions. On the contrary, the more approaches which are developed for analysing urban education, the more complete is our understanding likely to be. It has, however, been stressed that whatever approach is adopted, the wider economic, political and social forces which are operant in cities should not be ignored in discussions of urban education. As an alternative to methodological monism, it would be easy in this section to produce an educational research shopping list, everything that the authors consider needs to be found out about global urban education. There are certainly many issues in urban education that could be illuminated by international research. Studies of urban curricula and pedagogy and their relationship to state control and/or the needs of the developing patterns of international labour distribution might well be high on the list. The connections between urban social theory and urban education suggested in the section on sociological approaches above are also major outstanding tasks which require elaboration.

It is suggested here that these connections need to be traced not only within the framework of the unitary state but also in terms of international analysis. This analysis would centre on the ways in which the international movement of people, knowledge and capital articulates with expanding global urbanization and the part which urban educational institutions play in this process.

A starting point could be a recognition of the centrality of these international dynamics which act on urban education. The international approach would not be concerned with the activity of comparison for its own sake. It would draw on information from various cities and states in order to reveal the international forces which are operant in urban educational systems.

The twentieth century has seen unprecedented urbanization, the result of widespread intranational and international demographic movement. People have moved to cities such as New York, London and Paris from all over the world. One significant educational consequence of this movement of people is that some of the cities of Western Europe, North America and Australia have become linguistically, racially, religiously and culturally diverse, with the educational systems of those cities often being unwilling or incapable of adjusting to changed and still changing circumstances. In many other areas of the world, urbanization is still mainly intranational, heavily biased to the primate cities of particular nation states. But these cities too are increasingly affected by patterns of international movement. The effect of the demand for labour power generated by the South African economy, for example, is having a profound effect on the demographic pattern of the whole subcontinent. The Gulf oil states are providing a similar attraction within and beyond their region. Those nation states with mainly intranational migration are providing the examples of the most rapid growth; cities such as Jakarta, Cairo, Sao Paulo and Mexico City are likely to have populations in excess of 20 million by the end of the century and still be expanding rapidly. They will reach population sizes unprecedented in urban history. It is possible that a new form of social organization is about to come into existence, as different from the familiar Western megalopolis as that was from the nineteenth century industrial city.

On the surface there would appear to be considerable differences in the educational issues facing these different urban areas. In North American, Western European and Australian urban areas, it could be claimed, the issues are mainly concerned with the content and organization of education, whereas in many third world urban areas, issues relating to adequate resourcing might well be regarded as dominant. From the international perspective it is clear that this simple division is untenable. If there is a contrast it is more likely to be between the education provided for the children of the urban élites and that provided for the children of the urban masses. The issue of adequate resourcing continually bedevils those who plan the education of the urban masses, seldom those who plan the education of the urban élite. To this should be added the regional element, in terms of the differences to be found between urban and rural education both intranationally and internationally.

The urban-focused movement of people has clear implications for urban education, indeed this was a theme of earlier comparative approaches mentioned above. Less obvious, but interlinked and as important, is the relationship between movements of capital and knowledge to the development of urban education systems. The relations between states and between cities still seem to be dominated by the buying, selling and, too often, use, of military technology. This trade is part of a more general pattern of movements of capital and profits, especially between the metropolitan and peripheral states. International financial transactions and the operations of transnational corporations have developed a complex pattern of unequal interrelations which has important implications for urban education. A new international division of labour seems to be emerging where the subordinate classes are principally but not exclusively located in the peripheral states and the dominant classes are principally but not exclusively located in the metropolitan states. The rapid growth of urban areas throughout the world is associated with this growing global interdependence. The role of urban educational institutions in explaining and reproducing this pattern can best be understood in such international terms. As a starting point much could be learned from the way in which this pattern is explained, disguised or ignored within urban curricula at all levels in various regions.

An international approach to urban education could then be developed within a framework of the international movements and counter-movements of people, capital, produce, knowledge and culture. Such an approach would have at least three advantages. First, it would take account of wide social, political and economic forces within the contexts where they are increasingly tending to operate, those of international relations. Second, given the continuing rapid urbanization of the third world, such an international approach could escape the trap of Western bias. Third, the emergence of massive new urban areas in many third world states may well provide a crucial and challenging field of study, both as forms of social organization with their associated education provision, and in terms of their participation in those international educational exchanges outlined above. Thus, in view of the role of educational institutions in generating and transmitting knowledge, of the importance of educational and cultural legitimation for the existing political and economic order, and of the importance of technical knowledge to the process of industrialization, urban education is itself actually a crucial element in understanding the emerging pattern of international relations.

Acknowledgement

This chapter is based on a paper given to the British Comparative and International Education conference in London in 1988. Its subsequent development owes much to the helpful comments of members of the Urban Education Research Group.

References

Bash, L (ed) (1987) *Comparative Urban Education: Towards an Agenda*, London: DICE/UERG.
Bash, L *et al.* (1985) *Urban Schooling: Theory and Practice*, London: Holt, Rinehart and Winston.
Castells, M (1977) *The Urban Question*, London: Arnold.
Castells, M (1978) *Cities, Class and Power*, London: Macmillan.
Castells, M (1983) *The City and the Grassroots*, London: Arnold.
Castells, M (1985a) *High Technology, Space and Society*, Beverley Hills: Sage.
Castells, M (1985b) 'High technology, economic restructuring, and the urban-regional process in the United states', in Castells, 1985a.
Grace, G (1978) *Teachers, Ideology and Control*, London: RKP.
Grace, G (ed) (1984) *Education and the City*, London: RKP.
Halsey, A (1972) *Educational Priority, Volume 1*, London: HMSO.
Harvey, D (1973) *Social Justice and the City*, London: Arnold.
International Journal of Urban and Regional Research (1977 to date), London, Arnold.
Lauwerys, J A and Scanlon, D G (eds) (1970) *The World Year Book of Education 1970: Education in Cities*, London: Evans.
Miller, H and Woock, R (1970) *Social Foundations of Education*, Hirsdale: Dryden Press.
Park, R *et al.* (eds) (1925) *The City*, Chicago: University of Chicago Press.
Park, R (1952) *Human Communities: The City and Human Ecology*, New York: Free Press.
Saunders, P (1981) *Social Theory and the Urban Question*, London: Hutchinson.
Sharp, R and Green, A (1975) *Education and Social Control*, London: RKP.
Willis, P (1977) *Learning to Labour*, London: Saxon House.

2. Urban social theory and education

Leslie Bash

Introduction

This chapter is predicated upon the assumption that the task of theorizing about education in cities is contingent upon a satisfactory understanding of urban processes. Although this has conventionally not been the case, in recent years there have been attempts to correct this omission. In the context of urban education in the United Kingdom, the approaches adopted by social scientists in their analysis of urban life have been given serious consideration (see Bash *et al.*, 1985) while, in comparative perspective, Jones (1987) has sought 'to demonstrate the importance of urban studies for an understanding of urban education systems' (p. 1).

In so doing, these attempts to demonstrate the relevance of urban analysis in general for urban education in particular bring into focus the very nature of what may be termed urban social theory and the legitimacy of attempting to theorize about cities in the first place. For a good deal of European history, all social, political, and economic life tended to be defined in terms of the city; what lay outside was foreign, alien. But when city states gave way to nation states, urban–rural differences became apparent, even if they were not the subject of social analysis. The development of Western European social science, however, brought the city into the realm of intellectual debate, in turn privileging the development of urban social theory.

This chapter considers the current state of urban social theory in the light of past and recent debates and suggests how this may be linked to an understanding of educational processes in cities across the world. An overview of urban social theory suggests the pre-eminence of its eclectic character. There should be few apologies for this state of affairs: the 'urban' does not merely constitute a problematic concept; it necessarily invokes diverse academic disciplines. Geographers, historians, sociologists, economists and political scientists have all laid claim to the city as a subject for analysis, with implications for students of urban environments and urban policy makers. Some theorists, mainly geographers and sociologists, have attempted to provide a single explanatory framework for urban phenomena, frequently condemning alternatives as either inadequate or ideological. These attempts to establish some kind of theoretical hegemony, like many such attempts, are met with counter-factual arguments and some degree of academic hostility.

Cities and spatiality

There has apparently been little agreement regarding the role of spatiality in urban theory. Non-specialists might be forgiven for accepting that geographical space would unquestioningly play a fundamental role in urban social science. Since the spatial dimension is omitted from much of the classical social science of the nineteenth century save, for example, Engels (1969) in his descriptions of working-class life, and from a good deal of twentieth century sociology, this assumption might well be challenged. Following this, it would be helpful to explore some current views on spatiality, and its place in urban theory, before embarking upon an examination of the merits of urban theory as such.

Giddens insists that the analysis of social relations must proceed within a framework permeated by a space–time dimension. This can only be revealed through a dynamic view of social life where activities and events in institutional structures are built into space–time pictures. Linked with an ongoing structure of relationships is any number of other relationships situated spatially (and temporally). The process of regionalization of social life (as in the organization of a house into different rooms) and the establishment of 'back regions' where it is possible to escape (as inthe journey from classroom to staffroom), highlight time and space not as 'mere environments of action' but as a crucial dimension of social relations (Giddens, 1985, p. 265). Indeed, Giddens recognizes, in particular, the relevance of his thesis for the theorization of education in cities, given the emphasis placed upon space–time and the exercise of control. Here, the relative autonomy of schools is seen as a consequence of their 'enclosed nature' (Giddens, 1985, p. 289) and their insulation from those who would seek to control them from the outside (local authorities, central governments, parents) has prompted state action in some countries (such as Britain) to undermine that autonomy. This suggests that space (and time) are fundamental to social reality, especially in the contexts of power relationships. Urban theory must of necessity focus upon spatiality and Giddens proceeds to expound the view that modern urbanism, through its 'commodified time and space' articulates the very essence of the capitalist socio-economic order (Giddens, 1985, pp. 294–5).

Opposed to Giddens is the seemingly paradoxical thesis that for urban sociology to be meaningful it must be shorn of its commitment to spatiality. This is the view expounded by Saunders who considers that urban social theory, as applied to the contemporary industrialized world, is ultimately concerned with issues related to the social organization of consumption and that to dwell upon space merely obfuscates the analysis of such issues (Saunders, 1981; 1985). Consequently,

> the crucial theoretical concerns of recent urban sociology should be freed from the anachronistic, restrictive and ultimately futile preoccupation with spatial forms (1985, p. 86).

It would seem that the role of spatiality in (urban) social theory is now questioned because it exists rather uncomfortably alongside certain paradigmatic assumptions. Saunders' own urban analysis is located in a political sociology of a decidedly Weberian flavour. And yet, the genesis of urban theory lies in the concrete circumstances of urban, industrial society where the practical concerns with space were significant for the lives of its inhabitants. This is of fundamental importance for those who might attempt to investigate the urban theory/urban education nexus on the assumption that the legitimacy of such theory is in its dialectical relationship with the material world.

Agendas and paradigms

The phenomenon of modern urban industrialism was, thus, bound to give rise to recognizable, if contested, urban social theory. Much of this was grounded in classical social science: notably, that rooted in the positivism of social Darwinists and functionalists; the political sociology derived from Weber; and the many variants of Marxism. Parallel to such developments may also be observed the growth of urban empiricism, with its somewhat distinct agenda of social reform, and the growth of urban geography, with an emphasis upon environmental/economic determinism. The former has often utilized evidence from social and economic history as the backcloth to proposed policies of urban social amelioration. On the other hand, the ideological dimensions of the latter, frequently well hidden (as in central place theory and its assumption of rationally based market exchange), have served to render the urban a human, but, nonetheless, 'natural' phenomenon.

The pervasion of urban theory by social Darwinism during the late nineteenth and early twentieth centuries cannot be overstressed. Darwinism was far from being yet another hypothesis to be tested in the course of practice; it was much more a case of a 'scientific revolution' (see Kuhn, 1970) having ramifications well beyond the sphere of biology. It matched the 'evolutionary' approach of the classical sociologists (Comte, and, especially, Spencer) and the outlook of classical economies (especially in its *laissez-faire* guise) on the one hand; while, on the other, Darwinism prompted social reformers to recognize and attempt to deal with the inequitable outcomes of the evolutionary process. Thus, it might be concluded that:

> Although Darwin himself fiercely resisted such thinking, it was clearly tempting to make close analogies between the natural and social world (Dickens, 1990, p. 33).

The Chicago School was indeed quite explicit in its support for a Darwinian view of urban life. The borrowing of Darwin's terminology – competition, succession, adaptation – demonstrates the readiness with which a major Chicago theorist, Park, was able to state that:

> Competition operates in the human (as it does in the plant and animal) community to bring about and restore the communal equilibrium when, either by the advent of some intrusive factor from without or in the normal course of its life history, that equilibrium is disturbed (Park, 1957, p. 47).

While today there would probably be few who would uphold such a naïve view of social life in general or of city life in particular, the work of the Chicago School with its refracted Darwinism still haunts contemporary urban theory, for at the level of empirical enquiry, the concerns of Park, Burgess and their colleagues continue to be the subject of debate.

Elsewhere, cultural criticism (exemplified by the Frankfurt School and post-war neo-Marxists) has additionally provided a context for the debate on urban industrialism. Writers such as Marcuse (1972) and Adorno and Horkheimer (1973) sought to locate the apparent lack of revolutionary zeal among the European working class in the pre- and post-war periods in the capitalization of consciousness, shaped by the industrialization of culture, which has as its correlate what Harvey has termed the 'urbanisation of consciousness' (1989, chapter 8). The image of the city, as portrayed in print and on the screen, has, in becoming part of the social reality it purports to represent, been subjected to varying degrees of analysis, not least by Williams (1973). In consequence, the result of all these diverse contributions to urban discourse has been the generation of a considerable literature and a high degree of contestation. Above all, it has raised questions and exposed doubts about the validity of the 'urban' as a distinct unit of theoretical analysis.

Universalism and particularism in urban theory

At the same time, conventional urban perspectives have been subject to fundamental revision on account of their ethnocentrism. Urban industrialism is redefined as essentially a North American and European phenomenon. Commentators on the social and economic conditions in the less-industrialized societies (Frank, 1969; Lloyd, 1979) have attempted to rewrite the urban agenda to comply with prevailing views on dependency/neo-colonialism, and with the significance of authentic historical movements and events in the less-industrialized societies; hence the application of neo-Marxism in development theory on the one hand, and the recognition of such entities as the 'Islamic city' on the other. Even here, there is an underlying dualism in the process of theorizing about the urban: the 'third world' is understood within the context of Western imperialism, except in the case of, say, Islamic supremacy.

In this context it is appropriate to consider events of the last ten years or so in Eastern Europe and the Middle East, and their possible ramifications for urban theory and for urban education. Here, cities have frequently become metaphors for political movements and have roused much media interest insofar as they have been the sites of intense struggles for power. It could be argued that such struggles are quite separate from conflicts endemic to Western industrial urbanism. Conflict resulting from the drive for capital accumulation is replaced by the fight for political supremacy, or for ethnic domination, or for the hegemony of a religious ideology. Although the new international economic order will increasingly affect the functioning of such cities (with the multinational corporations seeking lower wage costs and fresh markets) the autonomy of much urban life, related as it is to broader cultural concerns, might need to be emphasized. This is, perhaps, more apparent in, for example, those regions characterized by a core Islamic culture than in regions having closer cultural (as well as economic) ties with industrial urban capitalism. Thus, it is possible to argue that in cities such as Bucharest and Teheran there have been struggles to replace one set of dominant symbols with another. The previous regimes of societies which have recently undergone radical change sought to saturate their capital cities with particular symbolic artefacts. Their overthrow, however, placed a heavy responsibility on educational institutions to be instrumental in the establishment of a new hegemony. The outcome in Teheran is fairly clear: Islamic schools function to reproduce the Islamic character of Teheran in an increasingly authentic Islamic Iran. In Bucharest, the schools have apparently had to dismantle the old ideological order and replace it with an order having greater legitimacy in the new Romania.

These general statements concerning urban theory, however, convey little of its significance for education in cities across the world and, consequently, further investigation is necessary. Such an analysis might begin with the juxtaposition of nineteenth century European urban industrialization and the development of the modern social sciences. The impact of positivism through nascent sociology, classical economics, and the theorizing of Darwin occurred at the expense of a deeper, historical understanding of regions and nations outside Western Europe. Imperialism appeared to be legitimated by the social sciences (especially, anthropology) with non-European urban forms attaining significance through their (political/economic) relationships with the colonizing countries. Tönnies' distinction between *gemeinschaft* and *gesellschaft*, with the former characterized by all-embracing social relations and the latter by rational, contractual association, is well known. As applied to the village and the city, respectively, 'gemeinschaft und gesellschaft' conceptualized and helped perpetuate:

> one of the enduring myths of Europeans: the contrast between idyllic rural life and urban corruption and alienation (Bash *et al.*, 1985, p. 25).

Moreover, his emphasis upon an urban/rural dichotomy, his romanticization of social relations in the village community as against the impersonal rationality of the industrial city, mirrored the imperialistic view of European/non-European societies. The social change dynamic in Tönnies' work, while parallelling other approaches (as in Marx and Durkheim) gave pride of place to European industrial urbanism and implicitly relegated other forms of urbanism to pre-history. The journey from Tönnies to the sociologists of the Chicago School in the 1920s is fairly straightforward, although by this time Darwinian ideology had been absorbed into an 'ecological' view of industrial urbanism, a view which also reflected what was later to be designated as structural-functionalism. Here, the city developed organically and differentially, serving the modern capitalist order, though not necessarily without negative implications for certain sectors of its population. The Burgess model, with its concentric zones, signalled a dynamic aspect: migration as a process of ecological invasion and succession. Urban groups, after a period of struggle, would settle in spatially-defined patterns. The presence of poverty, crime and other social ills, though seen as the 'natural' outcome of urban ecological processes may, nonetheless, have to be dealt with through the implementation of ameliorative social policies in order to prevent threats to the social order.

Urban theory and spatial divisions of labour

The Chicago School furnished twentieth century urban analysis with a model of the city which was to be taken for granted for a number of decades. Other theories could be incorporated within the Chicago paradigm, including those from geography, such as Christaller's central place theory (1966), or even the neo-Weberian ideas of Rex and Moore (1967). However, the Chicago paradigm tended to lose ground when faced with competing perspectives based on Marxist theory, and with evidence from regions outside Europe and North America. The early writings of Castells (1977), locking into the dominant brand of mid-1970s French Marxism, provided a *raison d'être* for radical urban social theory, and assumed the possibility of mass urban political action to combat the ills of the capitalist city.

Harvey's work has also reflected a significant move among many geographers towards a more heavily politicized view of human location. The dynamics of the Western industrial city, in this view, reflects the fact that capitalism 'has survived not only through the production of space . . . but also through superior command over space' (Harvey, 1989, p. 58). Harvey has documented his theoretical journey through liberalism to Marxism and his current position, though long-established, bears all the hallmarks of a recent convert. Although committed to 'Marxian meta-theory' in his work as an economic geographer this has not prevented Harvey from employing insights gained elsewhere in his analysis of urbanism. Simmel, Durkheim, Weber, Wirth, and others have made notable, though partial, contributions to an understanding of the twentieth century Western city; even empiricism has yielded data of some significance to neo-Marxist urban enquiry.

Yet these approaches to urban analysis did not always provide convincing explanations for the variability in the experiences of people living in cities in Western indusrialized societies, let alone the third world. Interestingly, Castells has recently been drawn back to one of the major concerns of the Chicago School: the process of urban segregation. The re-emergence of metropolitan regions as 'dual cities' under late twentieth century industrial capitalism reflects a mode of production in which information technology plays an increasingly vital role and

> refers to the process of spatial restructuring through which distinct segments of labor are included in and excluded from the making of new history (Castells, 1989, p. 228).

Moreover, the restructured international economy, with its restructured division of labour, has profound implications for the stability of urban environments as economic units since:

> it creates a variable geometry of production and consumption, labor and capital, management and information – a geometry that denies the specific productive meaning of any place outside its position in a network whose shape changes relentlessly in response to the messages of unseen signals and unknown codes (ibid., p. 348).

Massey (1984) has demonstrated that capital has the important role of ensuring a highly effective spatial division of labour and he goes beyond the neo-Weberian notion that differential location, functioning reproductively, simply reinforces status positions in the social structure. Here, different urban locales provide normative sub-structures for different occupational groups such that they promote the processes of *production* as well as reproduction. In the context of the UK, for example, London's Docklands could be said to provide appropriate normative protection for professionals working in the financial sector of the city centre, while a smaller urban academic environment such as Cambridge may be essential for those working in the area of research and development (Massey, 1984). The residential concentrations in such 'technopolises' tend towards homogeneity in terms of ethnic group (white) and occupational reference group.

The adoption of more structuralist Marxist perspectives in urban theory does not necessarily imply uniform effects as far as international capitalism is concerned. It is apparent, from this broad standpoint, that the role of the global economy and the new international division of labour has had marked – and diverse – effects on the fate of cities in the less-industrialized countries. Thus, in the case of Latin America, while cities such as Sao Paulo and Mexico City have benefited from the receipt of significant production segments in the activities of multinational corporations, others such as Lima have lost out (Wilson, 1987, p. 199). Here, there has been a rise in the production of 'non-traditional exports', with relatively high capital:labour ratios, while manufacture for the domestic market, with low capital:labour ratios, has declined sharply. The point is that Lima has remained marginal to the global economy since it has not been able to participate in the assembly activities of the multinationals. Its exports are little more than processed raw materials and, consequently, must be seen as a contributory factor to declining real income and rising unemployment and underemployment (Wilson, 1987, p. 209).

The historical relationship of Latin America with Western Europe and North America has been characterized by the deep penetration of multinational industry, and the consequent loss of indigenous productive capacity. The resulting development of informal city economies, squatter settlements and structures of social relations based upon conflicts over the provision of basic services have suggested support for Castells' thesis on urban social movements. Yet, in his later writings such movements are judged not to be especially radical in orientation; they are no more than 'symptoms of resistance to the social domination' (Castells, 1983, p. 329) which, although linked with the structure of economic relations, are a reflection of a set of goals defined by actors in an urban setting. Castells, thus, seems to have made the transformation from a theorist attached to a somewhat discredited structuralist Marxism to that of a decidedly more fashionable Weberian.

In his most recent writing, Castells has returned to the theme of the universal impact of capitalism upon cities, but this time in consideration of a new trend: 'the historical emergence of the space of flows, superseding the meaning of the space of places' (1989, p. 348).

This is an important shift of perspective since it allows for the normality of change in what may be termed 'post-industrial society' at the expense of the crude functionalism of place. For people, cities increasingly fail to provide the locus of meaning, since they no longer have an assured place in either the national or international economic structures. Urban movements become ever more reactive to the 'variable geometry' of the world economy and less expressions of social consciousness embedded in the structure of the city. It is not surprising, therefore, to find the emergence of localized urban cultures rooted in traditional, mythologized histories, expressed in ethnic and fundamentalist religious identities and, in the final analysis, powerless against international economic forces. As Castells (1989, p. 350) so aptly states, it is here that the 'globalization of power flows and the tribalization of local communities' become increasingly juxtaposed.

If Castells' current thesis gains currency in the area of urban social theory it offers a way forward for the theorization of urban civil society in general and urban education in particular. Cities must be viewed within the context of their ability to deal with the 'space of flows'; more specifically, of their continuing role in the sphere of social reproduction in an entirely new international framework of production. It is the nature of the links between cities at the level of civil society, rather than at the level of the economy, which now becomes significant. Likewise, the analysis of urban education in comparative perspective takes on a whole new dimension.

Urban theory and education in cities

The nature of the urban experience under Western capitalism, whether described in positivistic or in subjective, existential terms, or represented in art and architecture, can only be fully appreciated against an awareness of the struggle to command space. The latter, in turn, hinges upon an acceptance of a fundemental aspect of Western industrialism: the drive towards capital accumulation. It is only against this background, according to Harvey, that a meaningful discussion of the autonomy of urban processes can take place. Here, Harvey's views make urban education an important element of urban theory. Thus, within the urban region,

> institutions and the people who run them tend to coalesce, sometimes tightly and sometimes loosely but rarely without conflict, into a matrix of interlocking and interdependent social resources offering a specific mix of social possibilities . . . affecting the qualities of labor power in all their aspects (from skills to work attitudes), the condition of the industrial reseve army, and other crucial aspects of labor power supply. But it has equal significance for the reproduction of capital, affecting the production of scientific and technical knowledge and the evolution of managerial know-how and entrepreneurial abilities (Castells, 1989, p. 146).

Yet, urban social theory, however defined, has seldom been viewed as an appropriate basis for educational discourse, even in relation to the structure and processes of urban schools. Indeed, in seeking to throw light upon urban educational issues and to provide a measure of critical insight there has generally been a regression to conventional theoretical models and accepted modes of research, usually derived from the 'sociology of education'. Whatever constitutes the 'urban' has been taken for granted, whether in the context of schooling in Nairobi, Sao Paulo or London. The assumption that education in urban areas is essentially problematic, with an emphasis upon social divisions, poverty, and crime, has mostly clouded the view that the 'urban' itself is problematic. Cross-national analysis has tended to strengthen this view, given the diversity of urban experiences, as well as the complex relationships between cities and the broader national and international socio-economic structures.

However, urban social theory presents an opportunity to reconceptualize education in cities; notwithstanding Saunders' thesis, space becomes a crucial feature of urban educational analysis. Few would challenge the proposition that education incorporates a spatial dimension. For all practical purposes, the idea of peripatetic schools or other educational institutions need not be taken seriously. Insofar as demand for mass education is met in any society it is done in a relatively spatially-fixed manner. As such, it is also met in a highly differentiated way, contingent upon modes of access and the geographical location of residence. While age stratification shapes the pattern of entry to schools, and even though there is significant international recruitment to universities, education is commonly viewed as an item of consumption, provided in the main by the state for population located in particular geographical contexts.

However, while recent neo-Weberian and neo-Marxist writings place an emphasis upon consumption and differential access to education in urban areas, it is also important to note the role of education in the continual production and reproduction of the urban socio-economic order. Here, perspectives deriving from economics point to the supply of labour and the creation of human capital as part of the process of urban industrialization. Capital accumulation, as the driving force of contemporary Western urbanization, is the end product of differentiated and hierarchical urban education systems, together with distinct cultural correlates. Elsewhere, the twin processes of political and ideological domination, eclipsing economic considerations, are the preferred outcome of urban schools. Either way, urban theory must reflect a considerable degree of sophistication in the way in which social and economic processes in cities are conceptualized. So, the question remains as to how far cities throughout the world are structured through the processes of international capitalism. Furthermore, to what extent do cities operate (more or less autonomously) to reproduce the social and technical divisions of labour and to allocate individuals to positions within the socio-economic hierarchy? These questions, central to urban theory, are of fundamental importance to urban education, since they raise further questions concerning not only production but also consumption.

The Weberian tradition, together with the more recent writings of Castells, would tend to grant autonomy to the social relations of consumption, whether in the context of the allocative powers of 'urban managers', the formation of urban status groups (such as housing 'classes'), or the growth of 'urban social movements'. However, the urban is now essentially international: cities constitute, to a greater or lesser extent, actors in the international economic order, or they may become part of a transnational culture in resisting the effects of advanced capitalism. The 'socialist city', governed by strict planning principles, established during the Stalinist era (see Bater, 1980), now appears as a superseded category, but the Islamic city may yet remain as an example of a counter-cultural force, especially in the midst of a process of nation-state restructuring.

'global village' effects, it is possible that Castells' 'informational city' provides a relevant model for contemporary urban social theory, and one which may be helpful to the analyst of contemporary urban education. Here, cities are seen as increasingly socially divided, with the 'ghettoization', not of minority groups, but of the professional-managerial class becoming more entrenched. This class is not seen as part of the social relations of production in any one urban context:

rather it relates directly and indirectly to subordinate classes, and to itself, through exchange networks made possible by the new information technology. As a consequence, it is able to colonize:

> exclusive spatial segments that connect with one another across the city, the country, and the world; they isolate themselves from the fragments of local societies, which in consequence become destructured in the process of selective reorganization of work and residence (Castells, 1989, p. 348).

The contemporary Western city is a microcosm of modern capitalist society, characterized by a high degree of social atomization and monopolistic commercial practices. Where the industrial city, previously, had been the location of interdependent firms providing a web of employment opportunities in the context of national and international competition, the new city harbours tightly controlled, secretive organizations. It does not lock into an integrated productive community, with its corollary of reproduction through consumption; rather, it manifests itself as an agent for production and reproduction in any part of the world it may choose. Cities elsewhere may indeed function in ways which are at variance with the imperatives of the international economy and the new international division of labour with its social and cultural manifestation. If so, the consequences for schools in those cities will be in terms of localism, whether in the context of alternative economic systems or of alternative national, ethnic and religious identities. However, it is probable that the internationalization of socio-economic systems will be increasingly significant over the coming decades for people living and working in cities throughout the world. In large measure, this has already been recognized by those who have sought to revise urban social theory; it is now incumbent on those who intend to examine education in cities to take note of such changes and to incorporate them in their analysis.

Acknowledgments

My thanks to members of the Urban Education Research Group and Paul Machon for their critical comments on this chapter.

References

Adorno, T and Horkheimer, M (1973) *Dialectic of Enlightenment*, London: Allen Lane.
Bash, L *et al.* (1985) *Urban Schooling*, London: Holt.
Bash, L (ed) (1987) *Comparative Urban Education: Towards an Agenda*, London: Institute of Education, University of London.
Bater, J H (1980) *The Soviet City*, London: Edward Arnold.
Castells, M (1977) *The Urban Question*, London: Edward Arnold.
Castells, M (1983) *The City and the Grassroots*, Berkeley: University of California Press.
Castells, M (1989) *The Informational City*, Oxford: Blackwell.
Christaller, W (1966) *Central Places in Southern Germany*, Englewood Cliffs, NJ: Prentice-Hall.
Dickens, P (1990) *Urban Sociology*, London: Harvester Wheatsheaf.
Engels, F (1969) *The Condition of the Working Class in England*, Frogmore: Granada.
Frank, A (1969) *Capitalism and Underdevelopment in Latin America*, New York: Monthly Review Press.
Giddens, A (1985) 'Time, space and regionalisation' in Gregory, D and Urry, J (eds) 1985.
Gregory, D and Urry, J (eds) (1985) *Social Relations and Spatial Structures*, London: Macmillan.
Harvey, D (1985) *The Urbanization of Capital*, Oxford: Blackwell.

Harvey, D (1989) *The Urban Experience*, Oxford: Blackwell.
Jones, C (1987) 'Urban centres, space and education: A comparative perspective' in Bash, L (ed) 1987.
Kuhn, T (1970) *The Structure of Scientific Revolutions*, Chicago: University of Chicago Press.
Lloyd, P (1979) *Slums of Hope?*, Harmondsworth: Penguin.
Marcuse, H (1972) *One Dimensional Man*, London: Abacus.
Massey, D (1984) *Spatial Divisions of Labour*, London: Macmillan.
Park, R E (1957) *Human Communities*, New York: Free Press.
Rex, J and Moore, R (1967) *Race, Community and Conflict*, London: Oxford University Press.
Saunders, P (1981) *Social Theory and the Urban Question*, London: Hutchinson.
Saunders, P (1985) 'Space, the city and urban sociology' in Gregory, D and Urry, J (eds) 1985.
Smith, M P and Feagin, J R (eds) (1987) *The Capitalist City*, Oxford: Blackwell.
Smith, M P and Tardanico, R (1987) 'Urban theory reconsidered: Production, reproduction and collective action' in Smith, M P and Feagin, J R (eds) 1987.
Williams, R (1973) *The Country and the City*, London: Chatto & Windus.
Wilson, P A (1987) 'Lima and the new international division of labour' in Smith, M P and Feagin, J R (eds) 1987.

Part 2: Urban educational issues: national perspectives

3. Urban education in China

Zhang Li and Meng Qingfen
(Translated and revised by Huang Shiqi)

Introduction

Background

Chinese civilization is one of the oldest in the world. There are many famous cities with long recorded histories. However, during the four decades since the founding of the People's Republic of China, new cities and towns have constantly emerged beside the conspicuous expansion of old ones. According to the statistics for 1949, there was an urban population of 57.65 million, accounting for 10.6 per cent of the total population of the country, and there were 168 cities and towns with a population of 50,000 and over. By 1989 there were 450 large, medium-sized and small cities, and the total urban population reached 296.51 million, accounting for 26.2 per cent of the total population of the country (Population Research Centre, 1989).

Cities may be classified by size of total non-agricultural population into the following: unusually large cities with a population of over 1 million; large cities

Table 3.1 *Distribution of city dwellers among large, medium-sized, and small cities of China (1989)*

	Grand total	*Size of cities (inhabitants)*					
		More than 2 million	1–2 million	0.5–1 million	300,000 to 500,000	100,000 to 300,000	Less than 100,000
Number of cities	446*	9	21	28	54	218	116
% of China's city population	100	23.3	18.2	13.1	14.2	25.8	5.3

* not including Beijing, Tianjin and Shanghai.
Source: State Statistical Bureau (1990).

with a population ranging from 0.5 to 1 million; medium-sized cities with a population ranging from 100,000 to 500,000; small cities with a population less than 100,000, with details given in Table 3.1.

Large and medium-sized industrial enterprises in China are mostly located in cities, and the statistics for 1988 indicate that the number of urban industrial enterprises accounts for 42.8 per cent of the national total, and their total output is 71.1 per cent of the national total. In view of the fact that the urban economy is far more developed than the rural economy, being favoured by a higher concentration of professional and technical personnel, a comprehensive network of educational and cultural institutions, and a far higher population density than in rural regions, urban education is on the whole more advanced.

Table 3.2 *The number of urban schools of all types and levels, their total enrolment, and the number of full-time (F-T) teachers (1989)*

		National total (A)	*Urban total (B)*	*B/A in %*
Population (in '000)		1133683	296512	26.2
Kindergartens	No. of kindergartens	172634	31880	18.5
	No. of F-T teachers (in '000)	709.1	227.6	32.1
	Total enrolment (in '000)	18476.6	4530.9	24.5
Primary schools	No. of schools	777244	28671	3.7
	No. of F-T teachers (in '000)	5543.8	679.2	12.3
	Total enrolment (in '000)	123731	13333.6	10.8
General lower secondary schools	No. of schools	73525	6469	8.8
	No. of F-T teachers (in '000)	2426.6	471.2	17.4
	Total enrolment (in '000)	38378.9	6050.4	15.8
General upper secondary schools	No. of schools	16050	5207	32.4
	No. of F-T teachers (in '000)	553.9	189.6	34.2
	Total enrolment (in '000)	7161.2	2170.2	30.3
ASSs and VSSs	No. of schools	9173	2493	27.2
	No. of F-T teachers (in '000)	213.8	79.4	37.1
	Total enrolment (in '000)	2822.7	966.9	34.3
SSSs	No. of schools	3984		
	No. of F-T teachers (in '000)	228.5		
	Total enrolment (in '000)	2177.5		
SWSs	No. of schools	2940		
	No. of F-T teachers (in '000)	170.9		
	Total enrolment (in '000)	1492.9		
IHEs	No. of schools	1075		
	No. of F-T teachers (in '000)	397.4		
	Total enrolment (in '000)	2082.1		

Source: SEDC: *Educational Statistics Yearbook of China (1989).*

Diversity and advantages in China's urban education system

The level of development of education in a particular city is an important indicator of the degree of its modernization. The development of urban education at all levels and of all types has shown a diversified picture adapted to the needs of the country as well as the cities themselves regarding economic and social development (see Table 3.2 for some essential relevant data).

Primary education has been universalized in all the cities, as evidenced by the fact that the net enrolment rate of school-age (6–11) children has reached about 99 per cent. Also 94 per cent of the graduates of urban primary schools meet the requirements for graduation set by the state. During the period 1949–89, the percentage of illiterates and semi-literates among the urban work force has decreased from 60–70 per cent to 8 per cent. The number of drop-outs among the nation's primary school population was about 3.2 per cent during the period 1988–89, most of them rural pupils.

At the secondary level, as a rule, students enrolled in general lower and upper secondary schools receive their schooling in local schools. From the data given in Table 3.2, it can be seen that the share of urban upper secondary school population is higher than that of lower secondary school population among the total school population of the country (29.9 per cent versus 15.2 per cent), while the latter is higher than the share of urban primary school population among the national total (9.9 per cent). This means that lower and upper secondary schooling in the urban setting has an obvious advantage over that in the rural setting. The same can be said of the distribution of full-time teachers. At the secondary level, beside schools offering general education or academic programmes, there are agricultural and vocational schools, skilled workers schools (SWSs), and specialized secondary schools (SSSs) providing vocational and technical education of various descriptions. Agricultural secondary schools (ASSs) mainly cater to the needs of rural students, while urban vocational and secondary schools (VSSs) only admit city dwellers. SWSs and SSSs open their doors to all qualified students, urban and rural alike, through a process of unified entrance examinations, recruiting their students from designated regions (provinces, municipalities, etc.). These schools operate under the supervision of administrative bodies of large, medium-sized, and small cities, as well as county-level governmental bodies. In 1989, the percentage distribution of urban and rural students admitted to regular institutions of higher education (IHEs) stood in the ratio 54:46 (Department of Students, 1990).

IHEs are concentrated in cities, partly the result of the inadequate financial strength of the state, and partly out of the urgent necessity for IHEs themselves to be located in a milieu of higher culture, conducive for information exchange and their organic growth, and in a place favoured by convenient communication. Therefore, the degree of concentration of IHEs in cities is even higher than the degree of concentration of such economic factors as productive capabilities. To illustrate: in 1981, in Xi'an, the provincial capital of Shaanxi, 78 per cent of the province's college students were concentrated, compared with 43 per cent of the province's gross industrial output; the two figures for Nanjing, the provincial capital of Jiangsu, were 57 per cent and 14 per cent respectively. Both cities manifested a far higher level of higher education versus gross industrial output.

Table 3.3 *The distribution of tertiary enrolment in cities of various size, in % (1986)*

Grand total	Cities of more than 1 million	Cities of 0.5–1 million	Cities of 200,000–500,000	Cities of less than 200,000
100	59.6	16.1	14.5	9.8

Source: Zhu Tiezhen, 1987.

Looking at the grouping of cities by size of population, we see that the greater the size of cities, the greater the total enrolment of college students. In 1986, concentrated in 23 unusually large cities with a population of one million or more, was 60 per cent of the total tertiary enrolment, while in 260+ medium-sized and small cities with a population of less than 200,000, there was only 9.8 per cent of the total tertiary enrolment (see Table 3.3 for more details). Table 3.4 indicates that from 1978 to 1986 the average number of college students per 10,000 urban population increased from 59 to 78, while the average number of college students per 10,000 urban population residing in the unusually large cities of more than one million population increased from 95 to 179. The average number of college students per 10,000 in medium-sized and small cities is lower than the national average. However, with economic growth in these cities, a better provision of various modes of higher education, especially the short-cycle vocational IHEs directly serving the needs of local development, is to be expected in the years to come, together with further growth in secondary education.

There has been a phenomenal growth of adult education of various types and levels during recent years, and the proportion of the urban workforce undergoing job-specific training or on-the-job training in more advanced courses is usually much higher than their counterpart in the rural workforce. In 1988, the total enrolment of adult learners in various types of adult IHEs located in the cities accounted for 95 per cent of the national total. Various modes of delivery of adult education, including radio and television broadcasts, correspondence programmes, evening schools, etc., have been utilized to promote adult education in the cities.

On the whole, urban education in China has evolved to cater to the needs of urban economic development in general, with constant adjustments made to fit

Table 3.4 *The average number of college students per 10,000 urban population in cities of various size for 1978 and 1986*

Year	National average	Cities of more than 1 million	Cities of 0.5–1 million	Cities of 200,000–500,000	Cities of less than 200,000
1978	59	95	54	34	31
1986	78	179	94	36	21

Source: Ibid.

structural changes in industry and to meet the needs of social development, especially the provision of increasingly diversified educational programmes. It goes without saying that urban education is far more advanced than rural education, and some of the experiences accumulated in the development of urban education should be of value to the development of rural education in regions with different degrees of economic development.

Management and financing of urban schools

Administrative system of urban schools

As regards the basic structure of educational administration in China, there are four tiers of governmental bodies at the national level, the provincial level (provinces are understood here to include autonomous regions and municipalities directly under the Central Government), prefectural (municipal) level, and the country level, responsible for the administration and management of education at each level. At the same time, it is incumbent upon the governmental departments of planning, financing, labour and personnel to draw up essential regulatory instruments on educational financing, capital construction in education and certification and remuneration of teaching and other staff in close cooperation with the educational departments. Within the State Council is a ministerial-level State Education Commission (SEDC) responsible for the general supervision of educational undertakings in the country. Figure 3.1 indicates the vertical relationship between various kinds of urban schools and their supervisory bodies.

All educational institutions operated and managed by non-educational departments are subject to the guidance and supervision of educational departments of the corresponding level with regard to general policies of educational development, objectives and training, matters concerning instruction, and other relevant policies. In addition, a system of school inspection has been instituted to supervise the operation of general primary and secondary education, secondary teacher training schools, and vocational secondary schools. The educational departments at various levels authorize corresponding inspection bodies (inspectorates) to conduct school inspections.

Financing education in urban areas

Currently the main sources of educational financing are state budgets at both central and local levels. Generally speaking, educational undertakings operated and managed by local governments are financed by local financial appropriations; the financing of educational institutions run by SEDC and other central ministries and agencies depends on budgetary allocations from the Central Government, and the Central Government also allocates ear-marked appropriations to finance specific programmes of educational development. Educational finance is mainly composed of recurrent expenditures and capital construction expenditures. State budgetary allocations for education in 1989 amount to 37,299 million RMB yuan.

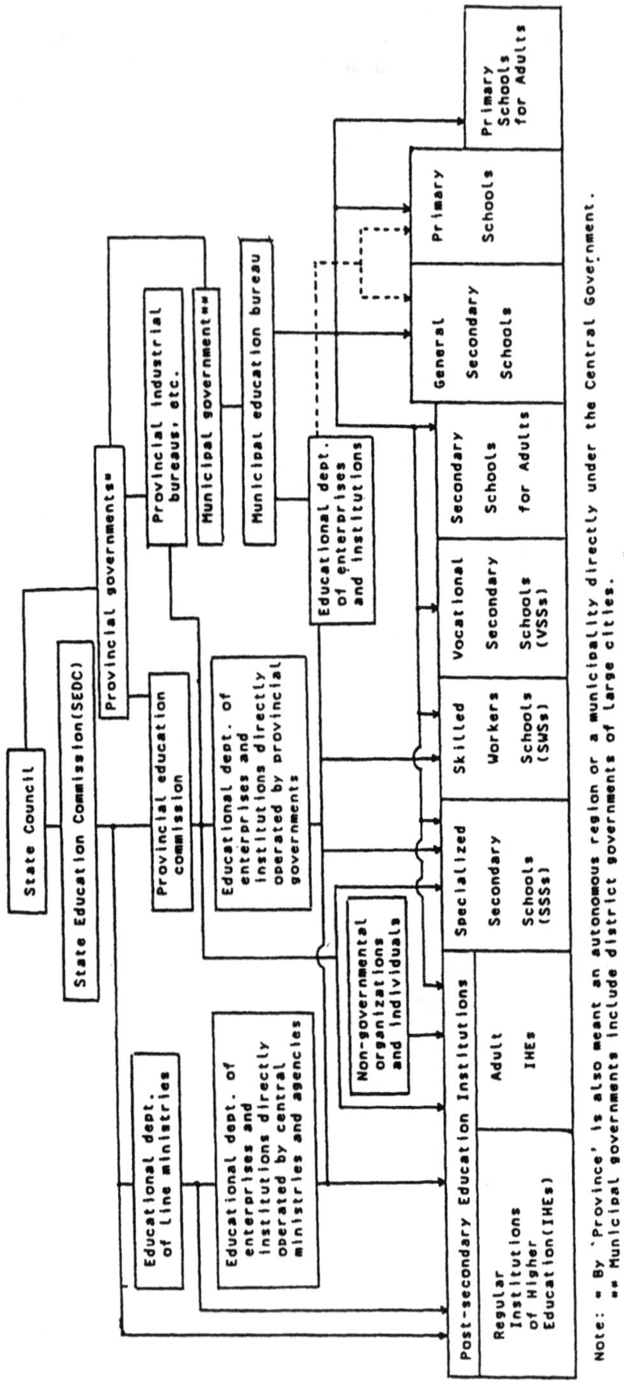

Figure 3.1 *Urban education in China – organization chart*

While urban education mainly depends on state budgetary allocations, efforts have been made to diversify sources of educational financing, including: 1) urban educational surcharges levied by local governments at various levels, generally charged as 1 per cent of industrial product taxes, added value taxes, and turnover taxes. In 1988 these surcharges amounted to 1021 million RMB yuan in the whole country. 2) Educational expenses borne by industrial and commercial enterprises, amounting to about 2300 million RMB yuan in 1988. 3) Donations from various quarters and individuals, amounting to about 450 million RMB yuan. 4) Special funds raised by regular IHEs and SSSs, totalling 800 million RMB yuan. 5) Miscellaneous fees collected by primary and secondary schools, and income earned by school-run enterprises and work-study programmes (no reliable data are available). These additional sources of extra-budgetary revenues added up to roughly 5000 million RMB yuan in 1988. In addition, foreign loans are also used as a source of educational financing; for example, loans provided by the World Bank on seven educational projects (partly used for urban education) amount to 866 million US dollars (Educational Fund Research Group, 1988).

Characteristics of urban education under different settings – a case study

We have selected relevant data from 68 large and medium-sized cities of Beijing (a municipality directly under the Central Government), Sichuan, Jiangxi, and Gansu (three provinces) and Inner Mongolia (an autonomous region) for analysis (see Table 3.5). From the data of the first six numbered columns, it can be seen that Beijing and Sichuan are regions of high population density, Inner Mongolia and Gansu are regions of very low population density, and Jiangxi occupies an intermediate position. With respect to the percentage of total urban population or non-agricultural population to total regional population, Beijing Municipality belongs to the type of unusually large cities, while the percentage of urban population in the other regions is not high; the share of urban gross industrial output of regional gross industrial output generally lies over 50–60 per cent, while the share of gross agricultural output is comparatively low, except in Gansu. Furthermore, Inner Mongolia, Gansu and Sichuan all belong to areas where people of minority nationalities live in concentrated communities. In these three regions there are 47 minority nationalities with a total population of 9.137 million, accounting for 6.3 per cent of the total population of these regions. The population of 15 minority nationalities accounts for about 90 per cent of the total population of the minority nationalities.

The data on these five regions indicates that the per capita gross industrial output of the cities is one to two times the average per capita value of the region, and there are some common features shared by educational development in these cities without obvious relation to the level of that economic development. For example, the institutions of higher education are all concentrated in the large and medium-sized cities of these regions, with the total enrolment of college students in the cities accounting for about 99 per cent of the total enrolment of each region, exhibiting no manifest relationship to economic, social and ethnic

Table 3.5 *(To be read across double page) Conditions of education in 68 cities of Beijing, Inner Mongolia, Jiangxi, Sichuan, and Gansu juxtaposed with some economic and social indicators of these regions (1987)*

		Total population	of which: non-agri. population	Density of population	Gross industrial output
		'000	'000	persons/km	billion Y.
Beijing Municipality	(i) 8 urban and suburban districts' total	6393	5111	4189	25.968
	(ii) Municipal total	10668	6010	587	35.723
	(iii) Share of 8 dist. in the municipality (%)	59.9	85	-	72.7
Inner Mongolia Autonomous Region	(i) 16 cities' total	5955	...	67	9.036
	(ii) Regional total	20536	6059	17	15.0884
	(iii) Share of 16 cities in the region (%)	29		-	59.9
Jiangxi Province	(i) 12 cities' total	6789.9	2988.2	434	11.828
	(ii) Provincial total	35589.5	6582.2	213	22.076
	(iii) Share of 12 cities in the province (%)	19.1	45.4	-	53.6
Sichuan Province	(i) 19 cities' total	16029.6	7248.4	582	33.853
	(ii) Provincial total	104584	15205	183	64.741
	(iii) Share of 19 cities in the province (%)	15.3	47.7	-	52.3
Gansu Province	(i) 13 cities' total	9528.7	2577.6	79	10.282
	(ii) Provincial total	21034.1	3364	46	15.305
	(iii) Share of 13 cities in the province (%)	45.3	76.6	-	65.2

Note: 1 billion = 1,000,000,000; Y = RMB Yuan; '-' = not applicable, and '. . .' = not available.
Source: *Statistical Yearbook of China for 1988, Socio-economic Statistics Yearbook of Beijing (1988), Statistical Yearbook of Inner Mongolia (1988), Statistical Yearbook of Jiangxi (1988), Statistical Yearbook of Sichuan (1988)*, and *Statistical Yearbook of Gansu (1988)*, all published by the China Statistics Press.

factors in these regions. Of course, there is a close correlation between the population of a city, and its school-age population, and the development of its primary and secondary education. The percentage of primary school population in the cities of the total primary school population of the region has a very good correlation with the percentage of the total urban population of the total population of the region. Similarly, the percentage of urban general secondary school population of total general secondary school population has a comparatively good correlation with the percentage of total urban population of the total population of the region. But the situation of rural education is entirely different from that of urban education. In 1987, we conducted a study of the relationship between educational development and economic development in 2000 counties and small cities, and found that in areas with per capita annual net income of 400 yuan or more there was an 81 per cent likelihood of universalizing primary education; in areas with per capita annual net income lying within 200–400 yuan, the likelihood declined to 55 per cent; and in areas with per capital annual net

Table 3.5 *continued*

Gross agri. output	*Per capita gross ind. output*	*Total enrolment in IHEs*	*Total enrolment in SSSs*	*Total enrol. in Gen. Sec. Schools*	*Total enrol. in VSSs/ASSs*	*Total enrol. in primary schools*
billion Y.	Yuan	'000	'000	'000	'000	'000
0.305	4062	136	. . .	270.5	43.2	381.1
2.16	3348.6	136	52.4	522.7	51.6	778
14.1	-	100		51.8	83.7	49
1.76	1517.3	31	44	431	. . .	605
8.774	734.5	31.2	44.4	1165.4	. . .	2434.6
20.1	-	99.4	99.1	37		24.9
1.408	1742.1	51.1	39.3	430.9	28.7	914.7
10.792	620.3	52.1	57.8	1783.5	108.5	5485.7
13	-	98.2	67.9	24.2	26.4	16.7
4.027	2111.9	125.8	68.5	140.2	57.6	1562.9
46.661	619	133.8	136	4033.3	150.8	12431.1
8.6	-	94	50.4	18.4	38.2	12.6
2.789	1079	32.9	39.4	562.9	28.2	1104.6
7.328	727.6	33	45.5	1114.1	. . .	2589.9
38.1	-	99.7	86.6	50.5		42.7

income of less than 200 yuan, the likelihood was only 27 per cent. Most drop-outs in primary and secondary schools have occurred in the rural areas. In contradistinction, urban education in China has advanced to a higher stage than rural education, showing more balanced development between cities of different types and located in different regions.

Prospects and developments in China's urban education in the coming decade

The development of urban education in China has been closely related to the process of urbanization. According to the prognosis made by some scholars, by the year 2000 China's urban population in various cities may reach 400 million, accounting for about 33–35 per cent of the total population of the country, and the number of cities may reach 600 odd (Wu Mingyu, 1989).

Different courses of urbanization could mean different modes of development for urban education. Among Chinese scholars there exist several schools of thought on the choice of different options in this matter.

According to the first school, in the light of the general course of urbanization in the world, in the initial and intermediate stages of industrialization, population tends to concentrate in cities continuously, owing to the demands of concentrated location of industrial facilities. Thus, small cities would develop into medium-sized ones, and medium ones into large. Only when the advanced stage of industrialization is entered into would the pattern of urbanization shift from one of a concentrated type to one of a scattered type. According to this line of reasoning, in case China's course of urbanization follows this course, there would be greater flexibility in the migration of the population in the years to come than heretofore. Accordingly, urban education would face the impact of newly increased population, ushering in a stage of development characterized by expansion of scales.

According to the second school of thought, in the light of the very large agricultural population of China and the realities of extreme unevenness in development between different regions, it is advisable to follow a course of integrated urban and rural development on the basis of developing the rural market towns, creating conditions for the transfer of rural surplus labour to nearby towns, thus alleviating the impact on existing cities produced by the migration of population. By so doing, in urban education priorities would be placed on the constant improvement of quality and the adjustment of structure, with the scale of provision comparatively stabilized; the intellectual resources possessed by urban education would be able to provide aid to rural education like a source of radiation.

According to the third school of thought, in the course of urbanization due consideration must be given to the regional disparities in development, and therefore, the poverty-stricken areas, the ordinary areas, the moderately prosperous areas, and the prosperous areas should not follow the same path in urbanization. Currently, there are some scholars forecasting or rather advocating that in the coming decade, priorities should be placed on the development of five types of cities: 1) great metropolises, comparatively few in number; 2) coastal industrial cities, with high levels of industrial development and vast potentialities in developing outward-looking economies, including the Special Economic Zones (SEZ) designated by the State Council and coastal open cities, such as Shanghai, Tianjin, Shenzhen, Dalian, etc.; 3) sightseeing cities, such as Hangzhou, and Suzhou, highly attractive to tourists; 4) central or pivotal cities, playing the role of an economic centre or the hub of communications, influencing several provinces, such as Shenyang, Chengdu, Wuhan, Zhengzhou, etc.; 5) satellite cities, such as Changzhou, Yangzhou, and Wuxi, which are medium-sized cities characterized by the coexistence of labour-intensive, capital-intensive, and technology-intensive industries, and playing the role of an interface between large cities and towns, facilitating the gradual adjustment of industrial structures. Corresponding to this framework, the main focus of urban education should be placed on the steady and sure elevation of the quality of education, and proper adjustment to the structure of educational provision to meet the needs of different types of cities.

There are sufficient reasons to predict that the process of urbanization in China will be comparatively slow. We think the third school of thought about urban development should be chosen. Within the next decade, the basic course of advance in urbanization is likely to be one characterized by diversified development and efforts focused on certain aspects of urban development in the light of local conditions. In deciding on the strategic options for developing urban education, due consideration has to be given to this basic setting and the trend of development. Looking forward to the end of the century and the early twenty-first century, the authors concur with the following predictions on the trends of development of urban education in China made by a number of scholars.

1) Generalization of nine-year compulsory education will be achieved in cities and towns, both quantitatively and qualitatively, with parts of the more highly developed large and medium-sized cities (such as Beijing and Shanghai) advancing to still higher levels, characterized by the popularization of education at upper secondary level (11–12 years of schooling), the raising of the quality of education, more rational location of schools, and improving the performance and cost-effectiveness of schooling.

2) The development of secondary vocational and technical education may basically meet the needs of providing the new workforce with initial vocational training, and there will be more vigorous development of post-secondary vocational and technical education. In urban areas, a system of vocational and technical education with the following features will have taken shape: rational division of functions between different industrial sectors and between different regions, closer articulation between initial (pre-employment) and on-the-job (post-employment) training, and diverse modes of delivery.

3) The provision of higher education by regular IHEs and adult IHEs will remain concentrated in large and medium-sized cities. Alongside a stabilized scale of operation (comparatively slow rate of growth), the main effort will be placed on raising the quality of education. Priorities will be placed on structural adjustment and reinforcing inter-city and inter-regional exchange and cooperation in the utilization of scarce resources of higher education and provision of programmes.

4) Effort should be made gradually to enhance the 'radiating' role of central or pivotal cities towards the counties and townships. The network of tertiary and secondary vocational and technical schools, and skilled worker schools located in cities would be the mainstay of vocational and technical education catering to the needs of both urban and rural areas of the region concerned.

In recent years in some coastal cities, there have been pilot experiments on building up an integrated system of community education combining the resources of urban centres and surrounding satellite cities and towns and rural areas, characterized by the complementary provision of education at various levels and with mutually supporting educational programmes. The subsequent interpenetration of urban and rural education thereby creates an indispensable

Table 3.6 *Number of minority students enrolled and F-T teachers in regular schools at various levels (in '000)*

1989	*Minority Students*		*Minority F-T teachers*	
	Number	% in total	Number	% in total
Regular IHEs	132	6.3	18	4.4
SSSs	73	3.4	14	1.3
General Sec. Schools	2835	6.2	174	5.8
ASSs and VSSs	137	4.9	10	4.8
Primary schools	10521	8.5	462	8.3
Kindergartens	627	3.4	25	3.5

Note: According to the report on the population survey in 1990, there was a total minority population of 91.2 millions, accounting for 8 per cent of the total population of China.
Source: SEDC, 1989.

infrastructure of intellectual resource, meeting the needs of local economic and social development. For example, in the southern part of Jiangsu Province, such urban centres as Suzhou, Wuxi, and Changzhou, have played a crucial role in the industrialization and urbanization of their adjacent countryside. In these localities, school districts have been mapped out according to townships and towns, and the location of general primary and secondary schools has been adjusted accordingly, alongside efforts to develop vocational and technical education and adult education to satisfy local needs. At the same time, the radiating role of the educational institutions located in the urban centres, especially IHEs, will be enhanced.

Recently, SEDC designated 15 cities and 100-odd large and medium-sized enterprises as the sites for conducting comprehensive reform experiments in urban education, covering a wide range of issues, including guiding principles of education, systems of administration and management, structures, content, and methods of education, constituting a multi-dimensional exploration of educational reform.

5) Now a comprehensive system of minority regions has been built up in China (see Table 3.6). But the level of economic and cultural development, the composition of population and the geographical environment vary greatly from region to region. Diversified modes of education should remain in the next decade. For example, the minority primary schools and secondary schools are set up independently in minority regions, although boarding schools for minorities are built up in thinly inhabited minority districts. The boarding classes for minority students are sponsored by urban schools. Although the ratio of minority populations moving into cities may not increase obviously, a greater learning opportunity will be provided continuously for minority students, especially those disadvantaged children and young people who live in mountainous or frontier regions.

The general goals of developing urban education in China are thus gradually to build up a socialist system of urban education which is adapted to urban functions, satisfying the needs of local economic and social development, being consistent with development at the national and provincial levels, and imbued with local characteristics.

References

Button, K J (1976) *Urban Economics – Theory and Policey*, London: Macmillan.
Department of Students, SEDC (1990) *The Handbook of Entrants of Regular IHEs*, Beijing: People's Education Press.
Digest (1990) 'The trends of urban development in China', *The China Industrial & Commerce Times*, No. 4.
Educational Fund Research Group, SEDC (1988) *Educational Fund and Teachers' Salaries*, Beijing: Education Science Press.
Hallak, J (1990) *Investing in the Future – Setting Educational Priorities in the Developing World*, UNESCO: International Institute for Educational Planning, Pergamon Press.
Hao Keming, Tan Songhua and Zhand Li (1989) 'The current stage, environment and trends of China's rural compulsory education', *Beijing: Educational Research* No. 10.
Hu Zhaoliang *et al.* (1987) *An Introduction to Economic Geography*, Beijing: The Commercial Press.
King, T (ed) (1980) *Education and Income*, Washington DC: The World Bank.
Li Fuzeng *et al.* (1987) *Skilled Manpower and Economic Development*, Beijing: China Zhanwang Publishing House.
Li Yingsheng (1990) 'Different development: the best strategic choice for the development of cities and countrysides of our country', *Future and Development*, No. 3.
Li Yuan (1986) *An Encyclopaedia of Cities in the World*, Beijing: World Affairs (Monthly) Publishing Company.
Liu Guoguang *et al.* (1989) *Lectures – The Strategies of Developing Outward-looking Economies in China's Coastal Zones*, Beijing: World Economy (Monthly).
Mao Guangru (1990) 'What is the content of the reform experiment of China's urban education?', *China's Education* (newspaper), 2 Aug., Beijing.
National Center for Education Development Research, SEDC (1989) *The Development and Reform of Education in China (1986–1988)*, Beijing: People's Education Press.
Piao Shengyi (ed) (1990) *Development and Prospectives of Minority Education in China*, Beijing: People's Education Press.
Population Research Centre (CASS) (1989) *Almanac of China's Population*, Beijing: Economic Management Publishing House.
Proceedings (1985) *Studies of Strategy of Urban Development*, Beijing: Xinhua Publishing House.
Report on Population Survey in China (No. 1, 1990), *People's Daily*, 31 Oct.
State Education Commission (SEDC) (1989) *Educational Statistics Yearbook of China (1988)*, Beijing: Beijing Polytechnical University Press.
SEDC (1990) *Educational Statistics Yearbook of China (1989)*, Beijing, People's Education Press.
State Statistical Bureau (SSB) (1989, 1990) *Statistics Yearbook of China (1989) (1990)*, Beijing: China Statistics Publishing House (CSPH).
SSB: Social Statistics Handbook of China (1990), Beijing: CSPH.
Socio-economic Statistics Yearbook of Beijing (1988), Beijing: CSPH.
Statistical Yearbook of Inner Mongolia (1988), Beijing: CSPH.
Statistical Yearbook of Tianjin (1988), Beijing: CSPH.
Statistical Yearbook of Jiangxi (1988), Beijing: CSPH.
Statistical Yearbook of Sichuan (1988), Beijing: CSPH.
Statistical Yearbook of Gansu (1988), Beijing: CSPH.
Survey Data of Incomes and Expenditures of Urban Families Collected During the Sixth Five-Year-Plan, Beijing: CSPH.
The World Bank (1986) *Financing Education In Developing Countries – An Exploration of Policy Options*, Washington, DC: World Bank.
Wang Xihong (ed) (1990) *Minority Education in Frontier Regions in China*, Beijing: Central Minority College Press.

Wu Mingyu (ed) (1989) *China and the World in the 1990s*, Beijing: China Finance & Economy Publishing House.

Zhu Tiezhen and Zhang Zailun (eds) (1987) *A Manual of Chinese Cities*, Beijing: Economics Publishing House.

4. Urban education in England and Wales

Geoff Whitty

Introduction

Writing about British education policy and inner cities in the mid-1980s, I suggested that, during the preceding decade, 'corporatist' and 'market' alternatives to traditional social democratic policies had been vying for position (Whitty, 1986). In the late 1980s, the British government and Mrs Thatcher, increasingly dominated by the 'New Right', displayed a clear preference for the market alternative. While state intervention rather than the vicissitudes of a capitalist market economy came to be blamed for the industrial decline and social dislocation that characterized the urban landscapes of England and Wales, the interventionist policies of left-wing local education authorities (LEAs) were blamed for the poor educational performance of inner city schools. Just as privatization was now seen as the key to reviving the economy, so the solution to the educational problems of urban areas was seen to lie in creating a market in education.

Many of the provisions of the 1986 Education Acts and the 1988 Education Reform Act were thus intended to enhance clients' rights of 'voice', 'choice' and 'exit'. It was claimed that they would give parents greater control over their children's schools, introduce more diversity into the system and make it more responsive to market forces. Referring to schooling in the capital city, the government minister responsible for the 1988 Act argued that 'choice and diversity are the key elements to improve the quality of education for all London's children' (Baker, 1990). In retrospect, even the earlier 1980 Education Act could be seen to prefigure some of the main elements of education policy under the Thatcher government, namely, the use of public money to support the provision of education by private providers and the attempt to make the public sector behave more like the private sector by encouraging competition and choice (Whitty and Menter, 1989). One commentator has suggested that, as a result of these various policies, 'the main configurations of formal schooling will be unrecognizable by the mid 1990s' (Johnson, 1989).

In what follows, I explore the nature and likely educational consequences of some of the key market-oriented policies of the Thatcher governments. In doing so, I concentrate upon those reforms which affect provision for children of compulsory school age (5–16) in England and Wales and those likely to have a particular impact on schooling in urban areas. Nevertheless, similar trends can be seen in other fields. For example, in the area of vocational training, government-sponsored training schemes expanded rapidly under the aegis of the Manpower Services Commission (MSC) during the 1970s. Under the first Thatcher government, there was a progressive increase in the amount of off-the-job training offered by private providers, thus forcing colleges of further education maintained by LEAs (for students aged 16 and over) to compete in the market. The subsequent demise of the MSC, the establishment of Training and Enterprise Councils (TECs), and the launching of a pilot training-credits scheme have marked a decisive shift away from the early corporatist policies of the MSC towards an overtly market-centred strategy to which LEA further education colleges have had to respond. Local Management of Colleges (LMC) introduced by the Education Reform Act and the complete removal of such colleges from LEA control, now being proposed by the Major government from April 1993, will force them to behave even more like private businesses.

Although the school-level reforms discussed in this chapter fall short of the wholesale policy of privatization that is being pursued in other areas of government policy, many of them can be seen as attempts to stimulate market forces at the expense of 'producer interests'. They pose a particular challenge to the centre-piece of British social democratic education policy of the post-war years, a system of comprehensive secondary education under LEA control. In reducing the powers of LEAs to engage in the detailed planning of provision, the reforms can also be seen as opening the way for a restructuring of the system as a whole and eventually the abolition of LEAs themselves. Alongside the apparent devolution of power to individual schools, there has also been a strengthening of the powers of central government, most noticeably in the establishment of a National Curriculum. At the end of the chapter, I suggest that the existence of this National Curriculum helps us to understand the limits to the government's commitment to introducing diversity and choice into urban schooling. Meanwhile, I examine in more detail some of the reforms that appear to enhance choice, namely the Assisted Places Scheme, open enrolment, local management of schools (LMS), city technology colleges (CTCs) and grant maintained schools (GMSs).

The Assisted Places Scheme

The Assisted Places Scheme, part of the 1980 Education Act, allowed the government to contribute on a means-tested scale towards the fees of children attending certain schools in the private sector. This was intended to help academically-able children from poor families to attend some of the country's leading academic independent schools which normally charge fees. Much of the rhetoric that surrounded the introduction of the Scheme emphasized the role it could play in the education of able children from inner city areas. Thus, in the week that the first assisted place holders entered the schools in 1981, junior government minister Rhodes Boyson claimed on national television that 'once again the boy or girl from an inner city area, where the aspirations and achievements of his (sic) local comprehensive school aren't such that he will be stretched the way he should be, can now once again join the ladders of social and economic mobility'.

However, at about the same time, the journal of the Headmasters' Conference (which represented the Heads of many of the schools involved in the Scheme) admitted that 'a Scheme designed to attract working-class children who would otherwise go to a poor neighbourhood comprensive [might] simply attract middle-class children who would otherwise go to a good comprehensive'. Our evidence, on the basis of an extensive evaluation of the implementation of the Scheme (Edwards *et al.*, 1989), is that this is precisely what has happened in many cases. Rather than being working-class pupils, the majority of beneficiaries of the Scheme are children from middle-class backgrounds, as is shown in Table 4.1.

Furthermore, the Scheme was found to have very few ethnic minority pupils in it and hardly any at all from Afro-Caribbean backgrounds. Those working-class children who were in the Scheme were not usually those who would otherwise have been trapped in poor neighbourhood comprehensives, but rather those whose parents or primary school teachers would have ensured that they attended one of the more successful comprehensive schools in the area. As this became clear, the government said less about the role of the Scheme in helping children from inner city areas and concentrated instead on the success of the Scheme in filling its places and on the fact that it was attracting children of families with low incomes, regardless of their social and cultural backgrounds. Many of the children in the Scheme came from single-parent families from middle-class areas, from families where the parents were in low-paid white-collar occupations or those where the main breadwinner was temporarily unemployed.

However, some advocates of the Scheme suggest that it will anyway contribute to the success of state schools by exerting an additional competitive pressure on them to improve their own standards. Not surprisingly, this view is not shared by the majority of Heads of academically successful comprehensive schools. Most feel that their capacity to attract the most-able students is inhibited by the existence of the private sector and that the Scheme is actually increasing the academic selectiveness of independent schools via a state subsidy

Table 4.1 *Occupational status of parents of assisted place holders*

	Service class		*Intermediate class*			*Working class*		*Not in paid employment*
	I	II	III	IV	V	VI	VII	
Fathers	11.9	38.1	10.2	15.3	8.5	6.8	2.5	6.8
Mothers	0	22.2	36.8	2.8	1.4	1.4	2.8	32.6

Note: figures are percentages. The occupational classification is based on that used in the Oxford Mobility Study: I Higher-grade professionals and managers; II Lower-grade professionals and managers; III Clerical, sales and rank-and-file service workers; IV Small proprietors and self-employed artisans; V Lower-grade technicians and foremen; VI Skilled manual workers; VII Unskilled manual workers.

Source: Edwards *et al.*, 1989, p. 162.

and thus enhancing their 'results' beyond what would have been attainable through the operation of 'pure' market forces.

Open enrolment to state schools

Meanwhile, the 1988 Education Reform Act has introduced a number of measures designed to introduce more competition directly into the state sector. The Act seeks to remove 'artificial limits . . . on the ability of popular schools to recruit up to their available capacity'. The abolition of the right of LEAs to set admission limits means that most schools may now recruit up to the level of their enrolments in 1979/80. It is claimed that this increases the chances that pupils, previously denied access to the most popular schools, will now be able to attend them. But, beyond these individual benefits, one of the ideas behind open enrolment is that it will lead to systemic benefits by forcing the less-popular schools to improve or, alternatively, to close.

A full assessment of the effects of open enrolment must await the implementation of Local Management of Schools (see below), which ties funding directly to pupil numbers. There are, however, some initial causes for concern about its impact on comprehensive education. Some of these arise from the fact that the Act represents an uneasy compromise between the arguments of the free marketeers and those with more traditional conceptions of educational planning. Pressure from the former to allow popular schools to expand without limits was resisted. Furthermore, few LEAs have entirely abandoned their traditional procedures and priorities, particularly for 11+ transfer from primary to secondary school. In practice, some parents continue to be denied their choice and others experience no real widening of it.

Even though overall enrolments in most LEAs are now well below the 1979 level, the fact that popular schools cannot entirely meet demand allows some other schools to remain open despite a drop in popularity. Although some schools have become literally full, while others have fallen well below their admission limits, the latter have not necessarily become unviable. Many such schools serve the dwindling populations of the inner cities. The Controller of the government's Audit Commission has suggested that the present policy will leave thousands of school places empty, rather than closing whole schools, and says that he can find almost no examples of open enrolment stimulating all schools to get better and hopeless schools to close (Bates, 1990). Meanwhile, popular schools, denied the opportunity to respond to their popularity by expansion beyond their 1979 level, are faced with the temptation of becoming covertly selective and thus, in time, using artifically boosted test scores to enhance their market appeal.

Another cause of concern is that the Labour Party's fear that 'these proposals will lead to educational apartheid and racially segregated schools' (quoted in Weekes, 1987) shows some signs of being realized. This concern arose partly from the experience of the 'Dewsbury Affair', where white parents had sought to enrol their children in a primary school with fewer Asian pupils than the one to which they had been allocated. It was alleged that the Reform Bill was a charter for racist parents, but (while denying that segregation was any part of the Bill) the government argued that they did not wish 'to circumscribe [parental] choice in any way' (Blackburne, 1988). The dangers of this became clear when, in 1989, the Secretary of State rejected the claim of the Council for Racial Equality that Cleveland County Council had acted unlawfully in allowing a parent to move her child on racial grounds. Although the details of the case were complex, it appeared to many people that the government was taking the view the Education Reform Act took precedence over the 1976 Race Relations Act (Hugill, 1990).

Local Management of Schools (LMS)

The Education Reform Act requires LEAs to devolve the bulk of their budgets to individual schools on the basis of age-weighted pupil numbers. This gives the Headteachers and Governing Bodies of individual schools considerably enhanced powers, while severely constraining the role of LEAs in the day-to-day management of their schools. There is already evidence that insufficient preparation has taken place in some areas and that governors are often far from clear about their new responsibilities. Nevertheless, the government feels that some LEAs could have devolved more of their funding to individual schools and has recently taken powers to force them to do so. Meanwhile, different schools are at different stages of development in exploring the possibilities and problems with which LMS confronts them. While some have barely changed their mode of operation, others have already introduced significantly new approaches to management and marketing. Knight (1990) suggests that LMS will produce greater differentiation between schools and that individual schools will seek to occupy different market niches.

The effects of LMS formulae on inner city schools have been a cause of considerable disquiet. The emphasis on funding via age-weighted pupil numbers is leading to the phasing out of even the marginal attempts at positive discrimination that had developed since the 1960s. An initial attempt by the national Department of Education and Science (DES) to discourage the introduction of additional factors and complicated formulae to follow for social need has made many LEAs reluctant to devise new forms of positive discrimination. Other elements of the government's approach to LMS will also have particular effects on inner city schools. A controversial decision to charge *actual* staffing costs against a budget based on *average* staffing costs has the dubious benefit of providing a budget surplus to inner city schools with a high staff turnover and numerous empty posts. But the effect of falling rolls in such areas had in the past also led to the merger of schools and relatively high staffing costs through the protection of posts and responsibility allowances after merger. Critics of LMS argued that this would place an intolerable burden on the delegated budgets of some schools, and the government has now accepted that such allowances cannot be phased out as quickly as originally envisaged (DES, 1991).

The overall effect of the formulae in some LEAs has been to move resources away from inner city schools or at least to give disproportionate benefits to suburban and rural schools. The draft formula originally produced for Avon, an LEA that spans all three types of catchment areas, was particularly criticized in this respect. Virtually all of its inner city primary schools and some of its most disadvantaged secondary schools in Bristol, stood to lose significant amounts of money under the proposals (Guy and Menter, 1990). Only a concerted local campaign, which was subsequently featured in the national press, produced changes. However, the same general tendency can be detected in other authorities, especially those with heavily contrasting catchments.

Some of those same authorities have also had cuts in their 'Section 11' funding (a national funding initiative), which has been used to put extra resources into schools in areas with substantial numbers of families who originated from the so-called New Commonwealth countries. A Home Office review of Section 11 funding has already produced some changes in the use of these funds. Although this is apparently designed to produce better targeting in terms of the original intentions of the legislation, and thus prevent LEAs absorbing the funding into their general budget, many commentators feel that this form of positive discrimination is also being squeezed by government policy. Members of the New Right close to the government have certainly argued for the scrapping of Section 11 funding on the grounds that it is being used for 'contentious anti-racist and multicultural education policies of leftist local authorities' (Dean, 1990a).

Another concern about LMS relates to children with special educational needs. The House of Commons Select Committee on Education, Science and Arts (1990) has recently argued that LMS, opting out and other provisions of the Reform Act are likely to undermine some of the progress made in integrating such pupils into mainstream schools. In addition, many of the special needs formulae adopted by LEAs are too narrow to bring into schools the additional resources to cope with the full range of special educational needs. Furthermore, even after some attempt by government to respond to such criticisms (DES, 1991), those needs that are recognized in the formulae may not offer sufficient enticement to schools to take pupils with special needs. Schools may well feel that the market consequences of doing so would be to make the school less attractive to those parents whose children still provide the bulk of the pupils whose numbers drive the funding formula (Gold *et al.*, 1990). In those circumstances, children with special educational needs could become concentrated in those schools which have difficulties in recruiting other pupils. These again may well be schools in the inner city.

City Technology Colleges

A crucial element of the Education Reform Act was to encourage the development of two new types of school, completely outside the control of LEAs. The first idea was for City Technology Colleges (CTCs), a 'new choice of school' for 11–18-year-olds, with a curricular bias towards science and technology. They had originally been launched at the 1986 Conservative Party conference when the Secretary of State announced that he was seeking to work with 'interested individuals and organizations to establish with financial assistance from the Department of Education and Science a network of [CTCs] in urban areas'. Many of the preferred sites were in or adjacent to areas of inner city dereliction, since 'it is in our cities that the education system is at present under most pressure' (DES, 1986). However, the plan to establish a pilot programme of 20 CTCs by 1990 was already in some difficulties before the scheme was given a legislative basis in the Reform Act and the wording of the Act itself represented some modification of the original proposal (Bristol Polytechnic Education Study Group, 1989).

Problems have continued to haunt the initiative and it now seems likely that only 15 CTCs will be established. Both sponsors and sites have proved difficult to find. While the failure to find appropriate sites, and the subsequent decision to accept sites in more suburban areas, could be blamed on obdurate Labour councils who refused to make inner city sites available, the problem of finding sponsors has been rather more embarrassing for the government. Not only were the costs of starting such schools 'woefully underestimated' by the DES, some major industrial companies like the multinational chemical conglomerate ICI very publicly dissassociated themselves from the scheme, preferring to make their contribution to education via existing schools. Initially, it was only companies and individual entrepreneurs closely associated with a Thatcherite style of capitalism who appeared to back the concept and there were persistent rumours of ministerial arm-twisting.

The various setbacks meant that, by September 1990, only 7 of the projected 20 CTCs were in operation. Two of these, in Croydon and Dartford, incorporated existing schools and were phasing in the CTC approach over the next few years. It is therefore difficult to tell in detail what CTC education will be like and whether there will be a distinctive and recognizable CTC ethos. When they were launched, it was claimed that

> their purpose will be to provide broadly-based secondary education with a strong technological element thereby offering a wider choice of secondary school to parents in certain cities and a surer preparation for adult and working life to their children (DES, 1986).

Their apparently modern and vocationally relevant curriculum was seen as part of the solution to the perceived failure of many urban schools.

Whether they will actually provide more genuine opportunities for disadvantaged groups and whether they will succeed in stimulating improvements in other urban schools is far from clear. The original plans for siting CTCs did suggest a concern with the particular needs of children in the inner city. Indeed, the decision to give CTCs defined catchment areas, at a time when other schools were losing theirs, almost smacked of discredited policies of positive discrimination and implied a concern to avoid this particular initiative being colonized by groups well-served by other schools. The staff of the few CTCs already open claim that their intakes meet the requirement that they are to be representative of their catchment areas, though a report drawn up for the DES apparently casts some doubt on this (Dean, 1990b).

Children at CTCs are not supposed to be selected on the basis of academic ability. Even so, traditionally disadvantaged groups certainly cannot expect to be favoured indiscriminately, but only to the extent to which they display the desired characteristics. These characteristics are broader than the purely academic ones that characterized the Assisted Places Scheme and emphasize commitment, orientation and motivation. The principal of Bradford CTC made this explicit recently in justifying a high acceptance rate for Asian applicants on the grounds that 'the strong work ethic associated with such families is exactly the sort of quality which we are looking for' (Lewis, 1990).

However, the strong competition for places that is already developing in some CTCs makes it difficult to predict what form selection will take in the future and the effects this will have on disadvantaged groups. On the basis of their observation at Kingshurst in the West Midlands, the first of the CTCs to open, Walford amd Miller (1991) argue that CTCs will undoubtedly successfully sponsor members of the working class (or the 'deserving poor' as they once might have been called) out of their environment, but that they will have little positive impact on that environment and some negative consequences for those who remain in it. They also feel that, as CTCs become increasingly popular, they will wish to move up the traditional hierarchy of esteem and thus 'deviate from [their original] role - as Kingshurst already appears to be doing'.

Meanwhile, the CTC concept has clearly had some effect on LEA provision. A few LEAs are establishing their own technology centres or considering reorganizing their own provision on a magnet school basis. Many more schools are rethinking their marketing strategy to attract pupils who might otherwise be tempted by the glossy hi-tech image and generous initial resourcing levels of the CTCs. But, at the same time, CTCs are exacerbating the over-provision of school places in certain areas and many people blame the closure of Simon Digby School in Solihull, near the Kingshurst CTC, on the decision to site that CTC in a previously closed maintained school in an area of falling rolls (Walford and Miller, 1991). Other LEAs, particularly some in south-east London, where there is a heavy concentration of CTCs, are worried about the impact CTCs will have on enrolment patterns in their own schools and on their plans for rationalization.

Nevertheless, the direct effects of 15 CTCs on the system as a whole are likely to be limited, especially if they continue to be perceived by other schools as resourced at levels way above those that can be achieved by LEA maintained schools. This is one reason why the government is now considering the establishment of voluntary-aided and grant maintained CTCs within the state sector (Hackett, 1991).

Grant maintained schools

The government claimed that the other new type of school introduced by the Education Reform Act, the grant maintained school (GMS), would 'add a new and powerful dimension to the ability of parents to exercise choice within the publicly provided sector of education' and that 'parents and local communities [would] have new opportunities to secure the development of their schools in ways appropriate to the needs of their children and in accordance with their wishes' (DES, 1987b). GMSs are existing schools which parents vote to take out of LEA control and receive their funding direct from central government. They were seen as a means by which schools could become more responsive to their immediate clients and also as a way of reducing the power of left-wing Labour LEAs, particularly in urban areas.

The overall extent of 'opting out' is difficult to assess at this stage. Mrs Thatcher's view was that the majority of LEA maintained schools would eventually opt out (Garner, 1987). However, although well over half the LEAs in England and Wales contained schools that had sought grant maintained status by April 1991, and over a third of LEAs contained at least one school where the change in status had been agreed, the 300 or so schools that had made moves in that direction represented only a small proportion of all maintained schools. Nor has the government's expectation that the first schools to opt out would be from Labour-controlled urban LEAs been borne out in practice. Less than a third of the first 72 schools whose transfer to grant maintained status was agreed were in Labour-controlled areas and Conservative-controlled shire counties have been amongst those most affected.

Parental votes in 50 schools have rejected plans to opt out and there have been other cases where LEAs (including left-wing urban LEAs) have persuaded school governing bodies not to proceed with a vote. On the other hand, some LEAs have argued that the government is bribing schools to go grant maintained by, for instance, granting GMSs 'over-generous initial capital grant allocations' compared with schools which remain in the LEA-maintained sector' (Halpin and Fitz, 1990). New incentives announced at the 1990 Conservative Party conference seem to bear out this view. The right to opt out, originally restricted to secondary schools and the larger primary schools, has now been extended to all primary schools. Accompanying this move, there has been a concerted campaign by ministers to encourage more schools to opt out.

Predictions that, if one school becomes grant maintained, others in the locality may be tempted to do so, are certainly beginning to be borne out in practice. Of the first 41 LEAs that had GMSs within their boundaries, 18 already have more than one. In situations where reorganization or school closure is planned, there is the possibility of serial applications for grant maintained status. The city of Bath is a classic case of the problems that GMSs pose to an LEA attempting to plan provision in accordance with its statutory duties and the directives of the Audit Commission about reducing surplus places. The LEA had sought to close one school and locate a sixth form college on its site. The school's parents voted in favour of opting out and the government accepted the application, while rejecting the LEA's own reorganization plans. The authority argued that this was to put the interests of parents at one school above the need to achieve economic and efficient education for the community as a whole. Nevertheless, the courts eventually upheld the government's decision and the fear on the part of another school that it would now be earmarked for closure led that school to opt for grant maintained status as well (TES, 1990).

The government originally stated that GMSs would not normally be permitted to change their character or admissions policies within five years of opting out. This has been seen by critics as a backdoor means of re-introducing selection and the government has recently said that it might allow this to happen in some schools in the future (Castle and Judd, 1991). Grant maintained status has already been used to keep existing grammar schools selective. Thus, LEA maintained selective grammar schools facing comprehensivization can immediately apply for grant maintained status and receive a decision before any reorganization proposals are acted upon. They can then retain their existing selective character if they are successful in their bid to change their status. Some of the earliest schools to opt out came into this category and 28 of the first 72 GMSs were selective schools.

Meanwhile, a debate is developing around the possibility of using the GMS regulations to fund minority schools, especially those for Muslim pupils (Cumper, 1990). At the time of the Reform Bill, the 'New Right' Hillgate Group (1987) argued that the government should encourage 'new and autonomous schools ... including Church schools of all denominations, Jewish schools, Islamic schools and such other schools as parents desire'. While their argument added to existing pressure on government to allow the development of non-Christian voluntary aided schools (Halstead, 1986), it came to be recognized that the same objective could be achieved either through state aid for independent religious schools or by the opting out of existing schools so that they could develop a religious or cultural distinctiveness. Marks (1990) argued the case on the grounds of 'natural justice' but a recent all-party attempt in the British parliament's House of Lords to allow it to happen failed to gain government support. Nevertheless, at a more general level, government ministers have expressed the view that the grant maintained school regulations should give 'schools freedom to develop individual character and compete for pupils on the basis of parents' preference' (TES, 1991).

However, there has been little evidence to date that grant maintained status is actually producing diversity in the types of schooling available. Indeed, if Walford and Miller's argument about popular CTCs seeking to emulate the existing high status parts of the system is also applicable to GMSs, then we can expect many of them to become increasingly academically selective in their intakes and conventional in their curricular approaches. Fitz *et al.* (1991) argue that, given the considerable number of 11–18, selective, voluntary and single-sex schools amongst the first GMS applications to be approved, the newly emergent sector as a whole may already be developing an image that appeals 'to parents seeking a "traditional" secondary schooling for their children'.

Diversity or hierarchy?

The government itself would like to characterize the drift away from comprehensive education towards more specialized and differentiated types of school as happening 'without any one being regarded as inferior to the others' (Dunn, 1988). More sociologically, the apparent diversity of modes of provision might be seen as reflecting some of the characteristics of post-modernity. Current developments might then be seen not merely as the product of the short-term ascendancy of a free-market ideology within the Conservative Party, but as a response to changes in the mode of accumulation, reflecting a shift from the 'Fordist' school of the era of mass production to the 'Post-Fordist school' (Ball, 1990). The physical appearance of some of the new City Technology Colleges, and moves towards 'niche marketing' of schools, might seem to support such a 'correspondence thesis'. A less economistic view might see the changes in schooling as a response to the complex patterns of political, economic and cultural differentiation in contemporary society which have replaced the traditional class divisions upon which comprehensive education was predicated. The shift might thus be seen as particularly appropriate to the apparently heterogeneous populations of Britain's urban areas.

The support being given to the diversification of provision and to local control of schools from a variety of political perspectives, as well as in other countries with different political regimes, should certainly caution us against viewing current reforms in Britain as merely an expression of New Right ideology, which will pass with a change of government. Many feminists have seen attractions in the shift towards pluralist models of society associated with post-modernism and post-modernity, and there are also some parallels in the educational policies currently being pursued by ethnic minorities. Social democratic policies have often been perceived as unduly bureaucratic and alienating by black parents, and some of them certainly welcome the new opportunities offered by the Reform Act to be closer to their children's schools (Phillips, 1988). Policies which seem to emphasize heterogeneity, fragmentation and difference may thus represent more than a passing fashion amongst neo-liberal politicians.

However, some of the groups which may benefit from the devolved and pluralistic patterns of educational provision which such thinking encourages themselves espouse philosophies that are rather more totalizing in their aspirations than the broadly social democratic ones which have dominated educational politics in the recent past. This is one argument that has been used against state funding of new religious schools in Britain, particularly Muslim schools with their assumed stance on the role of women (Walkling and Brannigan, 1986). However, this criticism can itself be seen as reflecting a prevailing stereotype of eastern culture which maintains the West's sense of its own cultural superiority (Parmar, 1981; Said, 1978).

More generally, the political implications of post-modernist tendencies and theories of post-modernity are notoriously difficult to 'read' (Giroux, 1990). Analyses that celebrate fragmentation and the atomization of decision-making at the expense of social planning and government intervention may merely be replacing one oppressive master-narrative with another, that of the market. Furthermore, the espousal of heterogeneity, pluralism and local narratives as the basis of a new social order is still seen by many sociologists as mistaking phenomenal forms for structural relations. Harvey (1989) sees post-modernist cultural forms and more flexible modes of capital accumulation 'more as shifts in surface appearance rather than as signs of the emergence of some entirely new post-capitalist or even post-industrial society'.

The early analyses of the effects of the market-oriented policies of the Thatcher government reported in this chapter would seem to suggest that, far from producing a genuine pluralism and interrupting traditional modes of social reproduction, they may be providing a legitimating gloss for the perpetuation of long-standing forms of structural inequality. The Education Reform Act cetainly seems more likely to produce greater differentiation between schools on a linear scale of quality and esteem than the positive diversity that some of its supporters hoped for. If so, the recent reforms represent a continuity with a long history in English education chronicled by Banks (1955).

Walford and Miller (1991) claim that, while comprehensive schools attempted to overcome the historic links between diversity of provision and inequalities of class and gender, 'City Technology Colleges have played a major part in re-legitimizing inequality of provision for different pupils'. Indeed, they argue that the 'inevitable result' of the concept of CTCs, especially when coupled with GMSs and LMS, is 'a hierarchy of schools with the private sector at the head, the CTCs and GMSs next, and the various locally managed LEA schools following'.

A leading spokesperson of the Labour Party has recently argued that this is a deliberate Conservative policy (Straw, 1991).

Overall, there is certainly little evidence that the Education Reform Act will provide a structure that will encompass diversity and ensure equality of opportunity for all pupils. Rather, there is some evidence that the reforms further disadvantage those unable to compete in the market. This will have particular consequences for the predominantly working-class and black populations who inhabit the inner cities. While they never gained an equitable share of educational resources under social democratic policies, the abandonment of planning in favour of the market seems unlikely to provide a solution. Indeed, there is a real possibility that an educational underclass will emerge in Britain's inner cities.

On this argument, whatever the intentions of their sponsors, present policies are as likely to increase structural inequalities as challenge them, while fostering the belief that their championing of choice provides genuinely equal opportunities for all those individuals who wish to benefit from them. For those members of disadvantaged groups who are not sponsored out of schools at the bottom of the status hierarchy, either on grounds of exceptional academic ability or alternative definitions of merit, the new arrangements are effectively just another way of reproducing deeply entrenched class divisions. At the very least, the reforms relate to a version of post-modernity that emphasizes 'distinction' and 'hierarchy' within a fragmented social order, rather than one that merely celebrates 'difference' and 'heterogeneity' (Lash, 1990). This is brought home most clearly when one looks at another element of the 1988 Education Reform Act, the National Curriculum.

Making sense of the National Curriculum

As I have argued at greater length elsewhere, the National Curriculum is the one element of recent reforms that, at first glance, seems to contradict the Thatcher government's espousal of market forces (Whitty, 1989). The National Curriculum established by the 1988 Education Reform Act specifies programmes of study and attainment targets for the three 'core' subjects of English, mathematics and science and seven other 'foundation' subjects. These must be followed by all children aged 5–16 receiving their eduction in state schools. While some of the extreme neo-liberals of the New Right would have liked to see the curriculum itself left to the market (Sexton, 1988), the government seems to have been more persuaded on this score by the arguments of neo-conservative wing of the New Right. One such pressure group, the Hillgate Group, argued that, even if market forces should ultimately be seen as the most desirable way of determining a school's curriculum, central government imposition of a National Curriculum on all state schools was a necessary interim strategy to undermine the vested interests of a 'liberal educational establishment' which threatened educational standards and traditional values.

The Hillgate Group was particularly concerned to counter the pressure for a multicultural curriculum that 'has been felt throughout the Western world, and most notably in France, Germany, and the United States, as well as in Britain'. It declared that it joined those 'who defend the traditional values of Western societies, and in particular who recognize that the very universalism and openness of European culture is our best justification for imparting it, even to those who come to it from other roots' (Hillgate Group, 1987). While happy to see the emergence of new and autonomous schools, including Muslim schools and such other schools as parents might desire, its commitment to market forces was clearly in the context of an insistence that all children 'be provided with the knowledge and understanding that are necessary for the full enjoyment and enhancement of British society'. 'Our' culture, being part of the universalistic culture of Europe, 'must not be sacrificed for the sake of a misguided relativism, or out of a misplaced concern for those who might not yet be aware of its strengths and weaknesses' (Hillgate Group, 1987). 'Choice' was only to be encouraged within limits and preferably only amongst those who had already internalized conservative values.

The Hillgate pamphlet thus worked both to acknowledge difference and to defuse its potential challenge to the prevailing social order. Given its influence on government policies at the time the Reform Act was being finalized, the reading of those policies with which we flirted earlier, seeing them as a reflection of the sort of post-modern society which celebrates heterogeneity and difference, becomes even more questionable. Furthermore, the alternative reading of those policies as legitimating existing inequalities is given added credence by the government's subsequent record on the implementation of the National Curriculum. In reviewing and revising proposed programmes of study in English, history, geography and the arts, it has consistently taken a Eurocentric view of the world. It has also sought to emphasize 'factual knowledge' at the expense of approaches to education that encourage pupils to explore a multiplicity of perspectives. There is clearly within the discourse of the Hillgate Group and the Conservative government a master-narrative that differentiates cultures on a hierarchical basis and which sees social progress largely in terms of assimilation into European culture. While it is now clear how a prescribed National Curriculum may be reconciled with the idea of an educational market within Conservative thinking, it is more difficult to regard policies informed by such views as adequately responding to the range of legitimate aspirations amongst the multi-ethnic urban communities of England and Wales.

Conclusion

To argue that the educational policies pursued by the British Conservative government in the 1990s are unlikely to enhance social justice within our urban communities is not to imply that an alternative blueprint is readily available. The British Labour Party has yet to move beyond critiques to develop a convincing set of new policies. Traditional social democratic approaches to education which favour the idea of a common school and, often, some version of a common curriculum (Lawton, 1975), are themselves faced with the need to respond to the social diversity of contemporary societies. Just as current discussions on the left about citizenship are seeking ways of 'creating unity without denying specificity' (Mouffe, quoted in Giroux, 1990), so will this be a challenge for future education policy for the cities of England and Wales. Donald (1989) has called for approaches which are based on 'participation and distributive justice rather than simple egalitarianism and on cultural heterogeneity rather than a shared humanity'. Whether or not Donald is right to argue that this puts a question mark against the very idea of comprehensive education, it certainly indicates the need for the left to challenge current policies with something more than a simplistic return to old orthodoxies.

Acknowledgements

Parts of this paper are based upon 'The Progress of Restructuring', a paper co-authored with Ian Menter and published in Coulby, D and Bash, L (1991) *Contradiction and Conflict*, London: Cassell. It also draws upon research carried out with Tony Edwards, John Fitz and Sharon Gewirtz under Research Grants C00230036 and C00232462 from the Economic and Social Research Council. I am grateful to John Fitz and David Halpin for access to their research data on Grant Maintained Schools (ESPC Award No. R000231899).

References

Baker, K (1990) 'A bright new term for London's children', *Evening Standard*, 30 March, p. 7.
Ball, S (1990) *Politics and Policymaking in Education*, London: Routledge.
Banks, O (1955) *Parity and Prestige in English Secondary Education*, London: Routledge.
Bates, S (1990) 'Unfilled primary school places cost £140m', *The Guardian*, 13 December, p.5.
Blackburne, L (1988) 'Peers back policy on open enrolment', *The Times Educational Supplement*, 13 May.
Bristol Polytechnic Education Study Group (1989) 'Restructuring the education system?' in Bash, L and Coulby, D *The Education Reform Act: Competition and Control*, London: Cassell.
Castle, S and Judd, J (1991) 'Clarke opens door for grammar school', *The Independent*, 24 March.
Cumper, P (1990) 'Muslim schools: the implications of the Education Reform Act 1988', *New Community*, 16, 3.
Dean, C (1990a) 'Right-wing group calls for repeal of race laws', *The Times Educational Supplement*, 3 August, p. 6.
Dean, C (1990b) 'CTC selectors face an "impossible task"', *The Times Educational Supplement*, 21 September, p. 1.
DES (1986) *City Technology Colleges: A New Choice of School*, London: HMSO.
DES (1987a) *Admission of Pupils to Maintained Schools*, London: HMSO.
DES (1987b) *Grant Maintained Schools: Consultation Paper*, London: HMSO.
DES (1991) *Local Management of Schools: Further Guidance* (Circular 7/91), London: HMSO.
Donald, J (1989) 'Interesting Times', *Critical Social Policy*, 9, 1.
Dunn, R (1988) Quoted in *Education*, 8 July.
Edwards, A, Fitz, J and Whitty, G (1989) *The State and Private Education: An Evaluation of the Assisted Places Scheme*, London: Falmer Press.
Fitz, J, Halpin, D and Power, S (1991) 'Grant maintained schools: A third force in education?', *Forum*, January.
Garner, R (1987) 'Mrs Thatcher enthuses over opting out proposals, *The Times Educational Supplement*, 18 September.
Giroux, H (ed) (1990) *Postmodernism, Feminism, and Cultural Politics*, New York: State University of New York Press.
Gold, A, Bowe, R and Ball, S (1990) 'Special Educational Needs in a New Context: Micropolitics, Money, and Education for All', paper presented to the Annual Conference of the British Educational Research Association.
Guy, W and Menter, I (1990) 'Local Management of Schools: who benefits?' in Gill, D and Mayor, B (eds) *Racism and Education: Strategies for Change*, Milton Keynes: Open University Press.
Hackett, G (1991) 'Major revives CTCs project', *The Times Educational Supplement*, 5 July.
Halpin, D and Fitz, J (1990) 'Local Education Authorities and the Grant Maintained Schools Policy', paper presented to the Annual Conference of the British Educational Research Association.

Halstead, J M (1986) *The Case for Muslim Voluntary-Aided Schools*, Cambridge: The Islamic Academy.
Harvey, D (1989) *The Condition of Postmodernity*, Oxford: Basil Blackwell.
Hillgate Group (1987) *The Reform of British Education*, London: Claridge Press.
House of Commons Select Committee on Education, Science and Arts (1990) *Staffing for Pupils with Special Educational Needs*, London: HMSO.
Hugill, B (1990) 'Government lets parents choose schools by race', *The Observer*, 22 April.
Johnson, R (1989) 'Thatcherism and English education: breaking the mould or confirming the pattern?', *History of Education*, 18, 2.
Knight, B (1990) 'Research on Local Management of Schools', paper presented to the Annual Conference of the British Educational Research Association.
Lash, S (1990) *Sociology of Postmodernism*, London: Routledge.
Lawton, D (1975) *Class, Culture and the Curriculum*, London: Routledge.
Lewis, J (1990) 'Bradford CTC responds', letter in *Education*, 1 June.
Marks, J (1990) 'Let natural justice be done', *The Times Educational Supplement*, 17 August.
Parmar, P (1981) 'Young Asian women: a critique of the pathological approach', *Multiracial Education*, 9, 5.
Phillips, M (1988) 'Why black people are backing Baker', *The Guardian*, 9 September.
Said, E (1978) *Orientalism*, London: Routledge.
Sexton, S (1988) 'No nationalized curriculum', *The Times*, 9 May.
Straw, J (1991) 'Quality Matters – a View from the Opposition', Address to the Secondary Heads Association 23 March.
TES (1990) 'Governors defy Avon in opt-out fight', *The Times Educational Supplement*, 3 August.
TEs (1991) 'Clarke senses a bloom time ahead', *The Times Educational Supplement*, 8 March, p. 3.
Walford, G and Miller, H (1991) *City Technology College*, Milton Keynes: Open University Press.
Walkling, P and Brannigan, C (1986) 'Anti-sexist/anti-racist education: a possible dilemma', *Journal of Moral Education*, 15, 1.
Weekes, W (1987) 'Tory fury at Heath attack on "divisive" schools Bill', *The Daily Telegraph*, 2 December.
Whitty, G (1986) 'Education policy and the inner cities', in Lawless, P and Raban, C (eds) *The Contemporary British City*, London: Harper and Row.
Whitty, G (1989) 'The New Right and the National Curriculum – state control or market forces?' *Journal of Education Policy*, 4, 4.
Whitty, G and Menter, I (1989) 'Lessons of Thatcherism: education policy in England and Wales, 1979–88', *Journal of Law and Society*, 16, 1.

5. Urban education in the Indian economy

Tapas Majumdar

Introduction

The process of urbanization in India, particularly in the second half of this century, can be seen as the result of industrialization taking place at a relatively accelerated pace, induced largely by centralized planning, rather than by the free forces of supply and demand. A consequence of this process has been a somewhat contrived emergence of the 'modern' segment of society in the urban sector standing in conspicuous contrast to the traditional rural society.

One pervasive feature of at least this phase of the urbanization process is the sharp accentuation of divisiveness on two different dimensions of Indian society.

The first dimension is sectoral: it is to be seen in the highly obtrusive rural–urban divide that looms large in all social policy debates in India and is a major factor in nearly all education issues. Since this divide is about the average characteristics of the two sectors, statistically it is also highly visible because achievement or deprivation can be immediately seen in terms of per capita entitlements of people to such components of the quality of life as incomes, economic assets, health (expectancy of life, mortality and morbidity), literacy rate and levels of education, and access to public goods like schools, hospitals or transport and communication services.

In terms of all these indices of the quality of life the average urban dweller is clearly far better off than the average villager. To take only a few examples, the per capita income in the urban sector of India is twice the per capita income in the rural sector; the urban literacy rate is 57 per cent, almost twice as high as the rural literacy rate which is around 29 per cent; nearly all the institutions of higher learning are concentrated in the urban sector and, compared to the average city or town school, the village school is an appallingly underprovided place of learning.

But what the urban–rural comparison of averages hides is that the worst in the urban sector is far worse than the average: the unemployed urban illiterates belong to the most deprived segment of Indian society and are amongst the poorest of the poor in terms of all aspects of life. The underemployed or underpaid working population employed outside the organized sector and living in the slums of the Indian cities have earnings far below the urban average and providing schooling for their children or literacy education for their adults are major educational issues that still defy solution.

The second dimension of divisiveness is then intra-sectoral: in this case, to be seen within the urban economy itself. Urbanization on this dimension is not, or rather has never been, the conversion of a socially whole people to a new culture brought about gradually over generations. It has rather been the result of flights of insecure individuals and unsettled communities into the towns and cities, fighting for a place in the sun with entrenched, less insecure individuals and better settled and better endowed communities.

Urban society in India is today very much split, and social issues, particularly educational issues, present completely different parameters to different clusters of urban people in terms of the incomes to spend out of or the loans to raise (both for making family investments in education), the schools to go to, the language of instruction to choose, the skills to learn, and finally, the jobs to look forward to. Though these differences are not brought out by the per capita sectoral figures, they are the ones that specifically affect the dynamics of urban education.

It is mostly by keeping this division and deprivation within the contemporary Indian urban society in view that the present account of the Indian perspective on urban educational issues is composed. It follows in four sections comprising (i) the demographic characteristics of the urban sector; (ii) the educational characteristics of urban Indians; (iii) the educational delivery systems in the urban sector; and (iv) India's national education policy and the urban education scene.

The demographic characteristics of the urban sector

Migration to the urban sector from the villages of India is probably no longer as large and visible a flow as it used to be in the past (not counting the now-rare famine-like conditions in the countryside when people flocked to the towns which are covered better by the public distribution system, and not counting flights of people from areas of civil strife and illegal migration of desperate people from across the borders). But evidence suggests that the inflow must still be considerable when measured over a reasonably long period of time. Table 5.1 gives a set of comparative figures from the 1971 and 1981 censuses that would indicate how the urban sector has grown in that decade both absolutely and relatively.

Table 5.1 *Urban and rural population of India (millions)*

	1971 Census			*1981 Census*		
	Total	Urban	Rural	Total	Urban	Rural
Total Population	548	109	439	685	160	525
Working Population	236	38	198	289	55	234

Source: Government of India, Registrar General's Office, 1975, 1985.

The census figures show that the urban population has grown over the decade 1971–81 from 109 million to 160 million, ie, by 46.8 per cent, while the total population has grown in the same period from 548 million to 685 million, ie, by only 25 per cent.

Thus, if we allow for the average growth of population in the urban sector by 25 per cent, we are still left with an excess population of over 23 million grown over the ten years. Much of this is on account of migration from the rural sector, the remainder being largely on account of rural areas being reclassified as urban.

The table also gives the growth of the working population in the urban sector from 38 million to 55 million ie, by nearly 45 per cent, while the rural working population has grown over the period from 198 million to 234 million ie, by only a little over 18 per cent. This fact implies that employment opportunities (of one kind or another) in the urban sector have grown much faster than in the rural sector, which partly explains why the cities and towns have continued to draw people in search of employment from the villages in large numbers. Provision of education, particularly provision of literacy to the incoming rural workers or elementary education to their children (when their families move with them) naturally poses a special kind of problem, accentuated when the migrant workers belong to different linguistic groups and face a communication barrier on top of having to cope with an unfamiliar (and often unfriendly) urban surrounding.

A remarkable feature of the growth of the urban sector in India has been its unevenness. That the sector has not grown uniformly but in concentrated 'agglomerations' is because the employment and other opportunities (including perhaps even access to education through one's own mother tongue) that attract working people and their families to the cities and towns are not to be found in all urban areas equally. A brief description of the unevenness of the concentration of India's urban population is given below.

A little less than one quarter (23.3 per cent) of the Indian population lives in urban areas (municipal corporation, municipal boards, municipalities, corporations and notified urban areas or a cluster of these forming an 'urban agglomeration'). While this is not a high proportion of the population compared to the proportion of urban dwellers in developed economies, its absolute size is very large. As we noticed in Table 5.1, it was 160 million at the last count (1981 census) which is larger than the total population of most countries of the world.

The urban sector in India has over 3,000 towns. Class 1 towns are those with a population of 100,000 and above and these are designated as 'cities'. There are around 200 cities in India where 60.4 per cent of the urban population lives.

Around 80 of these cities have populations of 250,000 and above. These are the 'principal cities' in which over 47 per cent of India's urban population live. Of these there are 12 big 'urban agglomerations' (UA) of populations of 1 million and above. Forty million people live in these 12 big urban agglomerations which is exactly 25 per cent of the total urban population of India.

Of these 12 big UAs the biggest are the four mega-cities: Calcutta UA (population 9.2 million), Greater Bombay (population 8.2 million), Delhi UA (population 5.7 million) and Madras UA (population 4.3 million).

Thus in the urban sector one actually finds several layers of concentration of population. Among the urban units people tend to concentrate in the cities, and among the city dwellers the concentration is in the bigger cities, then the big

Table 5.2 *Population profile of the mega-cities, 1981*

	Greater Bombay	*Calcutta UA*	*Delhi UA*	*Madras UA*
Population ('000s)	8243	9194	5729	4289
Male ('000s)	4652	5162	3169	2222
Female ('000s)	3591	4032	2561	2067
Literates ('000s)	5620	6020	3595	2892
Male ('000s)	3439	3661	2190	1670
Female ('000s)	2181	2359	1404	1222
Literacy Rate (%)	68.2	65.5	62.7	67.4
Male (%)	73.9	70.9	69.1	75.2
Female (%)	60.7	58.5	54.8	59.1
Homeless Population ('000s)	44	64	23	8
Slum Dwellers ('000s)	2831	3028	1800	1363

Source: Government of India Registrar General's Office, 1985.

agglomerations and finally just the four mega-cities in which over 27 million people or more than 17 per cent of the entire urban population of India crowd together.

The picture of the distribution of India's urban population would not be complete without a closer look at the population profiles of these four mega-cities which appears in Table 5.2.

One notable feature of Table 5.2 is the surprisingly low numbers of females recorded per 1000 males except possibly for Madras. India's overall female–male ratio itself is distressingly low (933 to 1000 by the 1981 census), but significantly higher than the following figures (females per 1000 males): 772 for Greater Bombay, 781 for Calcutta UA, 808 for Delhi UA. Only for Madras UA is it 930 which is not much different from the national figure.

The strikingly lower-than-average female-to-male ratios in the three metropolitan UAs of Calcutta, Bombay and Delhi probably indicate that in each of these there exists a large migrant population of unattached male workers and job-seekers who have to live away from the families they have back in their villages. If this indeed is the only or even the main explanation of this phenomenon, then calculating from the figures in Table 5.2 and after allowing for the all-India average female-to-male ratio, the size of this 'unattached' male population could be as large as approximately 0.78 million for Calcutta UA, 0.75 million for Greater Bombay and 0.4 million for Delhi UA. These figures give the broad dimension of a 'floating' population that perhaps exists in and around each of three major metropolitan cities – Calcutta, Bombay and Delhi – a population that might also prove more intractable for the purpose of the delivery of a basic service like an adult literacy programme than, for example, when there are whole families at the receiving end.

Out of the nearly 160 million people living in the urban areas of India about 55 million are 'workers' in employment (including the self-employed); about the same numbers are recorded as 'dependants and infants'. There are, in addition, probably over 20 million full-time students and about the same number of persons, almost all women, doing 'household duties'. There are also a few hundred thousand persons of independent means living on 'rents and interests'.

Besides these, there are several hundred thousand 'beggars and vagrants', one hundred thousand 'inmates of mental institutions' and perhaps still 2 million other people who are unspecified and presumably unemployed.

The educational characteristics of urban India

Table 5.3 gives information about the total and the urban populations by educational level. The urban literacy rate works out at 57.4 per cent as against the all-India rate of 36.22 per cent. Further information (not shown in Table 5.3) is also available about the 7 million urban Indians who are recorded as graduates and above. Of these, 1.1 million are technical graduates comprising 0.35 million in engineering and technology, 0.23 million in medicine, 0.03 million in agriculture and dairying, 0.01 million in veterinary sciences, 0.47 million in teaching and 0.01 million in other disciplines.

The educational attainment of urban Indians, as is only to be expected, varies considerably over the range of the cities and towns. For example, in the 82 principal cities and UAs that have populations of 250,000 and above, the literacy rate varies from as low as 38.7 per cent (for Srinager in the State of Jammu and Kashmir) to 78.5 per cent (for Cochin in the State of Kerala). Going back to Table 5.2 one can find the literacy rates of males and females in the mega-cities. While these are generally higher than in the rest of the urban sector except Kerala, gender discrimination also persists significantly in all the four mega-cities, the respective male and female literacy rates being 73.9 per cent and 60.7 per cent (Greater Bombay); 70.9 per cent and 58.5 per cent (Calcutta UA); 69.1 per cent (Delhi UA) 75.2 per cent and 59.1 per cent (Madras UA).

Educational attainments are also expected to vary considerably over income ranges. The relationship between the income group to which persons belong and the probable levels of education that they attain has not been well researched in India. But sufficient evidence exists to back up the intuitive

Table 5.3 *India's total and urban population by educational level (excluding Assam)*

	Total (mn)	*Urban (mn)*
Total Population	665.3	157.7
Literates		
Total	241.0	90.5
Primary	75.9	24.0
Middle	42.4	17.1
Secondary/Matric	28.0	15.0
Higher Secondary	9.8	6.0
Technical Diploma	1.14	0.64
Non-Technical Diploma	0.22	0.09
Graduate and above	9.5	7.0
Other literates able to read and write with understanding in any language	74.0	20.7

Source: Based on the 5 per cent sample data of Census of India, 1981, excluding Assam. (Government of India, National Sample Survey Organisation, 1988a.)

Table 5.4 *Per capita expenditure level and illiteracy 1981 all India: urban*

		Per Capita Expenditure in Rs per month			
		40–50	70–85	125–150	250–300
	Gender				
Illiteracy Rate (%) of	M	47.47	35.94	17.94	9.25
Population of age 15+)	F	74.70	65.46	44.21	23.68

Source: Government of India, National Sample Survey Organisation, 1988b.

hypothesis that the higher the income group, the higher would also be the probability of being educated up to any given level. Table 5.4 shows the relationship observed between per capita consumption expenditure in Rupees per month (a surrogate for per capita income) and illiteracy in the urban sector in an all-India survey (the Third Quinquennial Survey on Employment and Unemployment) conducted in 1981.

Two interesting features of Table 5.4 may be noted. First, the incidence of illiteracy in the urban sector is reduced sharply, even dramatically, as one moves from the lowest to the highest expenditure group observed, both for men and women. Secondly, and sadly, gender discrimination in providing access to literacy persists very perceptively even in the highest expenditure group though the almost constant gap between male and female illiteracy rates in the lower expenditure groups (about 30 per cent) is to some extend bridged in the highest group (about 15 per cent).

A later and much more detailed survey on the relationship between expenditure groups (divided into fractiles in the range 0–100) and three levels of education (not literate; below matriculation; matriculation and above) is now available from the 42nd Round of the National Sample Survey held between July 1986 and June 1987. This survey corroborates the presumption of the inverse relation between income and illiteracy and positive relationship between income and attainment of levels of education for groups of both men and women. The pattern holds for the rural sector also. One should perhaps add that the evidence also confirms the characteristic of the urban education sector noticed in Table 5.4: the gender differentiation persists but is mitigated in the highest income group in the case of access to education from literacy *up to* the 'below matric stage'. In fact, curiously there are actually proportionately more women in the below matric stage than men! It is at the stage of 'matric and above' that the large gap between men and women emerges again. This suggests that perhaps it is because of the presence of women who could have finished school and gone to college, but somehow were not able to, that women outnumber (strictly speaking out-proportion) men in the under matric group in the highest expenditure fractile.

The recent survey seems to give a slightly more reassuring profile of literacy of the urban Indian women for 1986–67 than did Table 5.4 for 1981. Though there can be no strict comparability, the rate of illiteracy for women in the highest expenditure fractile does show a distinct drop from 23.9 per cent in 1981 to 13.89 per cent in 1986–87 while the male illiteracy rate is about the same, around 9 per cent.

The educational delivery systems in the urban sector

The schools

The educational delivery system in urban India is as heterogeneous as the urban population itself. For the urban élite comprising the professional and business classes and the civil services, the system provides excellent pre-schooling for their children in the form of Montessori, Kindergarten and other types of nursery institutions run by private education societies. As is to be expected, in a free market situation and with relentless pressure of excess demand, many of the nursery institutions are, in fact, second-rate or even spurious. But there are some of high quality that would compare with the best in Western countries. These are highly priced and highly prized for they prepare children for entry into the best schools of India. These latter are all English-medium schools, though in some of them the language of instruction can be one of the Indian languages like Hindi, Bengali or Tamil up to a certain level.

Indian schools follow the usual classification: primary school (classes 1–5, age group 6–11); middle school (classes 6–8, age group 11–14); secondary (classes 9–10, age group 14–16); higher secondary (classes 11–12, age group 16–18); primary and middle together constitute elementary school. A good school invariably contains secondary or higher secondary but will have sections comprising the primary and the middle school classes also.

There are over 5 million primary schools and 1.4 million middle schools in the whole of India. Of these 50,000 primary schools and 20,000 middle schools are in the urban sector. Most urban primary schools have about 100 students each; more than 10,000 primary schools have above 250 students each. Most urban middle schools have above 300 students each, nearly 5,000 of them each having above 500 students.

There are about 7,000 secondary and higher secondary schools in India, most of them in the urban or semi-urban areas. There are about 18 million students in these schools.

The Indian schools are broadly of four types. The first type consists of the prestigious private schools (usually called 'public schools' following the old English convention) admission to which is difficult and highly valued by the parents. In principle, admission to the best privately run schools is open to all. The admission tests are in most cases fairly conducted in the sense that they are impersonally administered. But it is the expensive nursery institutions that are able to send their children to the best schools and thereby secure a head-start for the children of the élite classes. A sprinkling of high performing non-élite urban children whose parents are determined enough to bear the relatively high cost is also discernible in these schools. The success stories of the mechanic's son or the minor clerk's daughter making good in public schools are not unheard of. But the number of such stories, always applauded in urban Indian society, is not large.

Side by side with those highly regarded private 'public' schools are government schools. The second type are run by the central government and the third type by a State government. India, it must be remembered, is not only a mixed economy but also a federal polity.

The State government school will be affiliated to a State Board of Secondary or Higher Secondary Education set up by the State government concerned. Since school education has been a State responsiblity for a long time and the Centre has only recently entered the arena with concurrent jurisdiction, the number of State government schools is much larger than that of the Central schools. These latter are affiliated to the Central Board of Secondary Education set up by the Government of India.

Granting the certificate of passing a public examination, such as the school final after class XII, is the prerogative of only the School Boards in India (or, as a historical exception, the Indian Council Secondary Education or ICSE which is a descendant of the old Cambridge University Board). The private schools also have to affiliate themselves either to a State Board, to the Central Board or the ICSE.

The standard of the Central Board is often higher - usually much higher - than that of most State Boards, except the old established Boards of West Bengal, Maharashtra, and a few other educationally advanced States. It is to the credit of the Central Schools which have students from nearly all sections of the people as their fees are relatively affordable, that they often compete strongly with the prestigious private schools for the top positions in the Central Board Examinations.

Those who cannot get into the best private schools, the Central Schools or the State government schools have only the other, poorer schools left for them - which constitute the fourth type of schools in the sprawling education sector of urban India. They are numerous but mostly ill-equipped. The large majority of urban school children in India are forced to go to these institutions. Some of these schools do not even have such basic amenities as a lavatory or safe drinking water, as Table 5.5 shows.

It is clear from Table 5.5 that this appalling lack of basic facilities hits mainly the primary and the middle schools. The Fifth Survey of Schools (1986) did not give the urban/rural distribution in this respect but it is unlikely that the situation has improved much since even for the urban schools. It must be remembered, however, that the condition of the rural schools continues to be generally much worse.

The dimension of the task of providing facilities to the urban elementary schools cannot be conveyed by the percentage figures alone. In absolute terms, since there are approximately 50,000 urban primary schools and 20,000 urban middle schools in India, 16,000 of the urban primary schools and 3,600 of middle schools did not have access to drinking water facilities. Similarly, 22,500 of the urban primary schools and 5,200 of the urban middle schools did not have lavatories.

Table 5.5 *Urban schools in India having basic facilities (%)*

	Class of schools			
	Primary	Middle	Secondary	Higher Secondary
Facility				
Safe Water	68	82	90	96
Lavatory	55	74	92	98

Source: National Council of Educational Research and Training, 1978.

Vocational education

The tragedy about the hierarchy of schools described above is that as one goes down the ladder from the better-equipped to the practically unprovided schools, what changes is the quality of education imparted, the ability of the teacher to teach and the learner to grasp, but *not* the curriculum, which is still preparing for the Board examination, still trying to master the same subjects which are scholastic, non-practical and calculated to be unstimulating in all but the best teaching–learning situations. Thus it is that year after year streams of students come out of the school system, many of them both unfit for college and unready for the job market.

Vocational education, particularly to prepare students for urban industrial jobs after secondary school, was visualized by educational policy-makers as a parallel channel to the academic one, leading to college and university. It was estimated that gradually almost half the number of students finishing secondary school would be diverted to the vocational stream.

The results of the vocational stream experiment in the Indian schools have been unequivocally dismal except perhaps in the southern State of Tamil Nadu. While all educational institutions are encouraged to have the vocational stream at the plus-2 stage, the total number of institutions offering vocational courses at this stage in 1986 was only about 1700 for the whole of India. Of these, Tamil Nadu accounts for the largest number among all the states: 144. In the same year, the total enrolment in classes XI and XII in vocational courses at these institutions for the whole of India was a little over 126,500 – of which Tamil Nadu alone accounted for over 73,000 (58 per cent). Considering the fact that for the same year the total enrolment at the secondary and higher secondary levels for India was around 15 million, the vocational stream possibly accounted for no more than 2 per cent of the total plus-2 enrolment, a far cry indeed from the 50 per cent hoped for!

Non-school delivery systems

Non-formal education programmes in India have been mainly addressed to the rural sector and to the so-called educationally backward States. But there have been consistent adult education (including literacy) campaigns covering all the States and including urban areas. Even so, the coverage has been relatively small. In the whole of India the number of adult education programme centres operative in 1989 was approximately 250,000 with an enrolment of a little over 8 million. Not only is this a relatively small figure compared to, say, the total size of India's illiterate population (424 million, not counting Assam, in 1981), there have been persistent doubts about how effective the programme is even at this level.

Colleges and other institutions of higher learning

Any appraisal of the urban education situation would remain incomplete without reference to the higher education sector even though, strictly speaking, the picture here ought to be regarded as country-wide rather than urban/rural. But the fact is that it is in the urban sector where the nearly 6,000 general and

Table 5.6 *Unemployment by educational categories*

Educational categories	All India: urban (%) 1972–73 M	F	1977–78 M	F
Matric/secondary only	5.9	6.1	7.3	9.4
Graduate and above	6.8	9.5	8.2	15.7
a. General subjects	7.2	10.3	9.1	16.4
b. Technical/professional subjects	5.1	6.2	5.8	12.0

Source: Government of India, National Sample Survey Organisation, 1974; 1979.

professional colleges of India and over 160 universities and similar institutions of higher learning are mostly located. The large body of students of these institutions, even when they have a rural origin, become at last temporarily, and probably permanently, part of India's urban population. The students not only undergo the stresses and strains of the urban civil life, they actually add to them. Enrolment in higher education in India has gone on steadily increasing year after year. From a total enrolment of 2.4 million in 1975–6 it rose to about 3.7 million in 1986–7. Of this approximately 10.6 per cent are postgraduate (9.5 per cent) and research (1.1 per cent) students. Nothing can be more revealing of the frustration in higher education in India that is generated by these ever-increasing numbers than the phenomenon of educated unemployment. Table 5.6, based on two rounds of National Sample Survey (the 27th in 1972–3 and the 32nd in 1977–8) show the growth of unemployment at different levels of education in the urban sector in India.

One disturbing and regressive feature of the 1977–8 survey is that the position of women had sharply declined in the market for highly qualified labour, even in the technical/professional category.

Expansion of higher education has become, in the Indian economy, a major source of disappointment and of unfulfilled ambitions of young men and women, as many recent instances of unrest and disquiet in urban society in general and campus life in particular would show. This observation is not meant, however, to minimize the positive role of the radicalization of urban youth, brought about by these encounters with disappointments, in rebuilding urban society through social and political action.

The national education policy and the urban education scene

The rural–urban divide in India usually also encompasses the perception of deprivation of the scheduled castes (SC), the scheduled tribes (ST), and the other socially and educationally 'backward communities' ('the other backward classes' or OBCs) who largely belong to the rural society and also mainly live in the rural sectors. It is this perception that provides the main basis of positive discrimination in India's national education policy and there seems to be emerging a normative consensus on this amongst all the principal political parties. But, unfortunately, to the extent that the question of restoring the social balance in favour of the rural sector subsumes the question of restoring the balance in favour of the scheduled castes and tribes, the 'other socially and educationally backward communities' etc., education policy or for that matter, social policy, tends to underplay the relative deprivations within urban society itself. Thus it often happens that the blinkered advocate of social justice presses for norms of allocations of resources that would favour even the rural rich or the members of one of the 'backward communities' regardless of the income group they belong to, against the urban slum dwellers or the educated unemployed not belonging to the SC/ST or OBC categories.

The National Front government in Delhi that assumed office after the fall of the Congress Party government, had appointed a national committee under the chairmanship of Acharya Ramamurti to review the National Education Policy formulated by its predecessors in 1986. Though the Front government itself fell soon afterwards, the Ramamurti Committee survived. It submitted its final report in December 1990 which has been broadly accepted by the new government of Mr Chandra Shekhar.

The Ramamurti Committee too, underplays the relative unequalities in access to education within the urban sector cutting across castes and communities. However, two main emphases emerging in the report, if faithfully reflected in the allocation of resources and the formulation of programmes and follow-up actions, would seem to justify the claim that the new policy's 'basic thrust was to use education as a tool for an enlightened and humane society', thereby having a direct impact also on the urban education situation.

The first emphasis of the new education policy (Government of India Ministry of Human Resource Development, 1990), is on the building up of a common school system over the next ten years, both through persuasion and essential legislation – the objective being the promotion of social cohesion and national integration. As a first step the Committee recommends improvement in the quality of government (including local bodies) and government-aided private schools so as to transform them into genuine 'neighbourhood schools' good enough for all children. For this, obviously, there has to be an immediate and massive reallocation of resources.

The second emphasis of the Ramamurti Committee is placed firmly on productive education appropriate to an industrial society. Vocationalization is proposed no longer as an escape outlet at the end of high school (which few ever used) but as a component of all education from elementary onwards. In fact, the new idea is not to treat the formal school, non-formal education and adult education as separate and parallel channels, but to make the school (and the university) the centre for all the channels, so that they can play a part in upgrading the technology used by the surrounding community whether in the town or in the village. Since the present cohort of teachers may not be able to impart vocational skills, Acharya Ramamurti has even suggested co-opting craftspersons, local electricians and factory engineers to the education system as part-time teachers. The purpose is to ensure that employers in industry no longer will have to complain that students graduating from schools and colleges are unemployable because of lack of relevant modern skills.

To evolve a generally acceptable common school system and to re-orient schools towards productive education are both laudable tasks. But it is not the first time that these tasks have been perceived as important by the educational policy-maker in India. It may be recalled that both tasks were highlighted by the Education Commission (1964–6) headed by Kothari more than a quarter of a century ago.

The neighbourhood school, however, has been a non-starter. To find the resources for running neighbourhood schools that would be so good that no parents would hesitate to send their children to these rather than to the more expensive public schools has been impossible: plain economics or rather plain arithmetic would have ruled that out. On the other hand, to force parents to send their children to indifferent neighbourhood schools when they could afford to send them elsewhere would have been impossible too: plain politics would have ruled that out in a democratic society. But the more practical task of relating education and research to production, unfortunately, was never systematically undertaken in India whether in the rural or in the urban economy, though that was a major thrust of the Kothari Commission's recommendations.

Lack of vocational education on the one hand and educated unemployment on the other have remained two frustrating problems of the urban education sector of India and neither can be tackled except by relating education to production for all sections of the people and at all phases – from middle school to university. If this indeed is read as the message of India's new National Educational Policy, then perhaps the Indian education system might yet have a second chance of coming to terms with the process of the urbanization of the economy.

References

Government of India, Ministry of Education (1966) *Education and National Development: Report of the Education Commission* (Kothari Commission).

Government of India, Ministry of Human Resource Development (1986) *National Policy on Education, 1986*. (1986) *Programme of Action, 1986*. (1990) *Towards an Enlightened and Humane Society: Report of the Committee for Review of National Policy on Education* (Acharya Ramamurti Committee).

Government of India, National Sample Survey Organisation (1974) *National Sample Survey, 27th Round, 1973*. (1979) *National Sample Survey 32nd Round, 1978*. (1988a) *National Sample Survey 42nd Round, 1987*. (1988b) *Sarvekshana*.

Government of India, Registrar General's Office (1975) *Census of India, 1971*. (1985) *Census of India, 1981*. (1985) *Census of India, 1981, 5% Sample Data*.

Harris, N (1978) *Economic Development, Cities and Planning: The Case Of Bombay*, Bombay: Oxford University Press.

Kamat, A R (1978) 'Education and social change' in Shah, A B (ed) *The Social Context of Education*, Bombay: Allied Publishers.

Mohan, R and Chandrasekhar, P (1982) 'Morphology of urbanisation in India: some results from 1981 census', *Economic and Political Weekly*, XVII, 38 and 39.

Naik, J P (1975) *Equality, Quality and Quantity: The Elusive Triangle in Indian Education*, Bombay: Allied Publishers.

National Council of Educational Research and Training (1978) *Fourth All-India Educational Survey, 1978*. (1989) *Fifth All-India Educational Survey, 1986, Selected Statistics*.

6. Urban education in Kenya

Kevin M Lillis

Introduction

Since independence, there has been extensive population growth and urbanization in Kenya, although it remains essentially a rural and pastoral country. None of the multiplicity of tribal and ethnic groups is dominantly urban. Six urban areas in Kenya – the City of Nairobi and the municipalities of Mombasa, Kisumu, Nakuru, Eldoret and Thika (in descending order the largest towns in the country) – are responsible for managing their own systems of primary education. Whilst many of the other 90 or so urban areas manifest the same problems as these municipalities, writ small, the Kenya Ministry of Education considers them as rural areas. This chapter establishes some of the dimensions of urbanization in Kenya and, in particular, these six urban areas and reveals the constraints impinging upon attempts to resource educational development in them.

Urbanization in Africa

With less than 30 per cent of its population living within urban areas, Africa is the world's least urbanized region. However, it reveals the world's highest 'urbanization' rate. This averaged 4.6 per cent throughout the 1970s and will not drop back to 3.0 per cent until after 2025. None of the world's 'megacities' (of 20 million people) is located within the continent, although many of the rapidly expanding urban complexes, including the Kenyan capital, Nairobi, share the social and economic problems of those megacities. Table 6.1 illustrates the dimensions of several of the largest cities in Africa.

Recent demographic pressures in Kenya

Before dwelling on the growth of Nairobi, it is important to indicate the nature of the demographic pressures in Kenya. At independence in 1963, Kenya's population was 8,636,263. In the 1969 census it was 10,942,105; in the 1979 census it was 15,327,061 (7,607,113 males and 7,719,948 females) (see Table 6.2).

Table 6.1 *Growth of selected African cities, 1900–84*

	Population in '000s						*Growth %*		*Growth %*	
	1900	1930	1950	1960	1970	1983	1900/50		1950/83	
Nairobi	5	50	75	315	509	1314	70	1400	1625	1687
Dar es Salaam	17	23	69	129	273	770	62	306	701	1016
Kampala	3	5	22	123	331	400	19	633	438	1919
Cairo	570	1065	2091	3349	4220	5074	1521	267	2983	146
Lagos	42	130	270	670	1600	2200	228	543	1930	715

Source: Mulcansingh, 1987.

The estimated 1989 population was 23 million and a census was scheduled for that year. Importantly, at the time of writing, data from the much criticized and abortive Kenyan national population census of 1989 are not available to make accurate up-to-date observations on the nature of the population explosion in Kenya in general and in Nairobi in particular. Most authoritative projections (eg, Ominde, 1987 and Central Bureau of Statistics, 1986) remain based upon the 1979 census and these are also used in the discussions in this chapter.

The UN Fund for Population and Development estimates that the growth of Kenyan population (varyingly calculated at between 3.9 per cent and 4.12 per cent) will average 4.11 per cent between 1995 and the year 2000. This remains the highest population growth rate in the world. Despite ambitious, but relatively unsuccessful population control programmes, the planning and management of education in Kenya remains under the influence of this hidden population momentum. The trend reveals that the rate of growth increased from 2.5 per cent in 1948 (when the first census was conducted in Kenya) to 3 per cent in 1963, 3.3 per cent in 1969, to 3.9 per cent in 1979, when the last acceptable census was conducted.

The problem is more critical given that the Kenya fertility rate averages 8.12 - again the highest in the world: this, too, rose from 6.8 in 1963 to 7.6 in 1969 and stablized from 6.8 in 1979, although prognostication for the 1989 census suggested a fertility rate in excess of 10. There are regional variations. Central and Western Provinces reveal the highest birth rates and the highest percentages of their population below 15 – which is reflected in school enrolment rates.

Table 6.2 *Population data, 1948–99*

Year	*Population*	*% increase per annum*
1948		2.5
1963 (independence)	8,636,263	3.0
1969	10,942,105	3.3
1979	15,327,061	3.9
1989 (estimates)	23,000,000	4.2
1999 (estimates)	40,000,000	4.1

Source: Central Bureau of Statistics, 1986.

By contrast, Coast Province has the lowest birth rate and the smallest percentage of population under 15. At present over 50 per cent of Kenya's population is under 20 – reflecting the massive pressures on all levels of the system of education and training. Several policy statements have 'advised' Kenyans to restrict the number of children per family (to preferably three or less). However, no official population legislation is contemplated.

Successive Five Year Development plans since 1966 and the key Sessional Paper No. 1 of 1986 on 'Economic Management for Renewed Growth' articulated the importance of checking population growth, especially in view of the educational, social service and economic implications. However, policy and official pronouncements have addressed carefully the sensitive issues of family planning and the inherent socio-cultural practices in many parts of the country, where, as elsewhere, children remain considered as blessings, security, power and prestige. Obviously, this has massive implications for education, training and employment, especially in the urban areas which, as discussed below, reveal excessive growth rates.

By the year 2000 over 14 million will seek employment, ie 6.5 million more than in 1989. This requires the creation of 500,000 more jobs every year for the next 12 years to maintain employment levels in the year 2000 at 1989 levels – as well as the creation through education and training of the skills for employment. At the current rate of employment generation, only 1.4 million jobs can be created during this period, leaving a potential 5 million (or 40 per cent of the labour force) seeking non-existent jobs. This will again stretch the capability of urban authorities to provide education and/or social services and/or training.

Urbanization in Kenya

There has been no substantial study of education within urban areas of Kenya apart from Thuo's (1990) work in progress on the equity of provision in Nairobi. In contrast, Obudho (1974; 1979; 1982; 1986) and Obudho and Muganzi (1987) especially, have sought to explore the dynamics of urbanization in Kenya and in Nairobi. Equally, 'Nairobi and its Environs' was the theme of the first international conference on Urban Growth and Spatial Planning of Nairobi (Obudho *et al.*, 1990), although the educational issues were accorded only superficial recognition (Orwa, 1990).

Urbanization in Kenya, in the sense of population concentration in towns, has a long history in the coastal region where Kiswahili settlements date from the 14th century (Obudho, 1986; UNICEF, 1989). The interior areas did not undergo urban development until the colonial period of the late nineteenth century. The urban pattern which exists today by and large reflects the development of British colonization and trade rather than the traditional African population and agricultural patterns, which were (and remain) predominantly agrarian and rural. The colonial and pre-independence period evidenced slow population growth, slow urbanization and restricted growth of the educational system. By contrast, the overall rate of population growth in Kenya has been accelerating in the period since independence in 1963, as has the growth of the education system throughout the Republic. The national population growth rate has been matched by an even faster acceleration of

Table 6.3 *Kenya rural and urban population 1948–79 (population in thousands)*

Year	*Total*	*Rural*	*Urban*	*Urban as % of total*	*Number of urban centres*
1948	5406	5121	285	5.2	17
1962	8636	7965	671	7.8	34
1969	10943	9861	1082	9.9	47
1979	15327	13020	2307	15.0	90

Sources: Based on data from Republic of Kenya, Central Bureau of Statistics, Kenya Population Census 1948, 1962, 1969 and 1979, Nairobi, Government Printer.

urban growth which reached 7.9 per cent in the first two decades of independence (1960s and 1970s), when the share of the urban population increased from 7.8 per cent in 1962 to 15 per cent in 1979 (Table 6.3).

Table 6.4 shows the shift in the percentages of the urban population with projections to the year 2025. In 1959, it was 5.6 per cent. This increased to 10.2 per cent in 1970, 14.2 per cent in 1980 and 16.7 per cent in 1987. If this trend continues, it is estimated that by the year 2025 approximately 45.7 per cent of Kenya's population will be living in urban areas, with massive demands made upon the resources for education.

An important trend in Kenya's urbanization is the increasing numbers of women migrants. Many are wives accompanying their husbands but a large portion are women who have lost their land or will not inherit land due to sexual discrimination in traditional land inheritance practices (UNICEF, 1989). Their move to urban areas is, therefore, a permanent, or at least semi-permanent transfer of residence. This in part explains the predominance of women-headed households in squatter settlement areas with estimates ranging from 40–75 per cent. That the residence of such women in the squatter settlements of Nairobi (as well as other urban areas) may be 'semi-permanent' rather than permanent because they are forced to re-emigrate in the search for the scarce educational

Table 6.4 *Estimates of urban population share in Kenya, 1950–2025*

Year	*Urban %*	*Year*	*Urban %*
1950	5.6	1995	22.7
1955	6.4	2000	26.2
1960	7.4	2005	29.9
1965	8.6	2010	33.8
1970	10.2	2015	37.8
1975	12.0	2020	41.8
1980	14.2	2025	45.7
1985	16.7		
1990	19.2		

Source: United Nations, Department of International Economics and Social Affairs. Estimates and Projections of Urban, Rural and City Populations, 1950–2025: The 180 Assessment (New York: United Nations ST/ESA/SER.R145), pp. 28–9.

opportunities they cannot find in the urban areas is further discussed in Chapter 14.

Growth of urban centres

The growth over time of urbanization can be examined by identifying the number of urban centres (see Table 6.5). At the time of the first Kenyan population census in 1948, there were 17 towns of 2,000 or more people, with an aggregate population of 276,000. The urban population was small (5.2 per cent of the total) and disproportionately concentrated in Nairobi and Mombasa (73.9 per cent of the total urban population) as indeed it still is, although these patterns are changing. The majority of urban dwellers were foreign racial groups - Europeans, Asians, and Arabs. By the 1962 population census, the number of such towns had doubled to 34 and the urban population had increased to 671,000, with an annual growth of 6.6 per cent per annum. The growth of towns both in number and population accelerated after independence when the indigenous Africans were permitted to migrate to the urban areas without any of the legal and administrative restrictions that had constrained such migration in the colonial era. According to the 1962 and 1969 population censuses, there were 34 and 48 urban centres respectively, with the urban population growing from 67,000 in 1962 to 1.082 million in 1969 – at the rate of 7.1 per cent per annum. The 1979 census recorded 90 urban centres and an urban population of 2.3 million. Overall, the urban population grew at the rate of 7.9 per cent per annum during the 1969–79 inter-censal period.

The problems of educational provision were exacerbated mostly in the larger urban areas. The primary urban centres of Nairobi and Mombasa together accounted for 70 per cent to 74 per cent of urban population during the 1948, 1962 and 1969 censuses although only 50.7 per cent according to the 1979 population census (Obudho, 1982). The rate of annual increase of Nairobi has

Table 6.5 *Distribution of towns and population by size groups (population in thousands)*

Size group	*1948*		*1962*		*1969*		*1979*		*Growth rate of population in size groups*
	No.	*Pop.*	*No.*	*Pop.*	*No.*	*Pop.*	*No.*	*Pop.*	
Over 100,000	1	119	2	523	2	756	3	1322	5.6
20,000–99,999	1	85	2	65	2	80	13	568	13.9
10,000–19,999	2	29	3	44	7	91	10	140	7.1
5,000–9,999	3	20	11	70	11	72	27	154	4.8
2,000–4,999	10	23	16	49	26	83	37	123	5.7
Total	17	276	34	670	48	1082	90	2307	6.9
% Urban		5.1%		7.7%		9.9%		14.6%	

Source: Based on data from Republic of Kenya Central Bureau of Statistics Kenya Publication Census 1948, 1962, 1969, 1979, Nairobi, Government Printer.

always been higher than that of Mombasa, and is, of course, a major reason for the low gross enrolment ratios in the two places, as is discussed in Chapter 14. The rates of increases of all urban centres during 1969–79 were at least over 10 per cent per annum, except for Nairobi, Mombasa, Nakuru, Thika, Malindi and Nanyuki. High rates of increase were also recorded in the towns of Kisumu (16.8 per cent), Nyeri (13.6 per cent), Kericho (11.4 per cent) and Eldoret (10.7 per cent). The population of other towns grew by 15.6 per cent per annum, while their share of the urban population increased from 5.3 per cent in 1948 to 28.9 per cent in 1979 or doubling in the last decade. However, such data are deceptive, because of expanded urban boundaries during the census period. The number of Kenyan towns with populations of 10,000 or more had increased to 26 in 1979. These data suggest that urban growth in Kenya is becoming less polarized towards Nairobi, and that rural–urban migration in Kenya has become focused on the intermediate centres. However, Nairobi and Mombasa have continued to grow at the rate of 5.1 per cent and 3.3 per cent respectively and, predictably the capital reveals the greatest social, economic and educational problems.

Although, as suggested above, not yet one of the world's megacities, Nairobi manifests the global shift towards urbanization and the complexities of planning and management associated with it – especially social services and education.

Erstwhile small and compact, and still less than 100 years old, the city now reveals many of the phenomena, the major economic, social and physical problems of other larger, older cities. To a lesser extent, the five other major municipalities managing their own systems of education (as well as other urban areas in Kenya) mirror these problems, writ small:

- massive housing deficiencies and the increased squalor and poverty of an increasing number of slums and squats (including shelters of paper and polythene);
- increased homelessness;
- absence of basic health, clinic, hospital and educational infrastructures;
- the decay of the physical infrastructre, including water systems, sewage and sanitation systems, transport, lighting, electricity, roads, pavements;
- environmental degradation including pollution and urban waste (the city is increasingly corroded by a mountain of garbage accruing from the rapidly expanding population);
- massive unemployment; latent crime and corruption;
- hawkers and beggars; high numbers of disabled;
- an increasing number of female-headed households and single families (especially in third generation slum dwellers);
- an increasing number of street children and street gangs, disadvantaged, homeless, uncared for, unloved; increased vandalism and petty thieving and car thieving;
- massive urban migration, based upon the mirage of jobs available and the quality of life there.

The poorest of the poor live in an environment of extreme poverty, danger, threat, pollution, ill-health, limited social services and child mortality with an absence of decent shelter, the lack of all but informal sector employment (especially for women), basic infrastructures and environmental quality, including adequate food, clean water and safe sanitation.

By and large the urban authorities of Nairobi, together with the other five municipalities mentioned, cannot tackle the vastness of the problems, with consequent major threats to social stability, public health and safety and the quality of life. The quality of educational systems is especially at threat, but the notion of sustainable educational development within a framework of sustainable cities is not necessarily the leading developmental priority.

Future urbanization

The past and recent urbanization of the country is discussed in detail above. Here, however, it is important to re-stress the future intensified pressures of urbanization. Nairobi's population rose from approximately 600,000 in 1970 to 1.3 million in 1980. It is estimated to reach 5 million by the year 2000. Mombasa's population has risen from 314,148 in the 1979 census to 500,000 in 1989 and is expected to double by the end of the century. In the municipalities of Kisumu, Eldoret, Thika and Nakuru the growth is parallel and a number of other large concentrations are expected to develop and outgrow the capacities of their education and social services systems.

The urbanization of Kenya is estimated to grow from about 2.3 million in 1980 to about 8.6 million in 2000. If Kenya's urban areas continue to grow at the same rate as that of the 1970s, by the year 2000 they will have to accommodate 2.5 times as many people as in 1980. Thirty per cent of the total urban population will reside in Nairobi and its satellite towns – with attendant administrative and planning problems, and the provision of social services including education by already financially overstretched, and even bankrupt, administrations.

Financial viability of municipalities

Managed by municipal authorities and commissions, most of Kenya's urban areas are financially destitute, which adds to the all-pervading sense of urban crisis. Developmental priorities within this stark context include the search for adequate housing and social services of realizable standards to all residents. In reality, the scale of needs of the public housing and public services programmes, including education, extends beyond the scope of government, which calls for a pragmatic approach to self-help mobilization for housing, education and wider social services. The marriage of large-scale government funding and small scale ('harambee') grass-roots initiatives within the spheres of housing and education, although an appealing framework for action, appears unable to arrest the increasingly appalling, disparate and inequitable conditions within the urban areas and fulfilling the realistic basic human needs in shelter (first), education and employment (thereafter) as a framework for future development and the arrest of urban growth and decline. Whilst the urban housing needs of the future have been in part identified (eg, through the 1983 and 1990 housing surveys), the urban educational needs of the present and the future have not yet been clearly mapped.

The indebtedness and unmanageability of the urban areas is best illustrated through the case of Nairobi, although its parlous state is mirrored by other municipalities. The elected City Council was abolished by the Ministry of Local Government in 1983 and replaced by the appointed Nairobi City Commission. Although it spent Shs 15 million on education in 1989/90, this leaves much of Nairobi without educational satisfaction (in Jan 1991, KShs 42 = £UK1). The City Commission has enormous debts, as the Chairman of the City Commission disclosed in December, 1988. Parastatal organizations, including Kenya Railways, owed the Commission Shs 1.5 billion; the private sector owed Shs 400 million; government departments owed Shs 400 million (the Ministry of Local Government alone Shs 301 million for water, land rates and garbage collection).

The implications for educational resourcing can be illustrated within the other municipalities. For example, in 1990, Kisumu, too, like other municipalities, faced bankruptcy and the inability to administer its social services including education. In 1988/1989, its projected expenditure was Shs 78 million, its estimated income was Shs 24 million. (Nairobi's income from the service charge had been Shs 150 million over the period 1988/90, although how this was spent was a source of complaints to residents. Why not on education?) In 1990, the Kisumu Municipal Commission owed Shs 112.4 million to private contractors as a result of financing municipal housing projects. Equally, it owed Shs 1.5 million to suppliers of equipment to municipal primary schools (including: Shs 1.1 million to the defunct Kenya Schools Equipment Scheme for equipment supplied in the period 1981/1988 (!); Shs 231,958 to the parastatal books supplier, Jomo Kenyatta Foundation, for books during the period 1987/1990; a further Shs 53,182 to another parastatal, the Kenya Literature Bureau, for books supplied in the same period; and Shs 89,030 for school equipment obtained from local suppliers in the same period). The consequence of these debts, not surprisingly, was the decision of educational suppliers to stop the deliveries of all supplies to the municipality's 44 primary schools. These, in any case, were (in common with all schools in the country) already suffering severe materials shortages as a result of financial shortages and the resourcing demands of the national education reform ('8-4-4') introduced in 1985 (and discussed more fully in Chapter 14).

The reactions to the paralysis of municipal (and city) authorities have been dramatic, further paralysing their ability and capacity to improve the management of social services and education. For example, creditors sought to impound Kisumu Municipal Council vehicles. In May, 1990, armed police took control of the Kisumu Town Hall following the decision of the Ministry of Local Government to dissolve the crisis-torn Municipal Council, so that like Nairobi, it became managed by an appointed Commission instead of an elected Council.

The impact of the management and resourcing crisis upon education is a familiar one, repeated in all the towns. Although Kisumu's 1989/90 Budget of Shs 14 million for education was a 33 per cent increase from 1987/88 (and it could show Shs 688,600 from nursery school fee income), like elsewhere, Kisumu was unable to provide adequate schooling of adequate quality. For example, of 3,743 pupils who sought Standard 1 places in the town in 1989 (including children from the rural districts outside the municipality), only 2,528 secured places. The overspill either sought places elsewhere, putting pressure on other (probably rural) systems, sought places in a growing number of low-quality private schools or because part of the other familiar pattern of out-of-school street gangs.

The enormous pressures exerted by the rapidly escalating population exceeds the capacities of the municipalities to satisfy them and the fate of large groups of urban children hangs precariously in the balance. The specific dimensions of this are explored in detail in Chapter 14.

References

Central Bureau of Statistics (1986) *Urban Housing Survey, 1983, Basic Report*, Nairobi: CBS, Ministry of Planning and National Development.

Mulcasingh, VC (1990) *Growth of African Cities*, in Obudho *et al.*, op cit.

Obudho, R A (1974) *Development of Urbanisation in Kenya: A Special Analysis and Implications for Regional Planning Strategy*, New Brunswick, New Jersey, unpublished PhD Dissertation, Rutgers University.

Obudho, R A (1979) 'The Nature of Kenya's Urban Demography', *African Urban Studies*, 4.

Obudho, R A (1982) *Urbanisation of Kenya: A bottom up approach to development planning*, Washington: University Press of America.

Obudho, R A (1986) 'Urbanisation and spatial planning in Kenya; A case for bottom up approach to planning', paper presented at Silver Springs Seminar, Nairobi, April.

Obudho, R A and Muganzi, Z S (1987) *Population growth and urban change; a case study of Nairobi, Kenya*, paper presented at the third meeting of the International Geographical Union's Commission on Urban Systems in Transition, University College, Dublin, June.

Obudho, R A, Ondiege, P O, Krodha, G O, and Syagga, P M (1990) *Nairobi and its Environs: Proceedings of the First International Conference on Urban Growth and Spatial Planning of Nairobi, Kenya, December 13–17, 1988* Nairobi: University of Nairobi Centre for Urban Research.

Ominde, S H (ed) (1987) *Population and Development in Kenya*, Nairobi: Heinemann.

Orwa, W (1990) *Educational Problems and Prospects*, in Obudho *et al.* op cit.

Thuo, R (1990) *Education in Nairobi*, PhD thesis in progress, University of London, Institute of Education.

UNICEF (1989) *Situation Analysis of Children and Women in Kenya*, Nairobi: UNICEF.

7. Urban educational issues in The Netherlands

Theo Veld

The urban context: a case of educational inequality

Since the 1960s education in the urban context has captured the attention of the public, students of education and responsible authorities. The reason for this interest is that the urban microcosm demonstrates the wide gap in the welfare state between the actual functioning of education and the ideal of equal educational opportunities. Differences between urban primary schools, in the social composition of their school populations, as contexts for scholastic learning and in the school results they muster, make formal uniformity in education flimsy. Primary schools divide pupils unequally over the different types and levels of secondary education. The different secondary schools prepare their pupils for separate segments of the labour market and thus structure their future life-chances.

The societal and political processes that forge the educational system to reproduce the social divisions in society are not readily observed, not even in the urban context. In studies on education often only the outcomes are shown in the form of data on the social distribution of school entries and school results. In their daily routines teachers and policy makers are faced with the massive intertwining of these processes.

It becomes increasingly more difficult for municipal and state agencies to monitor welfare programmes and programmes to counteract social disadvantages in an efficient way. The official data and social statistics on which they rely very often do not adequately characterize the real life circumstances of the citizens. The process of individualization, the development of a grey or black labour market and lasting immigration have resulted in discrepancies between marital status, formal employment and nationality on the one hand and real economic dependencies and membership of ethnic minority groups on the other.

In Dutch social research on education there is no tradition of explicitly studying education in its urban context. The research on educational disadvantages, however, most often deals with schools and social categories that are overrepresented in the cities. This finding and the harsh school reality in the inner cities has led to a branch in educational policy geared to the so called 'plural determinants of educational disadvantages' in educational priority areas or problem cumulation areas. The purpose of this chapter is to describe the development and content of this policy. First, some indications are given of the concentration of social disadvantaged groups in the Dutch cities and on the poor educational results of their children.

Concentration of the disadvantaged in the cities

Urbanization patterns

The Netherlands has a population of 15 million. Some 6.8 million live in 21 urban agglomerates of a hundred thousand inhabitants and more. Almost 40 per cent of the population lives in commuter or industrialized districts and 10 per cent in rural communities. Despite its urbanized character Holland has only four agglomerates of more than half a million inhabitants; the central municipalities of these four agglomerates are Rotterdam, Amsterdam, The Hague and Utrecht. The cities of Rotterdam and Amsterdam have respectively 580 and 680 thousand inhabitants; including their suburbs each comes to just above one million. The ten agglomerates in the western provinces of Holland form together a belt of cities called De Randstad (in English: The Bandtown or Ring city).

The polycentric character of urbanization in the Netherlands is partly a result of the planning of space since the 1960s. This planning was not directed at organizing processes of social differentiation that normally go with urbanization. So, the upwardly mobile social strata flooded into the suburbs and commuter towns and the social composition of the former working-class neighbourhoods narrowed down to the lowest social strata. In the 1960s central and local authorities accepted the physical degeneration and social disintegration of the old working-class neighbourhoods and made plans for the reordering and rebuilding of the areas. Societal protest in the 1970s forced them to make a major effort for physical and social renewal of these localities. The effectiveness of that policy was undermined by the negative effects that growing industrial unemployment had on the life-chances of the unschooled and dependent people, especially in these neighbourhoods (Deben *et al.*, 1990).

Disadvantaged groups

The large towns in Holland have more than their share of the disadvantaged categories of the population: ethnic minorities, long-term unemployed, recipients of social security, pensioners and lower social classes. In the towns these groups are concentrated in the old working-class neighbourhoods. About 750,000 or 5 per cent of the population in the Netherlands belong to an ethnic minority group, ie a group with a non-indigenous culture and a low position in society. As in other countries, a large proportion of these immigrant groups were attracted by the opportunities the large towns offered to unschooled labour. Ethnic concentration and chains of immigration reinforced this tendency. In Holland the largest ethnic minority groups are from the former colonies: Surinam, the Antilles and Aruba and from the Mediterranean countries that provided foreign workers in the 1960s, especially Turkey and Morocco (WRR, 1989, pp. 65–9). Table 7.1 shows their disproportionate share in the population of the four largest towns.

Table 7.1 *The proportional distribution of minority groups as compared to the total population over types of municipalities in 1986*

Ethnic origin	*Four towns*	*Other towns > 100,000*	*Small municip.*	*Total*	*Abs.*
Turkey	37	30	33	100	177,000
Morocco	48	10	42	100	139,000
South-European*	43	12	45	100	58,000
Surinam	59	12	29	100	210,000
Antilles	32	21	47	100	66,000
Total population	13	12	75	100	14.5 million

* Italy, Spain, Portugal, Yugoslavia and Greece.

Source: Entzinger *et al.*, 1990, p. 101.

In the four main towns there are 29 neighbourhoods where ethnic minorities form more than one third, in six of them even more than half of the population. Most often they are working-class neighbourhoods built in the late nineteenth or early twentieth century. A few are recently built like the Bijlmermeer in the south-eastern part of Amsterdam (Entzinger and Stijnen 1990, p. 117).

In comparison with other countries Holland has a small labour force, mainly due to the low participation of women in paid labour. Nevertheless a high percentage of the Dutch labour force is unemployed – in 1989 a total of 13.8 per cent. Unemployment is concentrated in the four largest cities where especially the ethnic minorities and poorly educated are affected. In 1988, Amsterdam had the highest percentage of unemployed: 25 per cent of the working population. The percentages for the other three cities were Rotterdam 21, The Hague 20 and Utrecht 19. For minority groups in these towns the unemployment rates were around 30 per cent, except for Utrecht with 20 per cent. People who are unemployed for more than two years form the 'hard core' of unemployment. In 1988, 35 per cent of the Dutch unemployed belonged to this hard core, in Amsterdam 39 per cent, in Rotterdam 46 per cent and in The Hague and Utrecht 34 per cent and 35 per cent respectively.

As a consequence of high long-term unemployment and high divorce rates, many households in the cities are dependent on welfare. Of the main cities, Rotterdam has the largest number of such households. In 1989 about 30 per cent of its households had to live on welfare. Rotterdam households that had welfare as the only source of income were in 27 per cent of cases female-headed families and in 41 per cent households of single persons, mostly of pensioners (Oude Engberink, 1987, p. 170). Table 7.2 shows the income distribution in the four main towns of Holland compared to the national income distribution. Since the legally guaranteed minimum income in Holland varies with the composition of the household (roughly between 13 and 22 thousand florins), the income categories A and B are partly a reflection of the high proportion of welfare dependents in the cities. The high proportion of female-headed families among the welfare recipients is addressed by students of poverty through the concepts of the feminization and infantization of poverty. By these terms they draw attention to the risk of the perseverence of poverty among these families and to

Table 7.2 *Proportional distribution over income categories of the population of the cities as compared to the nation (at 1.1.1988)*

	A	*B*	*C*	*D*	*E*	*Total*
Amsterdam	25.6	23.4	19.6	17.2	14.2	100
Rotterdam	24.7	23.6	19.2	17.8	14.7	100
The Hague	21.1	22.4	19.5	18.2	18.8	100
Utrecht	24.4	22.6	20.2	18.0	14.8	100
4 cities	24.2	23.1	19.6	17.7	15.4	100
The Netherlands	20.2	19.8	20.0	20.0	20.0	100

Note: Income categories in FL: A = ⩽15.200; B = from 15.200 to 21.300; C = from 21.300 to 26.000; D = from 26.000 to 31.600; E = ⩾31.600

Source: Externe Commissie Grote Stedenbeleid, 1989, p. 18.

the possibility of transmittal of poor life-chances through education into the next generation (NRMW, 1988, p. 51).

There is a wide consensus in the Netherlands that the high level of unemployment is primarily of a structural type. It makes the creation of new jobs very urgent. New employment would at the same time diminish welfare expenditure and governmental deficits. Government cannot do much directly to further employment. A decrease in the relative price of labour, realized in the last decade, is hoped will stimulate economic activity. Frictions in the labour market play a secondary role in the unemployment rates. The groups with the lowest levels of education and training do not satisfy the rising qualification demands of the labour market. A better balance between supply and demand of labour is expected from a combination of policies: reorganization of the labour market agencies, coordination between these and municipal welfare agencies, the supply of a wide variety of training programmes and stronger incentives for accepting work. It is feared, however, that even with these policies the long-term unemployed will not be reached and that their marginalization will turn out to be irreversible.

Manifestations of educational inequality in the cities

It is well known that social disadvantages in families such as lower social class, ethnic minority origin and long-term unemployment correlate negatively with indicators of school results of children from these families. Though there is little systematic data on this, it is obvious that children of disadvantaged groups are over-represented in the urban context. For example, more than a quarter of the pupils in primary education in the four cities are from an ethnic minority background (Entzinger and Stijnen, 1990, p. 243). Comparative figures on educational participation of minority and majority groups shed light on inequality in school results in the cities.

In the Dutch education system the main division at the secondary level is between general and (pre-)vocational education. When pupils are around 12 years old and have had eight years of basic education, they have to make the decisive choice between schools for these types of education. In both types there is, after a transition class, a choice between a wider range of courses. So, in the second year, the school population is differentiated even more. The differentiation in the (pre-)vocational school mirrors the division of paid and unpaid labour: technical, agricultural, commercial, home economics, etc. The differentiation in the schools for general education is between junior-general, senior-general and pre-university education. Figure 7.1 shows the structure of the Dutch education system at the secondary and tertiary level; omitted from the diagram are adult and special education.

Choices in the education system are not irreversible; a pupil may transfer from one to another type of education. For example, more than one third of certificated pupils from junior general secondary education continue their education in the last classes of senior general secondary education. Apart from

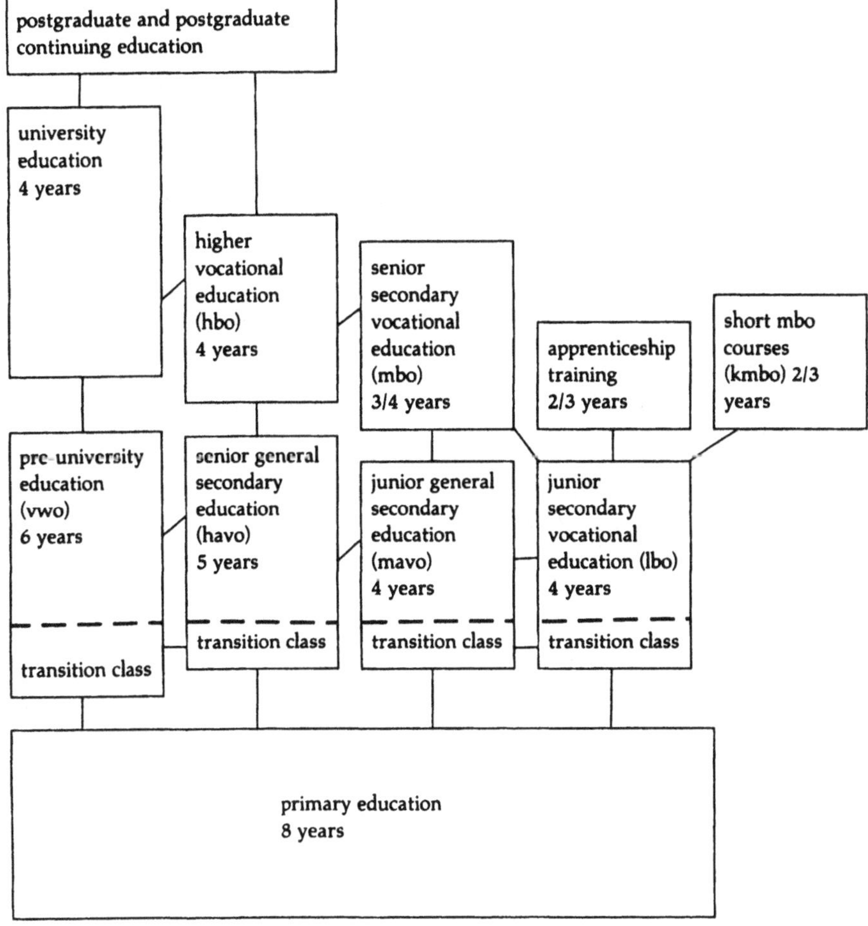

Figure 7.1 *The Dutch education system*

Table 7.3 *Proportional (percentage) distribution per ethnic group of pupils between 13–18 years over types of education*

	Primary school	*Junior education**	*Other types***
Morocco	19.8	69.4	10.8
Turkey	12.1	70.7	17.2
Surinam	8.6	61.7	29.7
Antilles	6.1	69.5	24.4
Dutch-indigenous	4.2	43.8	52.1

* junior general secondary plus junior secondary vocational education.

** senior general secondary plus pre-university education.

Source: WRR, 1989, p. 142.

this, upward transfers are quite rare, especially between junior general and junior vocational education. The Dutch law on compulsory education compels young people to attend school until they are 16. By that age they may have finished a junior school for vocational or general education. A lot of the young people attend types of secondary education that have a higher status: senior general secondary education or pre-university education. To get their certificate they stay in school until they are at least 18.

Table 7.3 indicates the types of education the school population of 13–18 years is receiving. It reflects large differences between ethnic groups at the age at which primary school is finished and in the types of secondary schools attended. The differences are the biggest between children of Dutch origin on the one hand and those of Turkish or Moroccan origin on the other hand. As in other indicators children of Surinam and Antilles origin are in the middle ground. A major reason for this is their better knowledge of Dutch, since it was used as the official language in their homeland. These figures do not show how many pupils of different ethnic groups are early school leavers. There are estimates that around 20 per cent of Turkish and Moroccan girls even elude the law on compulsory education (Vlug, 1985).

Table 7.4 shows the proportion of pupils per school type and ethnic group that were certificated. The figures indicate the type of school last attended. The contrasting percentages show the amount of school drop-out.

Table 7.4 *Percentage of certificated school-leavers per school type and ethnic group*

	Turkey	*Morocco*	*Surinam*	*Antilles*	*Dutch*
Junior secondary vocational	43	34	69	64	70
Junior secondary general	41	*	53	64	72
Senior secondary vocational	64	*	60	52	84
Senior general and pre-university	*	*	65	52	74
Higher vocational	*	*	75	71	84
University	*	*	77	74	87

* = less than 25 cases in the survey sample.

Source: Ibid, p. 144.

Educational policy and the educationally disadvantaged

Educational policy in Holland is a responsibility of the central government which, on the basis of statutory laws, gives detailed regulations for many aspects of school organization. Lower authorities have mainly a role in the management and administration of schools; for the public schools these tasks are performed by the municipalities, for the private schools by foundations or associations. All schools are subsidized according to uniform norms by the Ministry of Education that thus provides almost 100 per cent of their expenses. It will be obvious that this system has prohibited the development of any independent urban educational policy. An advantage is the equivalence it produces in schools, school equipment, curricular and certificates. It discourages, however, local initiatives for educational policies directed at specific problems and circumstances.

The forerunners of the educational priority policy

As in many other countries around 1970, the public and academic discussion on equality of education concentrated on deficits in the preparation for school resulting from the primary socialization in the lower social classes. Thus from 1972 onwards the Ministry of Education provided the financial basis for three large experimental compensatory and enrichment programmes. These programmes were of course situated in urban environments, in Amsterdam, Groningen and Rotterdam.

The programme (IPA) in Amsterdam provided extra facilities for innovation in the schools and for cooperation between schools and community welfare organizations. The methods and contents of the programme were directed at narrowing the gap between schools and families and at integrating school in the life of the pupils. Experiments included differentiation in the content of traditional core subjects, groupwork and thematic learning in the new subject of language and world orientation.

The programme in Groningen (GEON) was aimed at the transfer of teaching skills and course material that would enable teachers to support the learning of children from disadvantaged backgrounds. Under the OSM programme in Rotterdam, courses for more effective learning of the basics were developed and introduced into schools. A programme for stimulating parents to undertake school supportive activities with their children was included (Slavenburg *et al.* 1989). For a full discussion of the Rotterdam programme, see Chapter 16.

Summative evaluations on the first mentioned programme were published around 1980, on the longer lasting programme of Rotterdam in 1988/89. As in many compensatory and enrichment programmes in the USA, the mixed findings in Holland indicate the complexity of educational inequality and the difficulty in counteracting it. Relatively better school results were realized, but the improvement in the relative position of the children was lost when they no longer participated in the programme.

While these experimental programmes were under way, in 1974 the Ministry of Education introduced the Policy for Educational Compensation. It provided extra facilities for schools with large numbers of pupils with social disadvantages; as such it formed the basis for the lasting funding of the educational priority programmes.

In the 1970s the number of pupils from ethnic minorities was growing as the former colony Surinam became independent in 1975 and migrant workers from Turkey and Morocco reunited with their families in Holland. For those pupils who could not understand Dutch and were unfamiliar with the mores of Dutch education, intake/preparation groups were set up. The government started to subsidize Minority Language and Culture Teaching (OETC). Such courses of five hours a week were given partly during normal school hours by assistant-teachers recruited in the homeland. The official aim was to enhance the reintegration of the children to the land of origin when their families would remigrate.

The provision of OETC was only partly induced by a guideline adopted in 1977 by the EEC countries. The guideline says in its main article (Art. 3) that member-states in cooperation with the states of origin of migrants should develop a policy for the provision of education to migrant children in the language and culture of their homelands; this education should be given in coordination with the normal school programme. The verbal content and judicial status of the guideline is such that it leaves much discretion to the individual countries as long as they demonstrate steps being taken towards such a policy.

In Holland, professionals supporting schools with mixed populations developed a growing awareness of the ethnocentricity and prejudices imminent in the normal functioning of the institution and in the standard curricular materials. They became convinced that education ought to contribute towards a mutual understanding between pupils of different cultural backgrounds, preparing the new generation for living in a multicultural society. The professionals called for intercultural education as a principle under which all curricula and procedures had to be reconsidered. In practice, intercultural education gave birth to special projects in which the different cultures of the pupils were presented in the schools. Quite often the emphasis thereby fell on folkloric type of information (Fase *et al.*, 1989).

The Educational Priority Policy (OVB)

Around 1980 the government no longer took remigration, but lasting immigration as the departure point for its policies towards ethnic minorities. It had developed an awareness of the plural character of social disadvantages: social class, ethnic minority and gender. As a consequence, the programmes through which schools and welfare organizations tried to combat social disadvantages were widened to include not only the lower social classes, but also ethnic minorities and girls. The programmes were brought under the new heading of the Educational Priority Policy (OVB).

Three important instruments are used within the OVB. The first concerns school resources. When establishing staffing levels at primary schools the presence of educationally disadvantaged pupils is taken into account. Technically speaking, higher weights are ascribed to pupils with family backgrounds such as ethnic minority, lower social class, long term unemployment, one parent family, disabled parents. According to the weighted school population, extra staff may be provided. The same sort of scheme operates in secondary education.

The second instrument involves the creation of educational priority areas.

Areas designated as disadvantaged in socio-economic terms are entitled to extra support provided that educational establishments and welfare organizations in the area are prepared to tackle educational disadvantages jointly and systematically. Of course this instrument applies mainly to urban areas. At present 70 educational priority areas have been identified, of which 30 are in the four main cities. The 70 areas involve a total of 903 primary schools, 167 special schools, 388 secondary schools and 518 welfare organizations (Ministry of Education, 1989, p. 107).

The third instrument comprises support, in the form of provision of advice and information, curriculum development and training (including in-service training). The Ministry of Education intends to provide a statutory basis, particularly for the first two instruments, in the legislation on education.

Since 1987 the results of OVB have been systematically evaluated. On the whole the extra resources have not led to big changes in objectives and methods of teaching in the individual priority schools (Tesser and van der Werf, 1989). Still, the practices inside the priority areas are more goal-directed and innovative. This is probably partly a result of the fact that the status of priority area is assigned only on the basis of specific programme proposals. There are modest improvements in the proportions of pupils with an ethnic minority background that attend other types of education than junior vocational education. It is unclear how much of this effect is produced by the extra attention provided for under OVB and how much by the longer time the younger cohorts of ethnic minorities have lived in Holland.

Educational policy for the minorities

Since 1985 Minority Language and Culture Teaching (OETC) and intercultural education have been included in the Act on Primary Education. Intercultural education is prescribed as an aim for all schools and all subjects. In 1990 there were still hardly any specific curricula and materials developed in line with this perspective, so schools have to develop their own material and projects. A recent study estimated that 10 per cent of schools are actually implementing multicultural education, 19 per cent are willing to take steps to do so and 18 per cent are making preparations. The majority of schools have no intention of introducing multicultural education. In practice, schools with an ethnic mixed population must often try to implement this principle in their teaching (Fase *et al.*, 1989). Meanwhile specialists discuss whether true intercultural education ought to be antiracist and how ethnocentrism and cultural relativism can be avoided.

The official objectives for OETC are formulated as to teach pupils their native language, to familiarize them with their culture, to help them develop a positive self-image and healthy self-awareness and to diminish the divide between school and home. OETC is not offered to all minority groups. Courses are provided for children of Turkish, Moroccan and Moluccan origin, not for children from Surinam and the Antilles. The last groups are not entitled to OETC, partly because they are having fewer problems with Dutch as a second language. Other minority groups, for example the Chinese, do not make use of their formal entitlement to OETC.

OETC is becoming more and more the subject of controversial discussions.

Sociolinguists are criticizing the fact that OETC in most cases is teaching the official language of the country of origin which often differs from the mother tongue spoken in the family of the child. They plead for a genuine adoption of the transition-model, ie, starting education in reading and writing in the mother tongue and on that basis teaching Dutch as a second language. The discrepancy between ideal models and the everyday conditions under which OETC has to function leads some educationalists to a pragmatic position. They argue that the isolation of ethnic minority pupils for part of the school day has negative effects both on the integration of the heterogeneous school population and on the scholastic achievements of minorities in the regular programme. They are not convinced that the positive effects OETC can have on the cultural and individual identity of pupils outweigh the negative scholastic effects; they therefore plead for OETC in an extra-curricular form.

A readily visible aspect of segregation of the educationally disadvantaged is recently attracting much attention; it is the concentration of ethnic minority pupils in particular primary schools. It is labelled the problem of 'black' schools. In 1980, 227 of the more than 8000 schools had a majority of pupils with a foreign background, in 1984 the figure had risen to 368 schools (Entzinger and Stijnen, 1990, p. 143). In the same year there were in The Hague, Rotterdam and Utrecht 32 schools with more than 80 per cent of pupils from ethnic minorities. Dutch educational research is not conclusive on the negative effects of these concentrations on school results and self-esteem for the ethnic minority pupils (De Jong 1989). Policy makers hesitate to propose explicit measures for desegregation as free parental choice and a free admission policy for the high proportion of denominational schools are basic values in the Dutch educational system. The few local plans for enhancing desegregation of ethnic minority groups by an explicit housing policy were criticized for their alleged discriminatory character.

A more recent development is important with respect to segregation in education. Groups of parents from ethnic minorities are making use of the freedom in the Dutch educational system to provide schooling based on their own religious creed. As a consequence, the first Muslim and Hindu schools have qualified for subsidy by the Ministry of Education. Dutch society, until the 1960s, associated denominational segregation with social emancipation. It is as yet uncertain whether the dominant and minority groups are willing to accept a revival of this emancipation strategy.

Opportunities for an urban educational policy

It has been shown that the highly centralized Dutch educational system was in the last two decades under pressure to provide policies directed at disadvantaged groups and schools. The educational priority policy and educational policy for minorities exemplify this development. These policies differentiate on the basis of social criteria between formally equal pupils and schools. The same tendency of problem-orientation and differentiation can be observed in some late branches of the housing and labour market policies. This chapter mentioned the urban renewal policy; the policy of problem cumulation areas is another example. It subsidizes cooperative projects of labour market agencies, municipalities and welfare agencies directed at offering training and temporary jobs in the public sector to long term unemployed (VNG, 1989).

The centralized character of the Dutch state and of its policies have also come under criticism through the debate in the 1980s on the welfare state (eg, Ringen, 1989). Issues in that debate are the control and efficiency of public services and the public support for the welfare state. The criticism has fostered new ideas about forms of public administration: output-financing, earmarking of funds, deregulation and decentralization. Even new ways of producing public services are discussed: private–public partnerships and privatization of services.

The chances for an independent urban policy geared at counteracting social disadvantages and their manifestations in urban education will be enhanced by two forms of decentralization the central state envisages at this moment. The first is a system of lump-sum-financing in education. It will give the schools free decisions on the spending of a total amount of money while at the same time introducing control on output criteria. A difficult question will be what criteria will be used to determine the level of the individual lump-sums. The second form of decentralization is the policy for social renewal, introduced in 1990 (Commissie Sociale Vernieuwing, 1989). One can see it as the continuation in an integrated form of the policies for urban renewal, educational priority areas and problem cumulation areas. The sole administrative instrument of the state is a covenant with a municipality, whereby, the state offers a lump-sum in exchange for commitments by the municipality to a local programme to fight social disadvantages. The municipality stimulates the cooperation between agencies from different sectors of the public services, private institutions and businesses. Some towns hope that, under this regime, cooperation between public and private education will also develop. Critical to this social renewal policy is that the central state brings the parts of the budgets for sector policies under the heading of social renewal and suspends the many regulations involved.

The future will show whether these new strategies lead the way to policies for each town separately, directed at mastering its own social problems and setting free innovative social forces.

References

Commissie Sociale Vernieuwing (1989) *Het Nieuwe Rotterdam in sociaal perspectief. Rapport van de Comissie Sociale vernieuwing, ingesteld door CvB Rotterdam in oktober 1988, uitgebracht op 15 september 1989*, Rotterdam: Gemeente Rotterdam.

Calcar, C van (1977) *Innovatieproject Amsterdam*, Amsterdam; (Van Gennep).

Deben, L, Heinemeijer, W and v.d. Vaart, D (1990) *Residential Differentiation*, Amsterdam: U.v.A.

Eldering, L and Kloprogge, J (1989) *Different Cultures Same Schools. Ethnic Minority Children in Europe*, Amsterdam: Swets & Zeitlinger.

Entzinger, H B and Stijnen, P J J (1990) *Etnische minderheden in Nederland*, Meppel: Boom.

Externe Commissie Grote Stedenbeleid (1990) *Grote steden grote kansen. Rapport van de Externe Commissie Grote Steidenbeleid*, The Hague: Min. BiZa.

Fase, W, Kole, S C A, van Paridon, C A G M and Vlug, V (1989) *Vorm geven aan intercultureel onderwijs*, Rotterdam: RISBO.

Grace, G (ed) (1984) *Education and the City. Theory, History and Contemporary Practice*, London: RKP.

Jong, M J de (1989) 'Toenemende apartheid in het Nederlandse onderwijs: oorzaken, gevolgen en mogelijke remedies', *Pedagogische Studiën*, 66, 52–60.

Jong, M J de, Mol, A A and Oirbans, P (1988) *Zoveel talen, zoveel zinnen. De behoefte aan lessen in Eigen Taal in het V. O.*, Rotterdam: Vakgroep Onderwijssociologie en Onderwijsbeleid.

Leseman, P M (1989) *Structurele en pedagogische determinanten van schoolloopbanen*, Rotterdam: SAD/OSM.

Ministry of Education (1989) *Richness of the uncompleted. Challenges facing Dutch education*, Report to OECD. Reviews of national policies for Education, The Netherlands, The Hague: Ministry of Education.

NRMW (National Council for Societal Welfare) (1989) *Op zoek naar armoede en bestaansonzekerheid langs twee sporen*, Rijswijk.

Oude Engberink, G (1987) *Nieuw onderzoek naar de financiële situatie van de sociale minima*, Rotterdam: GSD.

Ringen, S (1989) *The Possibility of Politics. A Study in the Political Economy of the Welfare State*, Oxford: Clarendon Press.

Slavenburg, J H, Peters, T A, and van Galen, W L M (eds) (1989) *The Dutch Education and Social Environment Project: Closing Report*, Rotterdam: OSM.

Tesser, P and van der Werf, M P V (1989) 'Educational priority and school effectiveness', in Creemers, B, Peters, T and Reynolds, B (eds) *School Effectiveness and School Improvement*, Amsterdam/Lisse: Swets en Zeitlinger.

Vlug, I (1985) *Schoolverzuim van Turkse en Marokkaanse meisjes; een studie naar de omvang en de redenen van schoolverzuim en schoolverlaten van 12 t/m 16-jarige Turkse en Marokkaanse maisjes en het tegengaan daarvan*, Rotterdam: Vakgroep Onderwijssociologie en Onderwijsbeleid.

VNG (Union of Netherlands Municipalities) (1989) *Wijken in achterstand. Een beschrijving van het PCG-beleid in 18 gemeenten*, The Hague: VNG.

Wilson, W J (1987) *The Truly Disadvantaged, the Inner City, the Underclass and Public Policy*, Chicago/London: University of Chicago Press.

WRR (Advisory Council on Government Policey) (1989) *Allochtonenbeleid*, The Hague: SDU.

8. Urbanization and education in the nation city state of Singapore

Elwyn Thomas

Introduction

Singapore is a republic with an area not much bigger than Britain's Isle of Wight on which 2.8 million people live, all of whom depend mostly on the outside world for food, electricity, most of their fuel and water supply, and are thus very vulnerable to world market forces. The majority of the population are not more than a third or fourth generation and the whole population is composed principally of three ethnic groups, reflecting differences in religion, culture and language. There is little in the way of natural resources and the country has only been in existence as a total and independent entity since 1965, having undergone, previous to that date, colonial exploitation, devastation and defeat in World War II and later experienced a somewhat chequered path to full nationhood. Singapore is planning to be politically, socially and above all economically a fully modernized society before the turn of the century. Planning strategies are clearly related to a deliberate policy of urbanization and industrialization. Singapore, according to World Bank Statistics, has the second largest GNP per capita in Asia after Japan and, according to *The Economist* (1990), has had the fastest economic growth span over 30 years. It ranks among the top of the middle-income countries and has a standard of living comparable with that of Spain. There is little doubt that Singapore's economic success in the 1970s and 1980s is nothing short of spectacular and is likely to continue into the 1990s.

Economic success in Singapore is closely related to the impressive improvements in other sectors of the country's national development, especially education. This chapter will try to look into the future of education in Singapore as well as discuss past and present achievements.

Issues and basic assumptions

It is the view of the author that there are at least three crucial psychological issues concerned with the process of urbanization and education in Singapore. The first issue is concerned with people's rising expectations of their status, standard of living and related earning levels in a society that has limited scope to expand demographically. The second issue relates to the search for a Singaporean identity in the rapidly changing regional and global context. A third issue relates to the question of growing affluence and the pressure by the economic and political order of the nation to survive and the effect this pressure has on the moral well-being and mental health of Singaporean citizens, especially the younger ones. Broadly, the three issues represent different but related aspects of human behaviour. The issue of rising expectations is a part of a wider motivational issue and one that needs careful analysis on the part of all those responsible for planning national development into the 1990s and beyond. The issue of forming a national identity is ultimately political but there are vital psychological processes involved. Identity formation is primarily an individualistic developmental process and yet as individuals share life space with others, it assumes a social significance which becomes influenced by societal pressures. The search for national identity affects the goals and aspirations of religious, cultural and linguistic groups.

The third issue is perhaps the most difficult and challenging of the three raised in this chapter as it deals with controversial and sensitive aspects of human behaviour, namely moral well-being and mental health.

In examining the three issues, it is important to recognize that in predicting any outcomes and formulating any strategies, certain basic assumptions need to be made. First, the discussion that follows assumes that the level of population control will continue to follow the broad pattern it has at present; second, that present policies to promote economic and political stabilities will continue.

Scope and definitional concepts

In this chapter Singapore is considered as an island city state predominantly urban, although there are some tracts of nature reserve and a few existing Malay Kampongs together with some accompanying islands which form part of the republic. Furthermore, Singapore is described here as a series of urban districts which include the so-called new towns such as Ang Mo Kio and Toa Payoh, all of which are in direct communication with the central administrative, business, and shopping areas which could be called greater or central Singapore. The discussion concerned with education will mainly refer to the formal sectors and will make references to all levels of the education system.

Origins and development of Singapore into an urban and industrial society

The origin of Singapore goes back as far as 231 AD, when Chinese explorers reported that an island existed at the end of the Malay Peninsula called by the Malays Temasek, and by the Chinese Pu Luo-Chung. From 1819, when the ruler of Singapore, the Sultan of Johore, signed the treaty with Sir Stamford Raffles, up to 1959, Singapore was under the British Crown. After joining the Malaysian Federation in 1963, it took two further years for Singapore to decide to leave the Federation and to become completely independent.

In the 1950s, there were serious housing shortages and so the government set up the Housing and Development Board (HDB), whose brief was to provide low-cost accommodation in the form of flats for as many as needed them. By 1990 over 90 per cent were housed. The success of HDB is well documented in Yeh (1975) and Wong and Yeh (1985). However, while success is rightly claimed for solving the housing shortages and the creation of a more environment-friendly building programme, it has marked the onset of a fundamental change in family structure from the extended pattern of familialization to more nuclear familial patterns.

On attaining self-government in 1957, the Singapore government's main economic priority was job creation. Industrialization was the main strategy as the traditional entrepôt trade had little scope for further expansion. By the end of the 1980s Singapore's industrialized profile consisted of a dominant financial and business sector in addition to transport, communication and a flourishing trade, construction and manufacturing base. The drive to produce quality products and services meant that education and training had to improve significantly, and the further development of high-technology industries, eg, computer and biomedical products, has meant further demands on the educational system.

Another factor which needs to be mentioned in the drive for industrialization is the changing role of women. In 1960 only 12.6 per cent of the workforce were women; by 1980 it was 34.5 per cent. This increase has had a profound change on the role and status of women as wives and as mothers, and ultimately in the job market where women may be occupying more and more key positions. It is already evident that single women graduates are increasingly postponing marriage and having children later in order to develop their own career pathways.

Another effect of urbanization, especially up to the mid-1980s, was government control of the population. To avoid Singapore becoming overpopulated, the policy in the early 1960s was to give priority to extensive family planning programmes in order to reduce the fertility rate. By 1984, the fertility rate was 1.6 per cent, reduced from 3.6 per cent in 1960, an impressive reduction by any standards. However, as all three ethnic groups highly prize their traditions of having a large family and expecting the younger family members to look after the old later in life, it was not an easy task to convince the Singapore adult population to observe their policy of population control. By 1985 it appeared that the family planning programme had gone too far for some groups of the population, namely the young graduates. The government put into operation several programmes reversing the policy on family planning of the 1960s, by encouraging young parents, especially graduates, to have more than the token two children. This encouragement mainly took the form of tax incentives, and for unmarried young graduates a unit called the Social Development Unit (SDU) was set up to encourage contacts between eligible young people with the ultimate aim of marriage.

The present government, which has had an uninterrupted term of office since 1959, recognizes that in order to industrialize effectively, at least two major issues have to be addressed. First, it is essential to have a well run, relevant and effective public education system which gives equal opportunities of access for all school-age children. Second, any language policy in Singapore has to recognize the important role of English not only as an international language, but as an agent forging national unity between the three ethnic communities while retaining their own particular languages - Mandarin, Malay and Tamil.

Education policy since 1959

The 1960s witnessed major changes in educational policies embarking on an urgent programme to provide basic education for all. This involved an extensive school building programme and a determination to improve technical and vocational education. By the late 1970s, the Goh Report on Education Reform in Singapore set the agenda for pragmatic policy change, making the educational system more adaptable to the needs of Singapore's rapidly growing economy. By the end of the 1980s and the start of the 1990s the theme for educational development linked to economic growth was not just emphasizing better quality but the promotion of excellence in education (Ministry of Education, 1987; Yip and Sim, 1990). Industrialization has not only influenced education but also people's values. Features such as individualism, pragmatism and achievement motivation are vigorously encouraged, while the concept of the larger extended family is undergoing steady re-orientation and, in the case of the better educated, is even being eroded.

Seah and Seah (1983) point out that when Singapore gained its autonomy in 1959 and after its exit from the Malaysian Federation in 1965, education was seen as an agency 'for national integration and political purposes'. With the increasing emphasis put on economic development as well as nation-building after independence, the scene was set for education to play a much more focused role in these areas. In 1959, education policy aimed at equal treatment of Chinese, English, Malay and Tamil languages in the schools with Malay as the national language, in an attempt to unify the multinational character of the country. It also recognized the need to promote the status of mathematics, science and technical subjects in the school curriculum, so necessary for the development of skills in the commercial and industrial sectors. Finally, educational policy underlined loyalty to the state. The break with Malaysia meant, among other things, that the policy of making Malay the national language was substituted for a bilingual policy in which English was put on a par with the child's own local languages. This meant that more stress was put on English, consciously or unconsciously, at the expense of the local language. In 1966 bilingualism was introduced as an official policy, being made compulsory for all secondary pupils. By 1969 the second language had become a public examination subject, reinforcing the government's determination to satisfy local sensitivities and meet national and international needs.

The Chan Chien Kiat Report (1961) had indicated the need for a diversification of the school system in order to prepare for the future demands of Singapore's industrialization. The diversification policy set out the plans for technical and vocational streams to co-exist with general secondary education. By 1969 pupils could be streamed into academic, technical and vocational classes after their primary education. Between 1959 and 1978 the total number of students in all forms of education had increased from 302,866 to 501,416. By 1980, 85 per cent of those aged 6–17 years were attending school (Gopinathan, 1986). This was to rise to nearly 100 per cent by 1990. Unfortunately, due to the many pressures and claims made on the education system and the lack of enough qualified teachers, it was more than likely that the system was going to suffer from gross inefficiency.

In view of the special importance given to education and its crucial role in developing Singapore's only abundant natural resource, namely human resource, the Prime Minister, Mr Lee Kuan Yew set up an Education Study Team under the leadership of the Deputy Prime Minister Dr Goh Keng Swee, who in 1979 was responsible for the Goh Report.

The Goh Report identified five major problems which had to be addressed if the education system were to become more effective and efficient. These problems involved educational wastage, low literacy, ineffective bilingualism, uneven school performance and low teacher morale. There were also problems relating to poor administration of the ministry of education and the lack of any coherent education plan. The Goh Report laid the basis for monitoring as well as reducing pupil wastage by a system of streaming, which was to lead to the pursuit of educational excellence in the system by 1987. The work of the team was also responsible for launching the Curriculum Development Institute (CDI), whose main function was to develop quality curriculum materials for the schools, and to pioneer new projects such as the Monolingual Programme, Confucian Ethics and several programmes on Moral Education for primary and secondary schools.

The setting up of the Schools Council, where ministry officials and school administrators discuss education programmes and crucial issues such as bilingualism in the Republic's literary schemes, has attempted to meet the problems of the Ministry's inefficiency. However, major policy decisions are still made by a small committee of key government personnel in the Ministry of Education and the cabinet. In dealing with the problem of teacher morale and improving teacher quality, the Taylor Report (Taylor, 1980) provided a sound basis for improving pre-service education and training, as well as possibilities for improving in-service provision. In 1987 opportunities were opened up for independent schools to operate alongside the state system. This is seen as a move to improve the quality of secondary education and is in line with a stated policy of promoting excellence in education through an ethos of competition.

The official government statistics for education including the tertiary level (Ministry of Education 1989) (see Table 8.1) show the number of institutions, education offices and enrolments. By 1991, a new key tertiary education institution will be inaugurated (Ministry of Education, 1990) which embraces education, technological subjects and physical education. This development is an expression of the need to expand tertiary-level education in order to meet the demands of furthering industrial and commercial development of Singapore in the 1990s and beyond. In concluding this brief background sketch of educational policies since 1959 and up to the present, three trends appear to dominate policy-making in Singapore and influence the relationship between urbanization and education in this island city state.

The first trend may be termed the pursuit of economic development as a means of survival; urbanization and industrialization are an integral part of this development. Educational opportunity, diversity and efficiency are key tenets to any substantive educational support that is necessary to bring about Singapore's prosperity for the future. The recent drive to promote educational excellence is

Table 8.1 *Education statistics for Singapore 1989*

8.1a *No. of institutions*

	Pre-primary	*Primary*	*Secondary*	*Full school**	*Pre-university*
Govt.	20	158	103	–	38
Govt. aided	19	45	31	8	5
	39	203	134	8	43

Post school	*University*	*Polytechnics*	*Teacher education*	*Technical*
	1	3	1	–

8.1b *Enrolment numbers*

Pre-primary	*Primary*	*Secondary*	*Pre-university*
4,934	257,690	170,855	26,703

University	*Polytechnics*	*Teacher education*	*Technical*
20,600	25,311	1,078	29,604

8.1c *Staffing*

	Pre-primary	*Primary*	*Secondary*	*Pre-University*
Education officers including teachers, principals and vice-principals	232	10,309	7,877	1,536

Source: Ministry of Education Education Statistics Digest, 1989.

* Schools with a primary department.

an indication of this trend. A second trend is the need to develop a sense of 'Singaporeness' amongst a diverse population, by employing education as an agency to forge a national identity while promoting a bilingual language policy and other measures for encouraging ethnic variety. A third trend is in some respects linked with the second, in that it concerns the Singaporean as 'whole person' (Ministry of Trade and Industry, 1986). The limited success of programmes such as the 'Good Citizen', 'Being and Becoming' and 'Confucian Ethics' (Eng, 1989) were meant to make children and adolescents aware of their spiritual and moral needs and to reflect more deeply on this important part of their lives. In view of the ever-present challenges of a rapidly changing society and the conflict of roles that is likely to arise, adolescents, their teachers, their peers and their parents are understandably prone to stress threats to mental health. These trends will be discussed in the remainder of the chapter and linked to the three issues outlined earlier.

Expectations of urban youth: resolution and conflict

Singapore is a meritocratic society. An accompanying feature of such a society is that its youth are exposed and often subjected to a whole set of expectations dictated by others and eventually by themselves. Having expectations is a natural facet of human behaviour, and all of us either overtly or covertly experience making them a part of our drive to live and succeed. Expectations are also closely related to the realization of our goals. For most Singapore youth, exposure to high expectations begins at home with their parents and grandparents, and later on from successful siblings and other family members. It may be argued that this is not necessarily a feature unique to Singapore. This is of course partly true, but what makes Singapore and similar places, eg Hong Kong or Japan, different is the intensity and level of expectation. In Singapore, where human resource is the only abundant source of wealth, the will to survive becomes everyone's preoccupation.

The mix of demographic, topographic, psychological and cultural factors which are found in Singapore, as well as the existence of strong economic and political influences, provide a milieu in which parents and their children have their expectations already determined if they are to remain and earn their living in the island city state. The path to success in Singapore starts with access to pre-school, which is available for most children but is not mandatory. It continues, through various achievement filtering mechanisms such as the Primary School Leaving Examination (PSLE), to a variety of differentiated post-secondary education provisions.

The limiting factor of Singapore's urban environment, however pleasant, clean and orderly the authorities have made it, has a narrow channelling effect on how parents perceive their children's future. These perceptions in most cases rub off on the children. Research (Thomas, 1990) into pupils' perceptions of parental influences in schools show that about one third of parents are perceived consistently to expect their children to become doctors, engineers, bank managers or to be in other senior occupations. The findings also showed that even for pre-university students the influence of parents on their children's career expectations was high.

High expectations at school or technical college, if translated into good examination performance, can lead eventually to high school expectations which include an improved standard of living, higher and more stable salary scales, improved prospects for job promotion and generally a more comfortable life. Much store is set by Singapore adolescents in junior college and young adults in university, that on some future day when they have passed their examinations, vistas will open up in which they may have their own car, their own flat and perhaps even their own house. However, the process of urbanization linked to Singapore's industrialization on such a small land mass means a somewhat restricted future for most youth.

If present policies for education are followed, especially the emphasis on excellence, meritocracy will be carried a few steps further and with it the danger of social conflict. It is clear that however hard young people are going to be asked to work and raise their expectations, the sheer physical limitations of urban Singapore will stand in the way of realizing all expectations. Education alone cannot hope to solve this dilemma, but it should provide some possibilities for preparing Singapore youth for setting alternative goals for their future, that would go some way in resolving the possible social conflict.

A powerful factor in the non-realization of high expectations leading to low pupil self-concepts is that all high expectations are viewed ultimately only as academic. A major direction which education needs to take is to encourage teachers, pupils and their parents to develop attitudes which form equally high expectations for achievements in technical, aesthetic, physical educational pursuits and in community care. This is as much a job for industry, the arts and social welfare as it is for education.

Moulding a national identity as part of urbanization

Singapore, being a state as well as a city, has to ensure that its citizens are aware of a national identity and this role is taken seriously by government and citizen alike. Nowhere are there road signs which indicate city limits or city boundaries. Official correspondence is always headed or countersigned by reference to the Republic of Singapore. For the most part, Singapore is a series of districts and new towns without a mayoral system and tightly under the control of the cabinet. For all intents and purposes, Singapore is run as a nation state where urbanization is recognized as an integral part of national development.

Yet, one is constantly reminded of the rich human diversity that exists within the bounds of this island community. The diversity makes itself felt in the appearance of official government publications in the four official languages, Chinese, English, Malay and Tamil. The celebration of public and religious holidays, which the government has officially designated, serve to reflect ethno-religious sentiments, eg Christmas and Good Friday for Christians, Divali for Indians, Vesak Day for Buddhists and Hari Raya Puasa for Malays. These measures show how the government acknowledges the necessity to respect religious diversity. On the other hand, August 9th marking Singapore's National Day is aimed at putting this diversity into a uniform national context.

Those who are responsible for planning education and its implementation have a particularly difficult path to tread. They must engender values that underpin national identity while at the same time give opportunities for cultural diversity. There is always a danger when a society has a much larger proportion of one cultural group, in this case Chinese (76 per cent) and much smaller minorities of others, that the interests of minority groups could be swamped.

In making the meritocratic principle such a strong uniform feature of schooling, the authorities have not only made a commitment to improving quality in education, so necessary for their fast growing economy, but have also enabled all children irrespective of ethnicity to play their part in national development and eventually share a Singapore identity. The high achievement motivation promoted by home and school is accompanied by the patriotic rituals of saluting the flag and singing the national anthem each day, as well as the ethos of participating in National Day parades. These all serve to strengthen and build up an identity. However, which influences are the stronger in forging national identity is impossible to say, as there is little research on the subject. One thing is nevertheless plain: education has a very important role in the process. Throughout the whole of the urbanized island state of Singapore, we find schools occupying central places in the middle of new towns and other city areas. There is little doubt that the school has a dominant influence on urban life in

Singapore which the government hopes is a valuable ingredient in the development of a national identity.

Conclusion

In this account of education and urbanization of the nation state of Singapore, three issues have constituted the main discussion. The issues of rising expectations, forging a national identity and the promotion of an individual's well-being, are in one way or another the business of education. Education in its institutionalized form, eg, school or college, has as much of a function to promote the expectations of its clientele as to provide solutions to make the expectations realistic and fit in with the opportunities the world of work can or cannot provide. Again, formal education has a very positive role to perform in developing a proper balance between producing loyal Singaporeans and at the same time getting them to take pride in their own ethnic and cultural traditions. In other words, education in schools and elsewhere should have the function of providing a dynamic context between cultural diversity and national identity.

It is clear that the curriculum in its broadest sense is a major factor in meeting the demands that all three issues present. However, looking to the future, an essential element to bear in mind is what role education should have after school and when pupils enter the world of work, for all three issues are as manifest at this time as during schooldays. In many countries, such as the UK, the USA and Australia, the role of adult education has set the scene for the time when the working adults may plan how they can use the increasing amount of leisure time fruitfully and enjoyably. With the constraints that exist and are likely always to exist in urban Singapore, it is probable that, as Singaporeans become ever more affluent, the ethic of living to work will be questioned more intensely. That education in both its formal and informal manifestations has a crucial role to play in such changes is in little doubt. Singapore has, in its relatively short history as an independent urbanized state, had to face some real challenges, all of which ultimately relate to its survival. This small nation state so far appears to have weathered the storm. However, the challenge of the following decades is likely to be more formidable, in that satisfying an affluent population living in such restricted circumstances will require all the resourcefulness and imagination that the political leaders have shown both in the past and at present.

References

Chan Chien Kiat (1961) *Report of the Commission of Inquiry into Vocational and Technical Education in Singapore*, Singapore: Government Printing Office.

The Economist (1990) 'No love lost in Singapore', 316, 7667, p. 55.

Eng, S P (1989) 'Moral education in Singapore; dilemmas and dimensions', in Gielen, U and Miao, E (eds) *Proceedings of the Academia Sinica Moral Values and Moral Education in Chinese Societies* Taipeh, Taiwan: ICP–CCU Publication.

Goh, K S (1979) *Education Reform in Singapore*, Singapore: Ministry of Education.

Gopinathan, S (1986) Education in Singapore 1959–1984, in Ng Cheng Wang (ed) *Singapore Taking Stock*, Singapore: Federal Publications.

Kuo, ECY (1986) 'Confucianism and the family in the urban-industrial society', in Slote, W H (ed) *The Psycho-Cultural Dynamics of the Confucian Family: Past and Present*, ICSK Forum Series No. 8, Seoul: Yougin Compographic.

Ministry of Education (1987) *Towards Excellence in Schools*, Singapore: Ministry of Education.
Ministry of Education (1989) *Education Statistics Digest*, Singapore: Ministry of Education.
Ministry of Education (1990) *Upgrading and Expansion of University Education and Teacher Training*, Singapore: Ministry of Education.
Ministry of Trade and Industry (1986) *The Singapore Economy: New Directions*, Singapore: MTI.
Seah, C M and Seah, L S (1983) 'Education reform and national integration', in Chen, P S J (ed) *Singapore Development, Policies and Trends*, Oxford: Oxford University Press.
Taylor, W (1980) *Teacher Education in Singapore 1980: The Role of the Institute of Education*, Singapore: Institute of Education Publication.
Thomas, E (1989) *Stress Profiles of Singapore Adolescents: Trends, Issues and Implications Research Report*. University of London, Institute of Education/Institute of Education, Singapore.
Thomas, E (1990) 'Filial piety, social change and Singapore youth', *Journal of Moral Education*, 18, 3, pp. 192–205.
Wong, A K and Yeh, S H K (1985) (eds) *Housing a Nation, 25 years of Public Housing in Singapore*, Singapore: Maruzen.
Yeh, S H K (1975) *Public Housing in Singapore: A Multi-Disciplinary Study*, Singapore: Singapore University Press.
Yip, J S K and Sim, W K (1990) *Evoluation of Educational Excellence*, Singapore: Longmans.

9. Urban education in the United States of America

Roger R Woock

Introduction

The story of urban education in the United States in the 1970s and 1980s is one of decline and disarray. The current scene must be placed against deteriorating resources for urban schools and an array of urban social problems, most particularly racism and violence, which have both increased and become more widely visible over the past 20 years.

The evidence for the decline of urban education as a field of specialization is substantial. It includes a significant reduction in the number of subjects taught under this heading in graduate schools of education in major universities in the United States, the collapse of the membership organization for urban educators, and the redefinition of topics chosen for articles in the three journals which focus on urban education in the United States. For example, the July 1990 issue of *Urban Education* includes such articles as 'Students as Volunteers, Personal Competence: Social Diversity and Participation in Community Service', 'Organizational Rituals as Culture Markers of Schools' and 'Current Index to Journals in Education'; *The Urban Review* for March of 1990 includes 'Principals' Relationships with Parents: The Homogeneity Versus the Social Class of Parent Clientele', 'Factors Related to Persistence among Asian, Black, Hispanic and White Undergraduates at a Predominantly White University: Comparison Between First and Fourth Year', 'Vouchers are a Viable Option for Urban Settings: A Response to Andrew Sandler and David E. Keppel'. The themes dealt with in the last four issues of *Education in Urban Society*, a single-issue journal with a rotating editorship, are Reflective Practice in Education, Elementary Schools and Child Abuse Prevention, Issues Based Education and Cultural Diversity, and American Educational Visions of the Future. It is significant that the word urban, and the concept of a specifically urban analysis connecting to urban social theory or indeed to cities in any generic sense, is conspicuous by its absence.

The urban education perspective in the United States, 1960–80

While it is difficult to encapsulate the perspective held by those identified as urban educators in the 1970s and 1980s in the United States the following might serve:

1. The work has generally been ahistorical or where there has been history of urban education as provided by people like Saul Cohen, Michael Katz or Warren Button and their students, it is not linked to contemporary studies. By and large these historians (with the exception of Warren Button) see themselves as being outside urban education as a field of study. On the role of history in urban educational studies, see also Chapter 1.
2. The origins of urban education in the 1960s and its institutional attachment to large urban universities like the City University of New York or large state universities in the middle-west meant that, like other fields within the social sciences, urban theory was virtually absent from urban education. The assumption underlying the work might best be described as liberal, ie, American society in general was fairly benign, progress was perceived to be occurring and urban schools and their students were seen as problems that could be dealt with by systematic intervention. This intervention would take the form of new curricula, new organizational structures in urban schools or other moderate changes in the school system.
3. The view of schools held by urban educators was that schools were important institutions that had an impact on the life of students within them and thus by changing schools, life-chances could be directly affected.
4. Politically, urban educators in the United States were generally Democratic and saw the Democratic party, particularly through the imposition of Federal government policy, as an important vehicle for moving towards solving the problems of urban schools.
5. Urban educators viewed their work as being about the distribution of a good, namely education. Urban education was about the equity of resource distribution.
6. With few exceptions such as the development of the black power movement, urban educators as middle-class professionals saw students in urban schools as passive recipients of new programmes and newly organized structures.

The attack on the assumptions contained in the above perspective and the decline and dismemberment of urban education are important for international scholars and students to understand and it is to this conservative restoration that we will now turn.

The conservative restoration

Ira Shore in *Culture Wars* (1988) identifies three phases of this conservative restoration. The first phase, beginning about 1969, was the attempt to introduce the idea of career education into United States schools and programmes of teacher education. Shore sees the push for career education as one which was anti-liberal arts, anti-dissent, especially intellectual dissent, and also as a movement which depressed rising expectations, particularly from minority group youngsters.

Shore's second phase, from about 1975 to 1982, is characterized as the 'War on Illiteracy' by means of a 'back to the basics'movement. This movement, which of course continues today in North American schools, did not so much argue for reduced expectations as attempt to implement them by eliminating elective programmes in schools and concentrating on the 'three Rs'. Again, as with the earlier phase, the movement was done in the name of a crisis in education which was, and has not yet been, clearly proven or well established.

The third phase and the one which will concern us in more detail began about 1982. Shore characterizes this phase as the 'War for Excellence against Mediocrity'. His sub-title is 'Authority and Inequality Disguised as Excellence and High Tech'. It is this third phase of the conservative reaction which has produced a series of national reports on education which constitute in this author's view the most important and significant attack on urban education and its liberal assumptions. This War for Excellence has produced a rhetoric of crisis. Consider the following:

> Our once unchallenged pre-eminence in commerce, industry, science and technological innovation is being overtaken by competitors throughout the world. . . . If an unfriendly foreign power had attempted to impose on America the mediocre educational performance that exists today we might well have viewed it as an act of war. . . . We have even squandered the gains and student achievement made in the wake of this sputnik challenge. We have in effect been committing an act of unthinking unilateral educational disarmament (National Commission on Excellence in Education, 1983, p. 1).

In explaining the decline of urban education it is difficult to over-emphasize the importance of the collection of reports published in the mid-1980s. *A Nation Prepared* (Carnegie Forum, 1986), offers the following analysis in its executive summary:

> America's ability to compete in world markets is eroding, the productivity growth of our competitors out-distances our own, the capacity of our economy to provide a high standard for all our people is increasingly in doubt as jobs requiring little skill are automated to go off shore and demand increases for the highly skilled. The pool of educated and skilled people grows smaller and the back water of the unemployable rises. Large numbers of American children are in limbo, ignorant of the past and unprepared for the future. Many are dopping out, not just out of school but out of productive society. As in past economic and social crises, Americans turn to education. They rightly demand an approved supply of young people with the knowledge, the spirit, the stamina and the skills to make the nation once again fully competitive in industry and commerce, in social justice and progress and not least in the ideas that safe-guard this society (p. 4).

The main recommendations of this report include:

1. The creation of a national board for professional teaching standards to establish such standards and certifv teachers who meet that standard.

2. A restructuring of the teaching force and the introduction of a new category of lead teachers.
3. Requiring a Bachelors degree in the Arts and Sciences as a prerequisite for the professional study of teaching and developing a new professional curriculum in graduate schools of education leading to a master in teaching degree based on systematic knowledge of teaching, including internships and residency in the schools.

These recommendations, particularly the establishment of a national certification board with the concept of a lead or master teacher and the elimination of undergraduate teacher education are designed to appeal to teacher educators as well as the public at large. The claim of course is to increase the quality of teaching and hence the quality of learning that occurs in the school. The problem is that in the United States well over 90 per cent of teacher education programmes are currently pre-baccalaureate in nature, combining in one degree or, in some cases, two concurrent degrees, academic and professional study. It is also quite true that the national certification board and the various state tests which have been adopted in the United States discriminate against minority teachers and need to be examined very carefully indeed.

An important report which bears directly on the movement away from urban education and its concepts was *Tomorrow's Teachers*, the report of the Holmes Group (1986). Many of the goals of the report are useful, for example, a close connection between universities and schools. Other demands are more questionable, such as the need for examinations to accompany institutional accreditation, a sweeping recommendation to eliminate undergraduate programmes in teacher education, most of which occur in state colleges and non-élite institutions and a specially harsh critique of current programmes preparing primary teachers. All of these recommendations affect most directly those programmes with large minority enrolments and those which prepare teachers for urban schools.

The Governors' Report on Education (1986) introduced market forces directly into educational thinking, planning and development. It is perhaps surprising in what is after all an advanced capitalist society that this was a new development. The Governors' task force praises state initiatives like teacher testing, raising of test scores for admission to teacher education, career structure for teachers which includes notions of master teachers and the development of performance evaluation. The proposals which the Governors advance contain ideas from the other reports: the creation of a national board, the re-building of a system for teacher education and the elimination of undergraduate education majors. In another section of the report, the Governors recommend that where local districts fail to meet minimal standards of student performance, state education officials should be empowered to relieve both local boards or local professional educators and in a sense to take a school system into receivership.

The importance of the attack on undergraduate teacher education with regard to the development of urban education programmes cannot be overemphasized for it is the state colleges or branches of state universities that have carried the burden of preparing urban teachers and developing masters degrees and other urban-oriented graduate programmes. The sustained attack on undergraduate teacher education and indirectly on recruiting minority members into the teaching force are clearly part of the reason for the decline in focus on urban educational issues.

The Carnegie Forum on Education in the Economy and in particular its Task Force on Teaching as a Profession commissioned Lee Schulman and Gary Sykes of Stanford University to develop a detailed proposal for a national board for teaching. The Carnegie Forum at this stage has spent over 20 million dollars on this endeavour. In this proposal, the authors, in describing how one can develop a 'national standard setting body in education', identified two strategies through which this might happen: politics, and markets. Here is their comment on the political approach:

> the political strategy relies on the constitutionally based authority of the state to regulate their professions. The task is to convince policy makers in enough states that a new standard is politically and legally supportable, scientifically achievable, socially and educationally desirable and obtainable at a reasonable cost. Political strategy aims at securing the authority of state law to institutionalize a new standard on a uniform basis throughout the jurisdiction. Once state policy makers become persuaded that the new standard meets these criteria then the law gives rise to the compliance enabling actions which leads to realization of the law's intent (Schulman and Sykes, 1986, p. 18).

Contrast this with their analysis of the market approach to national standards:

> a market strategy seeks to create a demand for teachers at a recognized level of quality. A certificate serves as a signal in a market for services if buyers, in this case employers, develop a preference for board certified teachers then market pressures will be the principal mechanism for propagating the new standard. Eventually market pressures may legitimate the standards to such an extent that state agencies might choose to adopt it for a licenser (Ibid., p. 26).

While some of the reports identified make a passing reference to the need to encourage and recruit candidates for teaching positions for urban schools from minority groups, there is little in them that speaks to the concerns of equality. In fact any reasonably astute forecaster could have pointed out that closing down undergraduate teacher education programmes, whatever its effect on the quality of teacher education, would also have a dramatic effect on those institutions which serve minority and working-class young people educationally.

Urban educators respond

Given the complexity of the education industry in the United States it is not surprising that the above reports produced a large number of responses from the urban education community. Lytle (1990) has suggested that these respondents fall in two categories; the advocacy group and the establishment group. While this is an over-simplified dichotomy it does suggest that both left-liberal urban educators and urban establishment figures saw themselves as being directly under attack by the major reports issued in the middle 1980s.

The more interesting responses came from the critical or advocacy group. They provide a diverse, angry and penetrating view of the current situation in America's urban schools. The earliest of this group of studies *Barriers to Excellence* (NCS, 1985) is a clear response to *A Nation at Risk* and focuses on the millions of poor and disadvantaged children who are at risk as opposed to the nation's economic system. The study is very critical of the kind of schooling available to urban children and calls for significant increases in expenditure on a whole range of programmes. Similar views were expressed in other reports (eg, Carnegie Foundation, 1988; MDC, 1988).

Working in Urban Schools (Cocoran *et al.*, 1988) produced by the Washington-based Institute for Educational Leadership is one of the more interesting urban responses to the major conservative reports. It is primarily a devastating analysis of the working conditions of urban teachers. The report basically argues that no efforts to reform urban schooling will succeed without serious and sustained attention to the working problems of urban teachers. It recommends involving teachers in decision-making, more district level support and better resources, but particularly giving teachers more control over what and how they teach.

The serious analysis and recommendations of these reports is to some extent contradicted or at least muted by another group of reports which can be identified with the urban educational establishment. There is not space in this chapter to comment individually on each of these studies but taken together they constitute either a defence of current 'good' practice or a critique of current practice from the right. Both of these approaches significantly downplay the problems associated with urban education and indeed the problems of America's cities.

Schooling and work

Carnoy and Levin (1985) have identified a different perspective on the decline of urban education in the 1970s and 1980s which can be equated with the decline of democratic forces within education. Their analysis begins with the identification of a paradox in the relationship between schooling and work in the United States. This paradox is based on both similarities and differences. Schools and workplaces are organized in ways which are very similar. Both tend to be large, bureaucratic and impersonal, hierarchical and routinized. Both motivate performance with external rewards like grades and wages rather than depending on the value of the activity itself. Both school and workplaces are dominated by formal authority and in both, time is tightly allocated.

In spite of these similarities in structure and programme, schools do differ from workplaces. Even though education in advanced capitalist societies like the United States is marked by great inequalities, schools do more than other institutions to provide equal opportunities for participation and rewards. The large differences in status and competition between men and women in the labour force are not reflected in education. Women in tertiary education tend to be concentrated in non-scientific and non-technical fields but not to a degree that women are found concentrated in non-technical occupations within the labour force. Whereas the top 20 per cent of the US population in educational achievement received only about twice as large an educational investment as the bottom 20 per cent, the richest 20 per cent of income earners not only earned eight times as much as the bottom 20 per cent but owned and controlled about 95 per cent of the nation's capital. Schooling then, according to Carnoy and Levin, tends to be distributed more equally than capital income or employment status. In addition, many educators believe that what they are doing in the school has its own purposes and is more universal and in some sense more important than simply preparing young people for earning a living.

The paradox of more equal and more democratic schooling preparing youth for a highly structured economic system has influenced many analyses of education. The progressive educators from John Dewey to Holt, Kozol, Bourdieu and Passeron, Apple, Giroux and Aronowitz all argue that the school can create values independent of the workplace. For this group, which Carnoy and Levin call critical progressives, education shapes minds which in turn conditions social relations outside the school. On the other side, those who examine schools from a functional perspective such as Parsons, Dreben, Carnoy and Levin (in the 1970s) and Bowles and Gintis, argue that the structure of social relations in the workplace determines how schools will develop social roles for youth. Education, in this argument, is designed to develop values and skills to fit social relations outside the school. Both the traditional and the Marxist functional view play down the differences between schools and workplaces to argue that what happens in one is a function of what happens in the other.

The implications for urban education of this analysis are quite striking since an important aspect of the urban education perspective is that schooling may be used directly by poor young people as a means to increase earning and status and that urban schools are not a function of what happens in the workplace or on the city streets. Carnoy and Levin are arguing a historical and dialectical relationship between education and the larger society and a perpetual tension between capitalism and democracy. The forces tending towards the imperatives of capitalism on the one hand and democracy on the other may be stronger or weaker depending on a variety of historical or sociological factors. The historical decline of urban education then is caught up in this relationship between capitalism and democracy.

Urban education and young people

In *Turning Points: Preparing American Youth for the Twenty-First Century* (National Governors' Association 1989) a distinguished task force, which includes several urban educators, has published a curious report focused on an overlooked age group, that of adolescents between the ages of 10 and 15. Recommendations of the task force will be familiar to most readers of this chapter; they include:

> Create small communities for learning where stable, close, mutually respectful relationships with adults and peers are considered fundamental for intellectual development and personal growth. Key elements for these communities are schools within schools, students and teachers grouped together as teams and small group advisors that ensure that every student is known well by at least one adult.
>
> Teach a core academic program that results in students who are literate

> including in the sciences, and will know how to think critically, lead a healthy life, behave ethically, and assume the responsibilities of citizenship in a pluralistic society. Youth services to promote values for citizenship is an essential part of a core academic program.
>
> Empower teachers and administrators to make decisions about the experience of middle grade students through creative control by teachers over the instructional program, linked to greater responsibility for students' performance; governance committees that assist the principal in designing and co-ordinating school life programs and autonomy and leaderships between sub-schools or houses to create environments tailored to enhance the intellectual and emotional development of all youth.

Other recommendations include ensuring success for all students – staff middle-grade schools with teachers who are expert in teaching young adolescents – improve academic performance in fostering the health and fitness of young adolescents – re-engage families in the education of young adolescents – connect schools with communities.

This set of proposals sounds very much like many of the curriculum and school innovations tried in the 1960s and 1970s in urban schools, yet in the executive summary there is only one reference to urban neighbourhoods:

> The conditions of early adolescents have changed dramatically from previous generations. Today, young people enter a society that at once denounces and glorifies sexual promiscuity and the use of illicit drugs. They live in urban neighbourhoods and even in some small towns where the stability of close-knit relationships is rare, where the sense of community that shapes their identify has eroded. They will seek jobs in an economy that will virtually require all workers to think flexibly and creatively as only an elite few were required and educated to do in the past.

It is quite clear from the writing and the recommendations that the group of young adolescents identified as at risk are in fact members of urban racial or cultural minorities yet there are virtually no references in the document to either urban, minority, or working-class young people. It is also somewhat discouraging to note that no efforts are made to identify where resources needed to implement these programmes might be found, except to argue that state governments should take a larger role in funding the very expensive programme changes and developments argued for in the report. The report reads as if crack gangs, inter-group murders with automatic weapons and multi-million dollar drug businesses operated by teenagers do not exist and we are once again in the early 1970s.

Conclusion

There is no doubt that the tenor of this chapter is one of discouragement, if not downright despair for the state of urban education in the United States. In spite of the general accuracy of the analysis in the preceding sections, it is by no means true to say that there are not good people attempting to do good work in many urban schools and universities in the United States. What seems lacking now compared with the situation two decades ago is wide-spread support in the rest of the educational community and a more optimistic view of the possibilities of social change.

Perhaps the most disturbing intellectual development of the past 15 years is the 'unthinking excision of education from most studies of social policy and the welfare state'. In *Schooling for All* Katznelson and Weir (1988) argue that universalism, one of the central characteristics of the tradition of schooling for all, provides an important contrast to the categorical and efficiency-based features of most domestic public policies in the United States. In an important sense, education is different from other social services and if we take ideas of democratic citizenship seriously it must be a universally distributed good. In a sense then, the debates around urban education and the conservative restoration conform to the centuries-old debate about how and on what basis public goods are distributed in society. Given conflicts in the world, and the continuing pre-eminence of free market theory domestically, it is difficult to see how concerns about the universality of education and democratic citizenship will soon re-emerge as central concerns of American society.

References

Brimelow, P (1983) 'What to do about America's Schools', *Fortune*, 19 September, p. 1.

Carnegie Forum on Education and the Economy (1986) *A Nation Prepared: Teachers for the 21st Century, The Report of the Task Force on Teaching as a Profession*, Princeton, NJ: Carnegie Foundation.

Carnegie Foundation for the Advancement of Teaching (1988) *An Imperiled Generation: Saving Urban Schools*, Princeton, NY: Carnegie Foundation.

Carnoy, M and Levin, H M (1985) *Schooling and Work in the Democratic State*, Stanford: Stanford University Press.

Cocoran, T B, Walker, J and White, J (1988) *Working in Urban Schools*, Washington DC: Institute of Educational Leadership.

The Governors' Report on Education (1986) *Time for Results*, p. 37.

Holmes Group (1986) *Tomorrow's Teachers*, East Lansing: Michigan.

Katznelson, I and Weir, M (1988) *Schooling for All*, California: University of California Press.

Lytle, J H (1990) 'Reforming urban education: A review of recent reports and legislation', *The Urban Review*, 22, 3.

MDC Inc. for the Charles Stewart Mott Foundation (1988) *America's Shame, America's Hope: Twelve Million Youth at Risk*, Chapel Hill, NC.

National Coalition of Students (1985) *Barriers to Excellence: Our Children at Risk*, Boston, MA.

National Commission on Excellence in Education, Washington DC (1983) *A Nation at Risk: The Imperative for Education Reform*, Washington, DC.

National Governors' Association, Centre for Policy Research and Analysis (1989) *Turning Points: Preparing American Youth for the 21st Century*, New York: Carnegie Corporation of New York.

Research and Policy Committee of the Committee for Economic Development (1987) *Children in Need: Investment Strategies for the Educationally Disadvantaged*, New York: CED.

Schulman, L and Sykes, G (1986) 'A National Board for Teaching', paper commissioned for the Task Force on Teaching as a Profession, Carnegie Forum on Education and the Economy (Unpublished).

Shore, I (1986) *Culture Wars: School and Society in the Conservative Restoration 1969–1984* London: RKP.

Urban Education (1989) 24, 3, Sage Periodicals Press.

Urban Review: Issues and Ideas in Public Education (1989) 21, 2, Human Sciences Press, Inc.

US Department of Education (1987) *Schools that Work: Educating the Disadvantaged*, Washington, DC: US Government Printing Office.

10. Urbanization and education: the USSR perspective

Nikolai D Nikandrov and Mikhail L Levitski

Introduction

The urbanization processes in the USSR commenced before the revolution of 1917. In fact, we can well take the year of 1861 (the abolition of serfdom) as the beginning of the very noticeable growth of urban population and urban way of life. After that event peasants could leave their villages and go to live in towns if they so chose, and if they had someone or something to maintain them there. Some of them chose to go to the towns at all costs – and the cost was very often high, for they could only take up the meanest jobs or just beg in front of churches or pubs.

After the revolution and the end of World War I, former soldiers, who were for the most part peasants, flocked to their villages and were ready to settle on their newly acquired land. But the Civil War and the events that followed meant terrible suffering for the whole people. First came the devastation of the war. Then came 'collectivization' (setting up collective farms with very little or no property left to each family). In most cases it was also under pressure that the 'kolkhozes', the collective farms, were organized, and many peasants were forcibly removed from their land and sent to far off places for imputed sabotage or just for being a little better off than the others. In the late 1960s and 1970s many small villages were 'liquidated' as having no future. Some were left by their inhabitants (especially the young) in search of better living conditions and schools for their children. Migration to cities and the growth of urban population, then, have not been smooth processes.

Since the problem of getting food and other consumer goods has always been less acute in the cities and towns, the population migration was a one-way process. At the same time, it has always been a prestigious thing to have a 'datcha' (a country house) as well as a flat (or, less often, a house) in town. This is why the urban population has been constantly growing, as is shown in Table 10.1.

It goes without saying that the school population (the word being taken as a generic term to mean any educational establishment) has been growing correspondingly, though for obvious reasons (size of school) the number of primary schools in the country has always been greater than the number of secondaries. In 1988, for example, there were 130,557 schools in the country

Table 10.1 *Population growth and urban population growth of the USSR*

	1959	*1970*	*1981*	*1989*
Population	208.8	241.7	266.6	286.7
Urban population (millions)	100.0	136.0	168.9	188.8
%	47.9	56.3	63.4	66.0

which included 96,388 village schools (73.8 per cent) and 34,169 schools in towns (26.2 per cent). In the same year there were 43 million pupils in the country of whom 61 per cent went to urban schools and 39 per cent to village schools.

Managing and resourcing urban schools

Both rural and urban schools are now in the process of evolution or, rather, in the balance; for many would say that there is much discussion and little change in the way that education in general and urban education in particular is managed and financed. The overall tendency towards decentralization is supported by everybody (at least overtly, for utterances to the contrary would certainly be unpopular). Nevertheless, the delimitation of responsibilities at different levels of management (the country as a whole, the union republics, the autonomous republics, the cities) is not clear and the uneasy relationship between 'the centre' and the republics, and national conflicts in several regions do not make the task easier.

As it stands, the practical management of educational affairs in a city lies with the executive committee of the city's Soviet (local authority). The body which is responsible for education in the committee itself is called the Office or Department of education. In larger cities there are also Boards of education in each district. Until recently, however, local authorities had little power over educational establishments in their areas except for schools. Other institutions were directly subordinate to either USSR or republican committees for public education or to numerous industrial ministries. The only real power over these institutions in the cities belonged to the Communist Party, be it the city or the district committee. In this respect the situation has drastically changed, for the party has relinquished that authority to the Soviets, some of which were not prepared to take it.

If one judges by numerous legislative and administrative papers, local educational authorities (the city level) are supposed to administer the activities of educational establishments subordinate to them. They must take measures for the development and proper distribution of institutions in the whole area; help them develop the material and financial resources; promote universal secondary education and vocational training for youth; direct pre-school and out-of-school education; help parents bring up their children; assist educational establishments in selecting and properly placing teaching personnel; organize and control the free issue of textbooks to pupils; supply free medical care, public catering, and also the material supplies for schools, etc. This enumeration of responsibilities could be made much longer, but even the aforementioned shows quite well that little authority is left for the school (or, indeed, other institution) itself. At least it is open to question that educational establishments do really need 'help' in selecting and placing teaching personnel or that parents will not consider 'help' in bringing their children up as meddling in their personal affairs.

In 1988 there appeared a decree of the (then still powerful) Communist Party Central Committee Plenum to establish Educational Councils at all levels of management, to be elected by conferences at the appropriate level. The Councils were to include professionals as well as people interested in educational affairs. The Councils were indeed organized. Some started to work enthusiastically and some hardly met at all. But even now a reasonable distribution of functions between the Councils and other governing bodies of the more traditional sort has not been established in most cases. This is especially true as far as rural schools are concerned where the quality of education of many teachers leaves much to be desired. It is also true in urban schools.

Much hope was placed on school councils, which would include representatives of the school administration, teachers, parents and students, elected by school conferences. School conferences also elect school directors (principals) and approve the statutes (regulations) of the particular school. Again, some of the school councils are very active in all matters of school life, others not. Important functions of school councils are decisions on the content of education (the part of it which does not belong to the union and republican components), on differentiation of general education and vocational training, adoption of a timetable (including the 5- or 6-day school week which is an important issue), on accreditation and promotion of teachers, and on the use of school finances. Pupils can be elected members of the school councils from the 4th form (at 10 or 11 years of age onwards).

The school directors are the real managers of day-to-day school life as well as the prime movers in all decisions of a more permanent character. However, their power is now more limited than it used to be, the limiting factors being school conferences and councils. To help the directors in their work they appoint the so-called methods (or pedagogical) council to discuss curricula and syllabi, to share experiences in teaching and to assist teachers in their professional growth.

Schools in general and urban schools in particular have in most cases limited financial and material resources. The distinction between financial and material resources is an important one because of the weakness of the country's currency (the rouble) which means in real terms that even having money cannot ensure buying what one needs. But even this money is in most cases in short supply which results in the poor condition of school buildings and insufficient equipment. Suffice it to say that by 1985 when stock was taken of all urban school buildings in the country, 5 per cent were found 'dilapidated' and 23 per cent required overall repair. In smaller towns many school buildings have no central heating or sewage facilities. Urban schools are also overcrowded. In many cases 30 to 40 pupils are in one class, the norm being 25 or fewer. Because of the insufficient number of school buildings children learn in two or sometimes three shifts.

The situation is exacerbated by innovations that are to be introduced in schools but which require additional funding (beginning school education from the age of six, one additional year of schooling, coaching of under-achievers, elective courses, the right to change schools on one's choice, etc.). The minimally needed finance for all this is estimated at 1.5 to 4.3 billion roubles per year in addition to about 15 billion which is already allocated for schools. This additional funding does not cover further education and retraining of teachers for work under these new conditions or the bringing of teachers' salaries closer to the national average.

Schools are financed by the budget of the state in proportion to their size and the number of pupils. Since the local authorities are beginning to have more power, they are technically empowered to allocate more money and resources to schools. However, apart from rare exceptions, this is not likely because of the general financial situation in the country. Often urban schools are here at a disadvantage. In some comparatively rich rural areas the state and collective farms do have the money to give to the schools and the pre-school education centres. They also have the incentive to do that, since the institutions cater for the children of the farms' workers. In urban areas two more negative possibilities are likely: a particular school is in a district where there are no (or no rich) factories or firms, or none or few children of their workers go to the school. There is also another difficulty of a more general nature. Formerly, workers of state enterprises had no right to dispose of their own profit which automatically went to the state budget, or they could use it for anything but raising salaries. Now they do have the right and giving money to schools under these new circumstances is not very likely. This is why much hope is placed on schools earning their own money by different means: pupils' work during vocational training; lease of school premises especially in the evening; teaching services to adults or young people who come to learn of their own free will; donations from firms or individuals, etc. However, these mechanisms and channels do not always function properly and it will certainly take time to change the situation.

New institutional alternatives

Perestroika brought to life many attempts to make education more mobile and receptive to new initiatives, both in the channels of management and the types of schools. As to management itself, many schools make concerted attempts to take more power in their own hands on the content of education and the methodology of teaching. Sometimes this leads to the setting up of new types of school which are supposed to provide a better quality of education. Officially the Soviet school has been called 'the unified labour school of general education' since the beginning of the 1920s. Minor variations (special schools with advanced learning for specific subjects or schools for the handicapped) do not make much difference. However, many parents and teachers say that too much emphasis on vocational training results in poorer general education whereas vocational education proper hardly does what it is supposed to do. Few children take up professions acquired during vocational training and insufficient equipment in schools makes the training a mere formality. Another reason for attempting to change the unified type of school is the recognition – now almost universal – that the content of education should be more oriented towards the humanities rather than maths and science.

Lyceums, gymnasiums and sometimes colleges, types of educational establishments which existed in pre-revolutionary Russia or abroad, have become popular slogans to guide many teachers, parents and administrators to set up new schools. Lack of new premises usually makes it imperative to use the same school buildings, so the main changes are in the field of content and pedagogy, sometimes in the practice of selecting pupils. Formerly the only basis of decision to admit a pupil into a school was a catchment area. Now schools of the new types select pupils 'on merit', using either extensive talks with each individual child or (sometimes) a battery of teacher-made tests.

Lyceums are schools for pupils for 8–11 forms (14- to 17-year-olds) which are specifically for the 'gifted'. The content of education includes not only obligatory subjects but many electives as well as special preparatory courses for university entrance examinations. Lyceums usually work in tandem with universities and other institutions of higher learning which select their future students from among the pupils. We now have lyceums in Moscow, Riga, Odessa, Lvov, Barnaul and other cities. In most cases their profile is maths and science with a good representation of humanities.

Gymnasiums are schools for the whole age range of classes beginning with the first form (6- to 7-year-old children) until the end of obligatory schooling (11th form, young people of 17 to 18). Here again the emphasis is on selecting able students even if their early age does not allow one to speak about 'giftedness'. The idea is to give each child the maximum opportunity to get quality education via selection of elective courses, smaller class size, better teachers, etc. Pupils will also have the right to stay another (12th) year for profound study of a group of subjects and preparation for university entrance examinations.

It is, of course, too early to say what will come out of these alternative schools (which are as yet only urban schools). The difficulties, though, are already apparent. One of them is the need for additional money and other resources necessary for all innovations; another is getting better teachers who are able and willing to work harder. In some cases taking a new name for a school is actually nothing but a desire to change something for the better rather than a conscious choice of a new model.

Equality and/or quality

In the early days after the 1917 revolution the accent was certainly on equality, equal chances in education, and for good reason, for at that time 80 per cent of the Russian population and over 90 per cent of non-Russians were illiterate, the literate minority being among the upper classes. The idea of equal chances is still much in the minds of many people but new priorities are now appearing. Nowadays many would say that concern for equality has led to poor quality of education for all. Though educational statistics concerning quality are almost non-existent (objective testing, for example, has never been used on a noticeable scale) newspaper and magazine articles shock readers with horrifying figures such as the USSR being near the 50th place among all countries in the quality of education.

What is certainly true is a lack of interest in education among many young people since they do not see educational efforts as sufficiently rewarded, which is certainly true. At the time of writing, a trolleybus driver with a few months training gets more than a university professor and four times more than a beginning engineer after a five-year college education programme. In many cases education acquired and salary received are in inverse ratio, which hardly motivates people to assiduous study. It is all the more true when it is recognized that to get good results one must really work very hard. Overload is a time-proven refrain in any critical account of Soviet schools. To be precise, overload is experienced by about a third of the high achieving pupils who work hard. About 26 per cent of 9-formers and 37 per cent of 10-formers (that is school-leavers) spend 15 to 21 and more hours a week on home-work which makes 45 to 51 hours weekly study load. On the other hand, 38 per cent of 9-formers and 27 per cent of school-leavers spend 3 to 9 hours on home-work (the difference being then sevenfold between the extremes).

For many years teachers were, practically speaking, encouraged to give students higher marks than they deserved, otherwise a substantial percentage of underachievers would place them under severe criticism. Now this practice has been done away with, a more realistic picture of educational quality has been revealed. However, the statistics available are not large or reliable enough. Checks reveal, for example, that in a teacher-training college, second-year students are unable to solve problems designed for children of 11. Of course, this is not sufficient to give an accurate assessment of the educational system, but it is enough to level criticism against schools, teachers and, more often than not, educational researchers who do not give proper guidance to educational practice.

There is a certain discrepancy between general knowledge (as a rule, much greater among young people of today compared with earlier days) and achievement in school. The latter has substantially declined with over 60 per cent of schoolchildren hardly getting beyond a minimal pass-mark in most subjects. This is why alarm-bells are sounded by the press and the people at large. As a result, schools are urged to make a greater effort, encouraged to take special care of the 'gifted' with less talk about equal chances. As yet, results are not very noticeable. All innovations cost money, which is scarce. What is more, with all the talk about education as a number-one priority – much to this effect has been said even in parliament – public opinion polls do not corroborate this view. In any poll of recent times four priorities in the following order take the lead – food, housing conditions, medical help and the environment. With other priorities that vary, education takes 7th to 11th place. In other words, only about 11 per cent of the people are worried about it. Since today's parliaments and municipal councils have been elected much more democratically than at any other time and do reflect the will of the people, hopes for additional resources for education are not high.

As to equality in education, the prevalent understanding is that all people should have equal access to educational institutions – that is, in law. At no time in our history have we been closer to the ideal than today. Whatever discrimination existed earlier as to class origin, nationality and religion, it has disappeared. On the other hand, less is now thought about positive discrimination like giving priority to workers and peasants when entering university. This is steadily disappearing, giving place to selection on merit. The chances of children entering school to get quality education are certainly different. By and large, urban schools give better education, and schools in large cities are better than in smaller ones. In the new school regulations children (or their parents) have the right to choose schools and to change schools, even in the middle of a school year. How often and to what effect this provision will be made use of is not yet clear. The hope is that competition among schools will raise the overall quality of education while giving individual children better chances to get to a good school.

Education and youth

Two points are covered here – motivation for learning and the health issue. The USSR shares the problem of young people's declining interest in education with most other countries. It is exacerbated, though, as explained above, by the poor reward for education as far as salaries are concerned. This is why many young people only see communication with friends and evening and disco parties as the prime value of school life (86 per cent and 49 per cent of respondents respectively in a recent poll among school pupils). The 'yes' answer to the question if it 'is interesting to learn at school' was given by 12.8 per cent of 7-formers and 15.4 per cent of 10-formers of the city of Voronezh; a larger percentage in any other city would be highly unlikely. Twenty-three per cent of respondents who, as they admit, do not work hard, stated lack of interst as the main reason. In practical terms it means that the aims of education as they are understood by the state and/or educationists are not accepted by the young. Knowledge plus more knowledge with little or no material reward is not sufficient motivation for the young of today. There was hope that the study and production centres organized several years ago (mostly in larger cities) would help children choose and learn a trade. With rare exceptions they have failed since less than 3 per cent of 9 to 10-formers say they will take up the trade they have learned at the centres. Opinion polls show, too, that little correlation exists now between life-plans of the young and their parents' professions.

These young people who finish the complete secondary school are to a large extent orientated towards entering a higher school. However, only about 40 per cent of Moscow school-leavers and about 20 per cent all over the country do enter them, which is certainly a discord between life-plans and their realization.

As in many other countries, school is losing its influence on young people or, rather, the influence is taken over by other socialization elements such as the mass media. Many parents are also unwilling to do much about their children's education or they are too busy with their work to do so. Here it is important to add that most mothers work, and thus families' educational duties are delegated to schools and the mass media. Supplemented with the new sense of freedom in society at large, this leads to a noticeable upsurge in informal groups of young people, mostly in urban areas. Perestroika brought this to the surface which is perhaps a good thing except it has resulted in a loss of faith in many young people in the state, the Communist Party and the education system as represented by teachers and the parents. The vacuum that appeared was quickly taken by informal groups.

More specifically, research shows six reasons for the upsurge of informal youth groups' activities which have now resulted in the appearance of a sub (or counter) culture: first, little attention paid by grown-ups to the education of the young; second, loss of interest among young people for important changes and activities in society; third, lack of institutions that provide leisure for the young; fourth, the information explosion with many sources contradicting each other; fifth, weakened influence (some would say collapse) of the Young Communist League (the Komsomol) which was traditionally the most influential organizing force among the young people; sixth, generation conflict which is a comparatively recent phenomenon in the USSR – recent for the simple reason that formerly it was tightly controlled by the state and was hardly expressed overtly. Some of the informal youth groups are neutral or even positively attuned towards society (like the 'greens'); some, on the contrary, are antisocial and often manipulated by adults, some with criminal records. Society at large and educationists are now rather slowly learning to accept these groups as a fact of life and are trying to have some influence on them.

Alarm about children's and young people's health has been voiced by professionals for a long time, but only glasnost (opennesss) first showed the facts as they are. It appears that over half of our schoolchildren have poor health and a third have chronic diseases like neurosis, intestinal trouble, cardiovascular diseases, weak eyesight, etc. Children now have more trouble with their lungs and teeth. By the 8th form the percentage of these diseases grows 4 to 5-fold. What one can define as 'absolute health' is possessed by 3 per cent of the more fortunate school leavers.

It would certainly be false to place the fault for all that on schools or education; environmental factors, food and the style of urban life have their part, too. Little physical exercise is certainly an important factor but this cannot be developed only by the schools. A few years ago, urban children had poorer health than their rural counterparts. Now they are closer, with, unfortunately, children from rural areas showing a greater decline. The road-accident rate also, in urban areas is very high. Schools are required to have full-time doctors. In fact 86 per cent of schools do have doctors, but only two-thirds of them are full-time. We can quite truly say that there is no hunger in the country – very many people are overfed. But meat, fruit and vegetables are in short supply which leads to a poor nutrition structure. Poor food in school canteens is often mentioned as an important drawback in school life and lack of seating facilities makes the situation worse. Many older school buildings do not provide adequate facilities for study, sports and recreation. These conditions are especially felt by the very young; this is why the commencement of schooling at the age of six is only gradually becoming a fact of life accepted by society.

Conclusion

Any status quo exposition is naturally followed by the question of quo vadis – where are you going? Under the present very unstable conditions in the country even a tentative answer to the question will border on pure speculation.

The tendency of decentralizing education will possibly gain strength. It will find expression both in more power in educational administration being taken from the State Committee for Public Education and in more power being given to the republican and lower levels. There is a danger – some would not qualify it like this, but we do – of political pressures totally doing away with any central planning. We can only hope it will not happen, otherwise education will partly lose its unifying and peace-making influence on society. As yet we can say schools are much more peaceful than any other part of our society. Also, nationality issues are, as yet, not so burning a point in schools as they have become in society at large. But things are changing here too – some are even changing for the better. For example, more schools where teaching is in the native languages are organized both in the Union and in the autonomous republics (we keep the distinction though there is pressure to abolish it and some autonomous republics have already taken this decision). There are plans to organize confessional schools as well as Sunday schools. A notable point in this respect will probably be an Orthodox gymnasium in Moscow – Orthodox meaning, of course, the Russian Orthodox faith. But there is also a chance that too much political and national confrontation will come into schools. We can only hope it will not, but it is difficult to work against it since teachers may find it desirable.

Where decentralization will undoubtedly prevail is in the content of education. Work is now going on on various standards of the content designed for different levels. But schools and especially higher education establishments sometimes act quicker, taking the matter in their own hands. A notable part in any new content of education will be the adaptation of youth to market relations. However, nobody really knows what these are, so efforts to this effect bear a close resemblance to a Russian fairy tale in which the crux of the matter is 'go-I-know-not-where and find-I-know-not what'.

One other thing is almost certain to happen which will influence education: stratification of the population according to its level of income. Then only those who plan to enter higher education will finish complete secondary education schools. Others will drop out earlier and enter the world of work, often ill-prepared for it. It will change school enrolments as well as the content of education, since teachers will have to think about adjusting it to suit different groups of students. This means, too, that state run schools with free teaching will find it difficult to adapt themselves to the changes and some sorts of private schools will spring up. A disturbing possibility here will be that many of the better teachers may quit ordinary schools to get higher pay in the private sector. In the sphere of higher education we are already experiencing the brain drain where some eminent professors and expert young people go abroad – and the numbers may rise.

An appropriate question to some of the aforementioned facts and trends would be whether they all concern only urban education. The answer is yes, to a large extent. Large cities and conurbations are more susceptible to change, for better or worse.

References

Bestuzhev-Lada, I (1988) *Nash molodoi sovremennik. Dialoghi i razmyshleniya* (Our young contemporary. Dialogues and deliberations), Moscow: Mysl.

Gabdulin, G (1988) *Sovershenstvovaniye funktsiy upravleniya obsheobrazovatelnoy shkoloy* (Improving the functions of managing the school of general education), Moscow: The publishing house of the Moscow Pedagogical University.

Khromenkov, N (1989) *Chelovecheskiy faktor. Obshestvenniy progress* (Education. The human factor. Social progress), Moscow: Pedagogika.

Kozlov, A (1989) *Molodezh i obrazovaniye: problemi perestroiki* (Youth and education: problems under perestroika), Leningrad: Znanye.

Kugayenko, A and Levitski, M (1990) *Metody i modeli opredeleniya effektivnosti narodnogo obrazovaniya* (Methods and models of determining the effectiveness of education), Moscow: Prometheus.

Levitski, M (1990) 'Finansoviye sredstva obshcheobrazovatelnoi shkoli' (Finances of the school of general education), *Sovetskaya pedagogika*, 11.

Narodnoye obrazovanye i kultura v SSSR. Statisticheskiy sbornik (People's education and culture in the USSR. A statistical yearbook) (1989), Moscow: Finansi i statistika.

Narodnoye khoziaystvo SSR v. 1988 godu (People's economy in 1988. A statistical yearbook) (1989), Moscow: Finansi i statistika.

Philippov, F (1989) *Ot Pokoleniya k pokoleniyu: sotsialnaya podvizhnost* (From generation to generation: social mobility), Moscow: Mysl.

Philippov, F (1990) *Shkola i sotsialnoye razvitiye obshestva* (School and social development of the society), Moscow: Pedagogika.

Part 3: Urban educational issues: city perspectives

11. Urban Education in Beijing: an international perspective

Dong Jianhong and Cheng Tiying

Introduction

Area and population

Beijing is located in the northeast part of China. Historically, Beijing has been the capital as well as the political, commercial and cultural centre of several dynasties. Now it has a total area of 16,807.8 square kilometres, of which 62 per cent is covered by mountainous areas, 38 per cent by plain areas (750 km^2 belongs to the urban area) (Figure 11.1a). Beijing had a total population of 10.819 million people by 1 July, 1990, which represents all 56 nationalities of the country. About two-thirds of the population (6.3 million) live in urban areas and the rest (3.9 million) in rural areas (Figure 11.1b). The minority ethnic population of the city is around 414,000, accounting for 3.8 per cent of the total population (Figure 11.1c). The natural population growth rate decreased to 7.9 per cent in 1990, 1.37 per cent less than that of 1988. By the year 2000, the population group aged 15 and above will be expected to have reached 10 per cent of the total population, thus changing the population structure from a youth type to an aged one.

Administrative structure

Beijing is one of the three municipalities directly administered by the Central Government. The highest authority of Beijing is the People's Congress of Beijing and its executive body, the Beijing People's Government. Beijing is divided into 4 districts, which comprise the 'Old Beijing City', 6 suburban districts and 9 counties. The local government at the district/county level is the highest authority of the area concerned.

A division between the urban and rural areas is made by including the 4 districts and part of each of the 6 suburban districts on the urban side, and the 9 counties on the rural side. Unless it is specified otherwise, the statistics that come under the heading of 'urban education' in this chapter refer to all the 4 districts and the urban parts of the 6 suburban districts.

Economy

Economically, Beijing is characterized by a planned economy assisted to some

Figure 11.1a *Land resources*

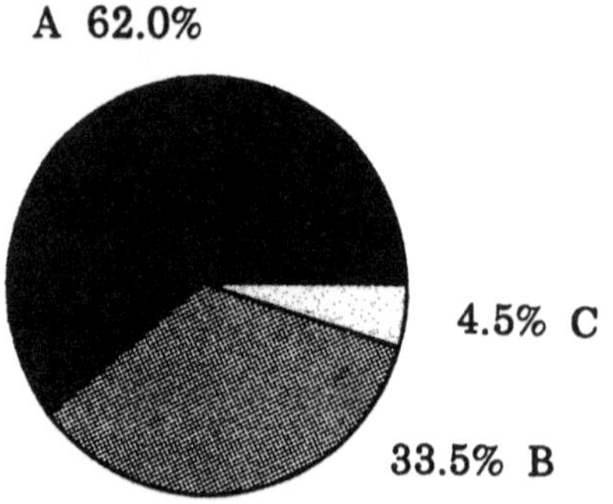

A: mountain; B: cultivated land; C: urban areas

Figure 11.1b *Population distribution*

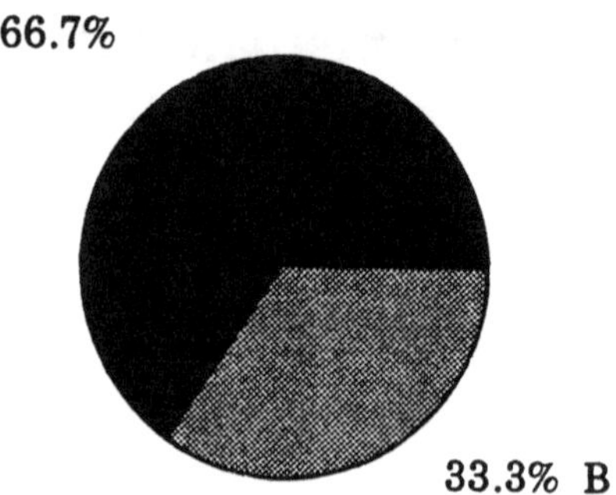

A: urban population; B: rural population

Figure 11.1c *Ethnic distribution*

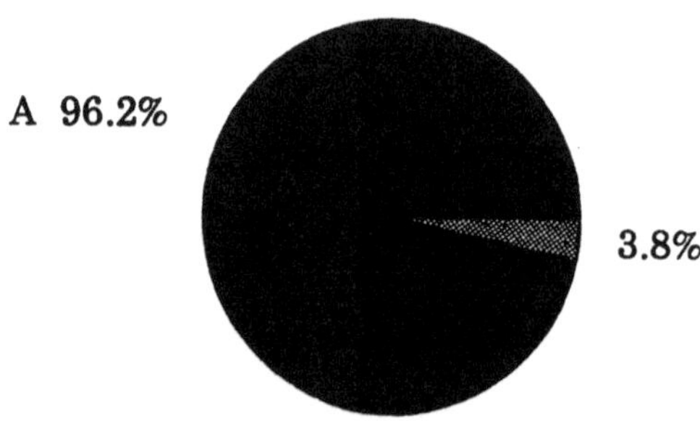

A: the Hans; B: minority nationalities

extent by the commodity economy. The economic development of Beijing has experienced five stages: the period of three-year economic restoration (1949–52); the period of the first Five-year Plan (1953–57); the period of the second Five-year Plan and three-year economic adjustment (1958–65); the period of the Cultural Revolution (1966–76); and the period after the downfall of the Gang of Four (1977 – the present).

According to statistics for 1989, all economic indicators for Beijing had increased compared to 1988, usually by a factor of about 5 per cent. In recent years, the municipal government has taken the initiative in transferring urban industries to the suburban and rural areas of Beijing. This has resulted in a change of agricultural structure in rural Beijing. The proportion of agricultural production in the whole agrarian economy has been reduced and the proportion of industry, construction, commerce and food production increased. In 1985, for example, 52.5 per cent of the agricultural labour force (from a total of 998,000 in rural Beijing) broke away from traditional agriculture and entered the secondary and tertiary sectors. This greatly speeded up the process of urbanization and had an enormous impact on education in Beijing.

Development of education

Before the founding of the People's Republic of China in 1949, education in Beijing lagged far behind. In the whole of Beijing, there were only 21 nurseries and kindergartens, 356 private and public primary schools (representing only 47 per cent of all the school-aged children at the time), 76 secondary schools (of which 80 per cent were private), and 13 higher education institutions. There was also a great disparity in school locations, with only a few schools in areas where the majority of poor people lived.

Since the establishment of the new China in 1949, education in Beijing has developed rapidly. More schools have been established for children from the most disadvantaged groups, and diversified forms of education have been provided in order to meet the demands of municipal economic and social development. All children in Beijing enjoy equal opportunities in education. Undoubtedly education has contribued a great deal to the construction and modernization of the city.

The development of education in Beijing can be roughly divided into four stages.

The years 1949–57 represented the first stage, when the old type of schools were taken over and reorganized by the municipal government. At this stage, major policies and strategies of education were to set up new schools in areas which were densely inhabited by working- or lower-class people, and to lower achievement scores on entrance examinations for children from working-class backgrounds and relax the age constraints on admission.

These measures provided easier access to primary education for those working-class children who had formerly been deprived of education. At the same time, many more institutions of higher education were set up in the city. In 1954, departments of education were established at both municipal and district levels in order to strengthen the leadership of education in Beijing.

The second stage was 1958–65, the period of revolution in education. In order to keep pace with the Great Leap Forward Movement, work-study programmes were introduced and experimental schools for part-work and part-study were set up. Many regular schools built up school-run factories as working sites for students. During this period, school activities were mostly devoted to political movements and productive labour rather than education, and this resulted in a low quality of education. In 1960, teaching reforms began and were implemented on a trial basis. The 9-year or 10-year schooling (namely, 5-year primary and 4-year secondary education or 5-year primary and 5-year secondary education) was also trialled in more than 20 primary and junior secondary schools in the city.

The years 1966–76 witnessed the disaster of the Great Cultural Revolution. During the Revolution, a large number of vocational schools, part-time and part-study schools were closed down, while an equally large number of senior secondary schools were set up. This unreasonable rejection of vocational and technical education and blind development of senior secondary education was the result of a lack of consideration for national economic development. It has led to a unitary structure of secondary education, in which little room was given to vocational and technical education. In the meantime, higher education was also seriously damaged. From 1966 to 1969, enrolment to higher education institutions was completely stopped. In 1976, 15 universities and colleges were merged and seven were moved out of the city. The number of university/college students was 50 per cent less than in 1965.

The final stage is from 1977 to the present. The municipal government has attached great importance to education. It has been declared that teaching order should be restored and school work would be concentrated on teaching and learning. Therefore, the administration and management of urban primary schools, which was once the responsibility of neighbourhood committees, is now the responsibility of the local education authorities. The Beijing Institute of Educational Research was created to strengthen study and research in education and the Beijing Education Administration Institute was set up to train and provide qualified administrators of education for the city. The present urban system of general schooling is 6+3+3, namely, 6 years of primary education, 3 years of junior secondary education and 3 years of senior secondary education; higher education is 4 years and above.

Education policies in Beijing

China is a centralized state in terms of its administration and Beijing is no exception. Educational policies in Beijing are developed and prepared in line with the national ones, although adjusted and updated in line with the socio-economic development of the city. It has been national policy that education should combine with production and that education should nurture a generation of qualified personnel characterized by high moral, intellectual and physical development to meet the needs of socialist construction and modernization. This policy has also been reconfirmed as the general objective for the city in the new period (1977–present).

Education expenditure

In recent years, the city government has taken steps to increase the funds for education. For instance, the municipal government and local administrations have collected 44,000,000 yuan through education tax, social donations and other channels in 1989. In the same year, the average educational expense per capita was the highest in the whole country, and educational expenditure took 20 per cent of the total financial expenditure of the city, which was a 15.6 per cent increase over the previous year.

Minority education

Ethnic minority groups in Beijing enjoy equal rights in respect to education. In order to develop minority education, the municipal government has developed special policies and strategies for the purpose of training minority cadres. Primary and secondary schools are specially set up in districts where minority people live, which give children from minority backgrounds easy access to education facilities regardless of their family backgrounds and religion. Children from minority backgrounds also enjoy other educational advantages. For instance, they can be admitted to university or college programmes with lower than average scores in the entrance examination. In terms of the language of instruction, a bilingual approach is adopted in minority classes, schools and universities where the common language is different from the mother tongue of the students.

Religion and moral education

Religion is not taught in schools, though citizens have the freedom to believe in any religion. Moral education, however, has been given great importance. It is offered either as an independent course or as an integrated part of other subjects, such as Chinese, music, history and geography, etc. Moral education includes social norms, cultural values, patriotism and the correct attitude towards manual labour and work, etc. At primary level, moral courses take one class hour per week, more at the secondary stage. In higher education, moral education is integrated into other subjects.

Pre- and primary education

By 1990, there were 3,824 nurseries and kindergartens, 41,314 working staff, and about 400,000 children, representing 84.5 per cent of all the urban children aged above 3 in Beijing. Among these institutions, 35 nurseries and kindergartens are solely set up for minority children and there is one special kindergarten for gymnastics. The main task of pre-school education is to develop the language abilities and general intelligence of children as a necessary preparation for primary education.

Table 11.1 *Pre-school education*

	Number of institutions	*Number of enrolments*	*Number of working staff*
1949	21	2,403	159
1957	863	66,577	13,852
1965	932	105,573	19,249
1978	5,074	235,923	39,982
1989	3,824	400,000	41,314

Source: State Education Commission, 1990.

According to statistics for 1989, there are 695 urban primary schools, 448,167 pupils, and about 24,641 full-time teachers. The respective numbers for the entire Beijing area, including both the rural and urban areas, are 3,703 primary schools (including 38 ethnic minority schools), 934,696 pupils and 49,022 teaching staff. Among these urban schools, 23 are for children from minority backgrounds. Since 1986, the starting age for urban children has been lowered from 7 to 6. Statistics for 1989 showed that the enrolment rate of primary schools has reached 99.5 per cent, the drop out rate 0.4 per cent, the retention rate 99.61 per cent and the graduation rate 98.18 per cent. The graduation examination for primary pupils has been abolished to reduce the heavy work load on pupils.

Table 11.2 *Primary education*

	Number of schools	*Number of pupils*	*Number of teachers*
1949	356	116,000	4,800
1957	1,249	468,000	13,700
1965	5,888	1,321,000	41,200
1976	4,892	892,000	43,300
1989	3,703	934,696	49,022

Source: Ibid.

In addition, 6 reformatory schools have been set up since 1955 to provide education opportunities for juvenile delinquents from the city. This type of school offers literacy and vocational courses over two years of schooling.

Secondary education

There are altogether 700 general secondary schools, 433,335 students, and 39,361 teaching staff in the whole Beijing area. Among them, 273 schools (including 8 for minority students), 211,853 students, and 22,515 full-time teachers fall in the category of urban Beijing. In the 1950s and 1960s, there were separate schools for girls and boys at the secondary level, but during the Great Cultural Revolution, the system was abolished and the co-education system was adopted.

Table 11.3 *General secondary education*

	Number of schools	*Number of students*	*Number of teachers*
1949	76	44,000	1,831
1957	133	170,700	6,702
1965	486	385,200	18,794
1976	1,200	1,232,300	51,210
1989	700	433,335	39,361

Source: Ibid.

Parallel to the general secondary schools are the secondary specialized schools, which emerged in the late 1950s in Beijing and which offer 4-year vocational and technical courses. These kinds of school enrol graduates from both junior and senior secondary schools, but their enrolment is strictly controlled by the state. In 1989, there were 122 secondary specialized schools, 59,316 students, and 6,698 teaching staff in Beijing.

At this point, one important distinction must be made between the key secondary schools on the one hand and the ordinary secondary schools on the other. A key school is usually well equipped, well staffed, and has a good record in terms of its enrolment rate to higher learning institutions – about 99 per cent or 100 per cent of its graduates enrol in universities and especially in key universities. According to the statistics for 1981, there were 63 key secondary schools in Beijing, most of them located in the central urban districts. Compared with the key schools, the ordinary and by far the majority of secondary schools are less fortunate in terms of their physical facilities, teaching staff, and educational allocations.

Table 11.4 *Key secondary schools*

	1953		*1963*		*1981*	
	Number	% of total	Number	% of total	Number	% of total
Number of schools	20	20.7	12	2.7	63	6.5

Source: State Education Commission, 1987.

Secondary education institutions, and especially the key secondary schools, have long been criticized as providing a service only to students who will and can enrol in higher learning institutions, in spite of the obvious fact that only about 5–10 per cent of all the secondary graduates can continue their education in higher learning institutions each year.

This misled objective of secondary education is due to, first, the traditional value which put scholastic learning above everything else, and second, the fact that higher education has been regarded by many people as one of the major means of social mobility. As a result, competition for enrolment in higher learning institutions has been extremely fierce among secondary school graduates. All the students, families, teachers and schools involved bear enormous social and psychological pressure. The content and methodologies of teaching and learning have also been led astray by this situation.

In order to provide more educational chances for the majority of secondary students and, most importantly, to keep education in line with the socio-economic development of Beijing by satisfying the urgent demands for medium-level personnel in all walks of life, great efforts have been made by the municipal government to reorganize secondary education. The most significant measure since 1980 has been the introduction into the secondary education system of a new type of school – the vocational high school.

Administered by educational departments or public enterprises, vocational high schools are open to junior secondary school graduates on a competitive basis. According to the needs and requirements of the labour market, various courses and specialities are offered within 3 or 4 years of schooling. Upon graduation, the students have a free hand to choose jobs they like. Since the school programmes are very work-oriented, they are well attended and the graduates are welcomed by society. In 1980, there were 52 such schools, providing 22 professional courses to 4,400 students in the whole of Beijing. Now, the respective numbers have increased to 131 schools, 232 specialities, 45,204 students and 7,084 teachers in the urban areas alone.

In the last ten years, vocational high schools have nurtured altogether 64,000 graduates, 95 per cent of whom are employed by government departments or

Table 11.5 *Specialized secondary education (including secondary technical schools and vocational high schools)*

	Number of sp. sec. schools	*Number of students*	*Number of voc. high schools*	*Number of students*
1960	110	59,435	-	-
1976	84	12,850	-	-
1980	113	21,892	52	4,400
1989	122	59,316	131	45,204

Source: State Education Commission, 1990.

other public authorities in Beijing. Some of the rest are self-employed and others have gone on to study in higher education institutions.

Special education

In 1949, there were only two schools for children with disabilities in the whole city. By 1989, this number had increased to 7. Besides, 10 special schools for children with severe learning difficulties have also been established and 56 such classes have been set up in regular primary schools. In urban areas, almost all the children with disabilities who are able to go to school can be admitted to such special education institutions. In addition to the literacy programmes, various vocational courses suitable to these children such as massage, typing and decoration are also offered at junior and senior secondary levels. These vocational courses have helped such children significantly in preparing for a more active part in social life.

Higher education

During the Great Cultural Revolution period, higher education in Beijing received the greatest damage. Many universities and colleges stopped enrolling students and many more institutions were moved out of the city.

After these setbacks, great efforts have been made to restore and develop higher education in the city. Five out of 7 of the universities and colleges that had been moved out of the city have returned to Beijing and more than 10 new institutions have been established. By 1989, there were 67 higher education institutions, 141,562 students and 37,108 professional teaching staff. These institutions account for 8 per cent of all the universities and colleges of China.

Table 11.6 *Higher education*

	Number of univ./colleges	*Number of students*	*Number of teachers*
1949	13	17,442	2,393
1957	31	76,700	11,425
1965	53	111,435	23,129
1976	24	46,016	17,693
1989	67	141,562	37,108

Source: Ibid.

By academic classifications, these institutions can be categorized as 3 comprehensive universities, 22 polytechnic universities/colleges, 3 agricultural and forestry universities/institutes, 5 medical universities/colleges, 3 normal universities/colleges, 7 language and literature institutes, 7 finance and economics colleges, 5 political science and law universities/institutes, 1 physical education college, 8 arts institutes, 1 nationality university, and 2 short-cycle vocational institutes.

Among these higher education institutions, 53 are administered by the related ministries of the state, and 14 by the municipal government. Among the 53 ministry-administered institutions, 22 are national key universities or colleges directly funded and administered by the State Education Commission – 23 per cent of all such institutions in the whole country. Graduates from universities or colleges in Beijing account for 10 per cent of the total number for the country.

Higher education institutions administered by the state enrol students from all parts of the country and assign all the graduates to posts in accordance with the national plan, while institutions run by the municipal government are open to students from the city and assign all their graduates to posts in Beijing. In addition to their regular educational programmes, key universities and colleges in Beijing also provide training for people from the minority regions so as to help with the socio-economic development there. Three classes with each having 30–80 students have been organized for ethnic minorities from educationally disadvantaged regions in three eminent universities in Beijing, namely, Qinhua University, Beijing University and Beijing Normal University.

Adult education

Since 1979, adult education has been restored and developed very rapidly in Beijing. In 1979, the municipal Office of Workers and Peasants Education (later renamed Beijing Adult Education Bureau) was set up. The Bureau is the highest authority responsible for the coordination, guidance and administration of adult education in Beijing. Sub-bureaux and departments of adult education have also been set up at district and county levels.

According to statistics for 1988, there are 1,349 adult education institutions in Beijing, which include 88 higher adult education institutions, 185 adult secondary specialized schools, 596 schools and training centres for employees, and 480 community schools, with 15,000 full-time teaching staff and around 1,000,000 adult learners each year. In 1990, adults who had received primary, junior secondary, senior secondary or university/college education accounted for 22.6, 30.6, 19.0 and 9.3 per cent respectively of the total population. The illiteracy rate of the city had been decreased to 0.16 per cent of the urban population.

Future development

Education is a future-oriented course, since the children who are studying in schools today will be masters of the next century. The general objective of education, therefore, is to cultivate people who will be able to make their contributions to the development of the whole of humanity in the twenty-first century. The future generation should be equipped with two very essential characteristics: a high sense of social responsibility, and an ability to make a contribution to society.

Urban education will continue its reforms and innovations at all types and levels of education in all fields. The key task is to improve its quality. In this regard, two changes are expected: one is the change from the traditional educational ideology which stresses enrolment rate of entering higher education levels to one which aims at the overall development of children; the other is the change in educational content from the emphasis on book knowledge to the emphasis on the moral, scientific and general capacity of the children. Therefore, the curriculum and courses will be more moral-oriented and work-oriented in future.

In terms of higher education, efforts will be made to increase the autonomy of higher education institutions under a strengthened macro-administration and to develop the cross-connections between these institutions and society to encourage a more responsive attitude of higher learning institutions to the socio-economic development of the city.

In the next century, the industrial structure, labour divisions, and the environment of work will undergo great changes. These foreseeable changes have already raised new and higher demands on education in terms of the moral, ideological, scientific, cultural, psychological and physical qualities of the future workforce. It is therefore expected that schools and society will be more closely linked, and that Beijing will become an educated society with a socialized education system.

References

Beijing Adult Education Bureau (1989) *Advancement of Beijing Adult Education*, Beijing: Legislation Press.

Beijing Statistics Bureau (1986) *Guidelines on National Economic and Social Development in Beijing*, Beijing: China Statistics Press.

Beijing Statistics Bureau (1990) *1989 Bulletin on Statistics of National Economic and Social Development in Beijing*, Beijing: China Statistics Press.

Beijing Statistics Bureau (1990) *Basic Strategies on the Development of the National Economy in the 90s*, Beijing: Finance and Trade Economy.

Department of Planning and Capital Construction, State Education Commission (1989) *China Yearbook of Educational Statistics*, Beijing: Beijing Industry University Press.

Jin Yiming *et al.* (1990) 'On several issues of introducing vocational counselling in regular secondary education', *Educational Research*, 4, Beijing.

Li Tieying (1990) 'On several issues of education in China', Beijing, *Guangming Daily*, 3 January.

Man Guifang (1989) 'Reforms in elementary education of the city', *Beijing Daily*, 15 November.

Man Guifang (1990) 'Maintaining on reforms and adjustment on production structure', *Beijing Daily*, 2 January

Man Guifang (1990) 'Achievements of school-run enterprises at primary and secondary education', *Beijing Daily*, 2 February.

State Education Commission (1983) *Big Events of China Education: 1949–1982*, Beijing: Education Science Press..

State Education Commission (1986) *Collection of National Working Meeting on Technical and Vocational Education in China*, Beijing: Beijing Normal University Press.

State Education Commission (1987) *China Education Yearbook: 1982–1986*, Hunan Province: Hunan Education Press.

State Education Commission (1990) *1989 China Yearbook of Educational Statistics*, Beijing: People's Education Press.

Wang Xiaohui (1990) 'Essential characteristics of combining education with productive labour', *Educational Research*, 5, Beijing.
Wu Zhong (1990) 'A review of the economic situation in Beijing', *Beijing Daily*, 2 February.
Yan Liqiang (1990) 'Achievements belong to innovations and reforms', *Beijing Daily*, 14 January.
Yang Lijun *et al.* (1990) 'Review and fugure orientations of Beijing's economy', *Beijing Daily*, 9 January.
Yu Fang (1989) 'Rapid development of elementary education of the capital in 40 years', *Beijing Daily*, 13 November.
Zhao Shiming (1989) 'Continuing completion of special education system in Beijing', *Beijing Daily*, 13 November.

12. Dogma, equality and excellence: education in London

Crispin Jones

Introduction

This chapter explores the ways in which an examination of the issues that face education in London exemplifies many of the issues prevalent in education generally in England as well as issues that are common to education in many other urban centres throughout the world. To contextualize such an exploration, the chapter starts with two brief descriptive accounts of London. The first is a socio-economic account of the city and the second a history of its education. Emerging from these two accounts will be the major themes that currently dominate educational debate and practice in London, and the discussion of these takes up the rest of the chapter. The aim of this approach is to illuminate both education in its contemporary setting and some of the more general themes in urban education that are discussed in the first section of this book.

London's rise and fall

When Dr Johnson, of English Dictionary fame, stated that 'by seeing London, I have seen as much of life as the world can show', he was talking of an eighteenth century city from the centre of which it was still possible to walk into open country and back within a day. Yet already, London was one of the largest conurbations in the world; more, as Dr Johnson's comments makes clear, its citizens were already as 'Londoncentric' as they have remained to this day. Its size and domination of Britain was coupled, for much of the nineteenth and early twentieth century, with a domination of much of the world. Thus London grew and became rich and powerful as a city, due to the immense revenues that accrued to Britain generally, and London in particular, from trade and colonialism. As Joseph Chamberlain put it in 1904, London had become 'the clearing house of the world'. But even as Londoners preened themselves on hearing such words, the economic basis of London's (and Britain's) prosperity was slipping away as Europe blundered slowly into the catastrophe of the Great War of 1914–18.

In historical retrospect, the rise and fall of the British Empire was a rapid event, with the seeds of Britain's economic decline being visible as the British

Empire was in its seeming heyday towards the end of the nineteenth century. However, Britain's relative economic decline, and that of London also, accelerated after World War II and, with minor ups and downs, continues to this day. Some of this decline, however, is masked. London remains a major financial centre and still, as the centre of a region (the South East of England) is, generally speaking, more prosperous than much of the rest of the British Isles.

London's overall population has declined to about 7 million, but this is partly due to the expansion of the exurbs at the expense of the inner city. It has the most diverse population in Britain, perhaps one of the most diverse in the world: over 170 languages are spoken in the Inner London schools (ILEA, 1989); it has extremes of wealth and poverty, increasingly exemplifying Galbraith's view of the modern capitalist city as exhibiting the contradiction of private affluence coexisting alongside public squalor. It is also a poorly administered city. The strategic authority for the city, the Greater London Council (GLC), was abolished by central government in the mid 1980s, many of its responsibilities being given to the 32 smaller local authorities, most looking after populations of between 150,000 and 250,000 people. Education in the inner 13 boroughs remained the responsibility of a unitary body, the Inner London Education Authority (ILEA), but that too was abolished by the 1988 Education Act with the individual boroughs becoming responsible for education. Thus today, each of the 32 London boroughs is responsible for education in its area, within broad guidelines set out by central government.

Despite such changes, the social conditions in which many London pupils live remain the same as they have done for many years. Within much of inner London and in many of the outer London boroughs, particularly those to the north and east, many of the pupils are from poor, working-class families. The prosperity of the South East has passed many of them by. Moreover, they are likely to remain relatively poor. Poor quality housing, both local authority and private, poor jobs or no jobs and a deteriorating standard of public services, including education, are likely to continue for the foreseeable future.

Some examples make this level of poverty easier to understand. Tower Hamlets, a borough immediately to the east of the City of London has, for hundreds of years, been a centre for migration into London. Tower Hamlets, and the East End of London generally, has traditionally been poor, disregarded by central government and often the focus for xenophobic sentiments in the majority population – a recipe for a demanding educational task. For example, in London generally, 16 per cent of white people are unskilled manual workers. The comparable figure for the British Bangladeshi population is 68 per cent, most of them living in Tower Hamlets (Home Affairs Committee, 1987, para. 14). Half of the population lives below the poverty line, with 19 per cent of households in 1985 having a gross income of under £2,600, approximately a quarter of the national average at that time. Furthermore, although unemployment is slowly declining in the borough, it remains, at 17.4 per cent, the highest in the whole of London (London Borough of Tower Hamlets, 1988, pp. 5–6).

Housing is similarly an area of extreme and concentrated difficulty. The demand for housing in the 1960s and 1970s led to the building of unsuitable and unsightly tower blocks across London. Tower Hamlets, like many other working-class boroughs in London, became full of badly designed and poorly constructed local authority housing. Despite changes in housing policy at the national level that have encouraged the sale of council properties, some 48,000 of the total housing stock of some 62,000 dwellings in Tower Hamlets remain in council hands (ibid.). There are also over 10,000 people on the housing waiting list, with little hope of being housed. In addition, despite public statements to the contrary, the borough was found to be practising racial discrimination in its housing allocation policies (Commission for Racial Equality, 1988).

Such concentrations of poverty, discrimination and disadvantage present particular difficulties for schools. The ILEA's own Educational Priority Area indicators for 1987 confirm this. Tower Hamlets came out as being the most disadvantaged area in London in terms of the number of children having free school meals, coming from large families and coming from homes where the wage earners were unemployed. On a more positive note, it is worth recording that there were fewer children in care or from single parent families than anywhere else in Inner London, perhaps reflecting the stable family structure of the Bangladeshi community (ILEA 1988).

Such social conditions, in Tower Hamlets and elsewhere in London, require the very best in administrative structures if their worst effects are to be compensated for. Yet the search for appropriate administrative structures in London, including those for education, has too often been submerged under different political agendas. The abolition of the GLC, the last central administration for London, broke a chain of government that was over 100 years old. As part of that broken chain of administration, the education service in inner London is attempting to come to terms with the changes introduced by abolition of the ILEA in 1989, one amongst many dramatic educational changes brought about by the 1988 Education Act (see also Chapter 4). The adjustment to the abolition of the ILEA is the more difficult given the long, and, in the main, successful history of a centralized education authority within inner London. This history is the concern of the next section.

The development of education in London

Mass education is a peculiarly urban phenomenon. In London, its history can be traced back over many centuries. However, the date traditionally seen as being that on which legally enforced education for all children in London was introduced is 1870, with the passing of the Education Act of that year. Locally elected School Boards were established to oversee the provision of education in their areas. Very quickly, the various strands of educational opinion became embroiled in struggles to control such Boards. In London, the radical and liberal strands tended to dominate, with conservative opinion huffing and puffing its indignation from the political sidelines. Outside London, the rapidly growing, more affluent and conservative suburban populations organized School Boards of a more conservative type. Conflict between the radical London School Board and more conservative opinion in central government was a constant feature of late Victorian education in London. At this time, compulsory education was only provided at the elementary or first level. Radical attempts by the London School Board to extend the period of schooling for academically successful working-class children were ruled illegal in the 1899 legal case referred to as the Cockerton Judgement. Such attempts to enhance the quality of mass schooling in London were frequently to lead to conflict with central government, which remained more conservative in its approach to issues of urban working-class education.

The days of the School Boards were, partly as a result of events like the Cockerton Judgement, numbered. Central government did not like their independent and sometimes oppositional stance. The 1902 Education Act abolished the School Boards, and responsibility for education in London passed to a newly created body, the London County Council (LCC). This body was to control education in London until 1965. The LCC is generally considered to have been a successful education authority, undertaking pioneering work in many areas of city based education. Its fame and popularity amongst teachers made it the most sought out authority for teachers to work in, enabling it to ensure that its schools were both well and fully staffed, a condition that is a distant dream for many schools in London today.

However, it too was abolished, again for broader political reasons. In 1965, the central Conservative administration, wishing to improve the strategic administration of the London area and fearing a seemingly permanent Labour party domination of the LCC, sought to change it so as to ensure a clearer strategic direction of London services, hopefully under permanent Conservative control. The outer suburbs of London, mainly Conservative controlled, were brought into the new and larger strategic London body, the Greater London Council. Although reluctantly willing to join the new body, the outer London boroughs were successful in insisting that they retained their existing control over education. Thus, the GLC's responsibility for education was limited to Victorian London's boundaries, the London area that had been controlled by the LCC and which was increasingly becoming the poor inner city. This new authority, technically a committee of the GLC, was called the Inner London Education Authority, and it ran education until 1989, when, as mentioned above, it too was abolished by central government action, education being devolved to the individual boroughs.

ILEA's achievements were many, in particular its work in the areas of curriculum reform and resourcing, where some of its pioneering work had an influence that went far beyond its boundaries. It was also, contrary to the views of many of its opponents, well administered. In 1980, the Conservative government sent in the independent national educational inspectorate (HMI) to investigate the quality of schooling provided. Their report, probably to the government's surprise and displeasure, was generally favourable, their main concern being the quality of the secondary education being provided. The HMI report concluded:

> The picture that currently emerges is of a caring and generous authority with considerable analytical powers to identify problems, the scale of which is, in some cases, unique in this country. . . Performance in nursery and primary education and in further and higher education is generally sound and improving. In secondary schools and special education, performance is much patchier; it calls for the same kind of fine handling which has improved the other sectors (DES, 1980, 21.16).

What raised Conservative concern about the ILEA to fever pitch was not, however, the measured concerns of the HMI. It was the range of policy initiatives that the ILEA, along with other Labour controlled boroughs in London such as Brent and Ealing, had started to introduce into their schools from the mid-1970s onwards under the general title of 'equal opportunities'. These policies had two main aims. The first was to combat racism, sexism and class prejudice in schools and society at large and the second was to enhance the learning of all children by eliminating the negative consequences of these societal structures and personal behaviours in the schooling system. At a time of increasing right wing domination of the national political debate, such aims were seen, correctly, as oppositional.

As well as being oppositional, the renewed emphasis on equality revealed that despite the concern and effort to ameliorate the worst consequences of poverty on educational attainment over a hundred years of mass education in London, such attempts had, in the main, failed. Perhaps such a judgement is harsh, given the fact that the schooling system by itself can do little to alter more fundamental inequalities in society. Certain key left wing politicians did not, however, perceive the role of education as an agent of social transformation in such a modest light. If there had been failure, it was thought, it was a result of delivery rather than of conceptualization; at their most simplistic, such views held that it was the innate conservatism of teachers and administrators that was responsible for the continuation of racist, sexist and class prejudices within the schooling system.

The popular right wing press had a field day with what they perceived as the most extreme of these equal opportunities policies, ridiculing efforts to bring about greater sexual equality and describing a race equality curriculum development programme in the London Borough of Brent as being the imposition of 'race spies' onto the local schooling system. Although this particular development project had been approved by central government and was being funded by them, the media publicity encouraged central government to end the scheme, which they eventually managed to do after several unsuccessful attempts.

These and other equal opportunity programmes often suffered from being too ambitious in their aims. Many London schools, like many other institutions in Britain and elsewhere, are indeed sexist, racist and class prejudiced. In general, that is not greatly in dispute (DES, 1984). What is in dispute is the extent to which schools can, first, reform themselves and second, reform the wider society. School reform is difficult and many of the advocates of equal opportunities policies in London in the 1980s seemed to think that theirs was a moral crusade that needed conversion rather than planning. As for using the schools as agents of wider social change and transformation, there is little evidence to support their efficacy in this role. At the moment of its abolition, the ILEA appeared to recognize this, saying that it

> was always conscious of the limitation of its powers even under previous legislation and understood that the implementation of its policies, including the practical applications necessary to achieve and change, depended on persuasion rather than coercion (ILEA, 1989, p. 3).

However, their practice was certainly more interventionist, at least in intent, in the early 1980s when they were introducing their radical equal opportunities policies. Nor were they alone. Similar policies were put in place by other London local education authorities (LEAs), with little thought being given to the practicalities of implementation. Existing, widely recognized equal opportunity issues, such as those relating to the educational needs of bilingual learners, remained mainly unresolved, because they were unaddressed. One consequence of this was that many teachers felt that policies were being forced upon them with little consultation and little sensitivity to the realities of inner city teaching. They resented this, little knowing that central government was thinking of an even greater imposition upon them, albeit from a different political perspective. Finally, a series of teacher strikes over pay and conditions alienated many parents, so that when the ILEA was attacked by the central Government with its proposals in the 1986 Education Bill, there was no constituency of support powerful enough to resist. The ILEA was abolished with less fuss than might have been expected, and the powers of other local education authorities in London (and throughout England and Wales) were severely undermined by other clauses in the 1988 Act.

This brief and curtailed administrative history of London education is important for at least two reasons. The first is that it shows that the capital's education has traditionally been a highly politicized area of British education. The second is that there remains no concensus as to the most effective administrative structures to adopt so as to provide effective and quality education to the children of Britain's largest city. In saying that, a further, more speculative point may be put forward, namely that capital city education in most mature capitalist cities remains in many cases administratively intractable and politically contentious.

Education in London in the 1990s

Given such a difficult recent history, what are the principal concerns of those responsible for running London's education system in the 1990s? In the immediate future, the major concern is likely to be the struggle to maintain the schooling system in the light of the mass of changes, many of them disliked by teachers, brought about by the 1988 Education Act.

Amongst the most significant of these changes in London was the abolition of the ILEA and the setting up of 13 new Local Education Authorities in its place. Each of the boroughs was required, by the 1988 Education Act, to produce an Educational Development Plan for the new LEA. Their purpose was to provide a detailed blueprint for the new LEAs, and as such they had to be approved by the Secretary of State. These Plans make interesting reading as no British LEA had previously been asked to provide a detailed account of its activities. In microcosm, they present a picture of the variety of responses to similar issues that the British education system encourages. The political persuasion of each of the new LEAs is clearly demonstrated, usually in debates about equality and excellence or about finance. In addition, the Plans give a detailed picture of the socio-economic circumstances within which they had to prepare a new educational administration and these statistics, more than the policies put forward, reveal clearly the daunting task that was facing the new LEAs.

The rapid rate of educational change that has followed the abolition of the ILEA has made many of the proposals in the Plans irrelevant, as the LEAs struggle with the swift pace of events. They were written as the Education Act of 1988 was being enacted, and few in education then had a clear idea as to how this would actually affect education. (For a broader discussion of the 1988 Act see Bash and Coulby, 1989 and Coulby and Bash, 1991.)

What the plans do reveal is the enthusiasm that Labour, Liberal and Conservative local councils brought to the idea of running their own education system. This new enthusiasm probably reveals just how much power local government across London (and, indeed, across Britain) has lost in other fields during a decade of Conservative central government. The new inner London authorities saw a new role for themselves, although the Plans also reveal that they had yet to realize the diminution of their educational role that full implementation of the 1988 Act would bring about.

Sadly, the new LEAs' enthusiasm for control of education in their area too often contrasts with their comparative lack of commitment to maintaining those cross-authority services that ILEA provided but which no single new LEA has the resources to maintain by itself. Such cooperation as did exist has been sorely tried as budget cuts grow greater and greater as poll tax capping (central government's latest control on local spending) takes its toll.

Another aspect of difficulties over cross-borough services continues to be argued in the courts. This is in relation to the provision of school places for out-of-borough children. Given contracting budgets, many LEAs wished to give priority to their own borough's children over children from other boroughs. A series of High Court decisions over the last few years has thrown LEA planning into further chaos as the legal judgements place the desires of the parents above the wishes of any LEA to give priority to children living in their borough.

The diminution of cross-borough cooperation pales in comparison with other issues. Staffing and financial issues are discussed later in this chapter, but there are many other significant issues facing London's schools. In particular, the whole range of issues that are demoralizing their colleagues up and down the country as a result of the 1988 Education Act are a further imposition on many inner city teachers. The changes brought about by the Act are enormous – the introduction of the new National Curriculum, particularly its assessment, the chaos of individual school budgetary control under Local Management of Schools (LMS) and open enrolment. Additionally, the national government announced in 1991 that it was introducing a major overhaul of all post-16 further and higher education in the country. For the inner London boroughs, the difficulty presented by all these radical changes is that everything seems to be happening at once, with a financial crisis and a teacher shortage to add on top.

Furthermore, such reforms have to be implemented in an intercultural, multilingual schooling environment. The teaching of English to speakers of other languages in London is, at best, patchy. Teachers with the specialist skills required to work effectively in this area are still few and far between; indeed, at times it appears as if the education service in London, after over 20 years of expressions of concern on this subject, is quite unable effectively to rise to this challenge, save at the level of rhetoric. For example, with over half the school population in Tower Hamlets having a home language other than English, the schools are under immense resource pressure to provide adequate language teaching. Yet, despite the funding of some 300 extra teachers by the Home

Office under special legislation known as Section 11 provision, the needs of many such bilingual pupils have continued to be inadequately met, due to an unfortunate mix of inadequate resourcing, poor planning and lack of educational and political determination to get the matter sorted out. The position is perhaps at its most severe in Tower Hamlets, but a similar long-standing pattern of inadequacy in relation to effective provision is to be found across London. Despite excellent and committed teachers, a similar picture is found in most British cities.

As the inadequate provision in relation to language indicates, the major negative pressure on the education service in inner London is resourcing. Just four days after the abolition of the ILEA, some of the poorest of the new authorities, all Labour controlled, were poll tax capped, forcing draconian budget cuts on them, including educational cuts. In addition, as the newest element within the inner London boroughs, many of the newly appointed education officials were unused to the bureaucratic in-fighting over budgets that are an integral part of local authority life. So, in a sense, education was penalized twice, first by the central government and then by the boroughs. Add to this a high level of inexperience in financial matters within the new LEAs and one has all the potential ingredients for a financial disaster. During 1991, such financial disasters began to occur, hitting the poorest boroughs first. So bad has the position become in some LEAs that it is likely that central government will have to intervene to ensure a legal minimum of provision. Even the better off LEAs are finding it difficult. For example, in Camden, the ILEA budget at abolition was £64.7 million. Central government, through the Department of Education and Science (DES) estimated a budget for 1990/91 of £52.77 million, which with short term transitional relief of £6.78 million, still left a gap of some £2 million (London Borough of Camden, 1990). There is a transitional element of relief for five years but the cracks in the financial wall are already clear and when the transitional relief disappears, the whole edifice may well collapse, if it has not done so sooner. Thus, the effect of the implementation of the 1988 Education Act, taken alongside the parallel legislation on the poll tax has been to decrease the amount of money available for the education of children and young people in those areas of inner London which have the highest concentration of social and economic disadvantage.

A sad irony of this contraction is that it has removed another issue from London's education agenda, namely teacher shortage. Until the cuts started to bite there was a serious and increasing teacher shortage in the schools of inner London, particularly at the primary level. The shortage remains but is disguised by the budget cuts. So class sizes are steadily rising, despite evidence that smaller class sizes are essential in such difficult learning environments. Taken with the poll tax, this aspect of the 1988 Act may be seen as an attack on the education of some of the most disadvantaged children and young people in England and Wales. Local governments in many of the boroughs, like the ILEA before them, find themselves as the defenders of working-class educational entitlements. The conflict with central government, having been seemingly resolved by the 1988 Act in favour of the DES, is still likely to continue. The issue of resources is likely to be the important component of this conflict. Whether the boroughs also find themselves in ideological conflict with central government over issues such as equal opportunities policies remains to be seen. Were this to be the case, being small and divided they might not be seen to manifest such a strong challenge as the disbanded ILEA.

It is important to put these serious concerns alongside some of the more optimistic perspectives held by many in the administrative and political structures of the new LEAs. Here, the argument is made that despite considerable difficulties facing the new LEAs, the fundamental issues remain the same in inner London's schools and are slowly being effectively tackled. Thus, although the schools continue to fail working-class children in large numbers, educational standards in the ILEA were slowly rising and will probably continue to do so in many of the new LEAs. Major initiatives undertaken by the ILEA, such as the successful pupil profiling London Record of Achievement, its pioneering Compact scheme, its anti-racist and anti-sexist policies, its ambitious induction and INSET programmes, show what can be done in adverse circumstances. The new London LEAs, in other words, have a firm base of achievement and a commitment to excellence and equality which may yet see them through their initial difficulties.

References

Bash, L, Coulby, D and Jones, C (1985) *Urban Schooling: Theory and Practice*, London: HRW.

Bash, L and Coulby, D (1989) *The 1988 Education Act: Competition and Control*, London: Cassell.

Commission for Racial Equality (1988) *Housing and Discrimination. Report of a Formal Investigation into the London Borough of Tower Hamlets*, London: CRE.

Coulby, D and Bash, L (1991) *Contradiction and Conflict: The 1988 Education Act in Action*, London: Cassell.

Coulby, D and Jones, C (1990) 'Teacher Retention in Urban Primary Schools', unpublished paper.

DES (1980) *Report by HM Inspectors on Educational Provision by the Inner London Education Authority*, London: HMSO.

DES (1984) *Education for All* (The Swann Report), London: HMSO.

Hall, P *et al.* (1971) *The Containment of Urban England*, London: Allen and Unwin.

Home Affairs Committee (1987) *Bangladeshis in Britain*, Session 1986–87, First Report, 96–1, London: HMSO.

Home Office (1981) *The Brixton Disorders* (The Scarman Report), London: HMSO.

ILEA (1988) *Deprivation Indices 1987*, London: ILEA Research and Statistics Branch.

ILEA (1989) *Prospects for Education in Inner London after 1990*, London: ILEA.

Jones, C (1989) 'The abolition of the ILEA', in Bash, L and Coulby, D (1989) *op cit.*

Knox, P (1982) *Urban Social Geography*, London; Longman.

London Borough of Camden (1990) *Camden Education News*, 1, February 1990.

London Borough of Tower Hamlets (1988) *Getting it Right: Draft Development Plan*, London: London Borough of Tower Hamlets.

13. A social geography of educational outcomes in Melbourne

Richard Teese

Introduction

Spatial inequalities in education are a feature of all Australian cities and have been extensively documented. Over the last two decades in particular, researchers have studied the links between residential segregation, unequal provision, and various measures of educational activity and achievement (Fisher *et al.*, 1973; Claydon, 1973, 1975; Johns, 1976; Neutze, 1978; Walker, 1979; Burnley, 1980; Newton and Johnston, 1981; Stimson, 1982; DEET, 1987; Linke, 1988; for more general studies on residential segregation see Stilwell and Hardwick, 1973; Logan *et al.*, 1975; Maher, 1982).

The evidence of social area disadvantage has played a prominent role in redirecting government programmes towards positive discrimination (Australian Schools Commission, 1973, ch. 9). However, the geography of educational success and failure has altered little over these decades and the weakening social trend on some broad indicators, such as school participation rates, conceals deeper structural problems which government policy has either not tackled effectively or has even aggravated.

This chapter uses original evidence of examination results to explore the interactions between urban social space, selective secondary schooling, and school organization and to model the distribution of success and failure across Melbourne.

It is argued that there are three sorting processes at work within the urban system: residential segregation on social class and ethnicity lines, the unequal location of selective schooling (and the differential effects of selective schooling according to social area), and academic selection within schools themselves.

Interactions between these processes occur within a framework of centralized curriculum control. This reposes on an uneasy relationship between the statutory agency responsible for subject accreditation and student assessment on the one hand, and a cluster of more or less powerful universities and colleges of advanced education on the other. The higher education institutions are each free to decide their own admissions policies, selection practices, and course prerequisites. Depending on their prestige and the market value of their courses, the universities in particular have been able to exercise a very strong influence over curriculum. However, this has been contested by teachers through their membership of the Victorian Curriculum and Assessment Board (VCAB), their professional associations, and their industrial organizations.

Despite growing tensions and open public conflict, the framework of centralized curriculum control has nevertheless been a source of stability. A full explanation of success and failure at school needs to take into account the role of centralized curriculum control, for it is through accreditation and assessment at this level that the mass of secondary school pupils who are otherwise divided by administrative and geographical boundaries are drawn into the one field of comparison and exposed to formally the same set of scholastic demands. However, in this chapter this framework of overarching political control is taken for granted.

After a brief sketch of Melbourne and an historical review of its secondary school system, a social area analysis of examination results is offered. The data are from the Higher School Certificate examinations conducted in the state of Victoria in 1985. However, results from a social survey conducted in 12 Melbourne Schools are also used in order to illustrate differential access to the curriculum as this occurs within schools (Lamb, 1991; Teese, 1991). Following this, an attempt is made to provide an integrated view of the effects of residential segregation, selective schooling, and school organization on the distribution of achievement in Melbourne.

Melbourne – dimensions of urban stratification

Founded in 1835, Melbourne is the second largest population centre in Australia and capital of the southernmost mainland state, Victoria. It is a widely-dispersed city of generally low population density, with about 3 million inhabitants. By the 1880s a distinctive pattern of residential segregation had been established in Melbourne. Working-class suburbs of high density developed to the north and west of the central business district, where manufacturing industry was located. The east and south were settled by professional and business families as well as Melbourne's middle classes – clerical and office workers, junior public servants, shopkeepers and traders.

Prior to World War II, the social space of Melbourne was divided primarily along occupational and status (including religious) lines. Non-British immigration had been restricted, and for Victoria as a whole, the population born in non-English speaking countries had fallen from 3 per cent in 1901 to 1.9 per cent in 1933 (Broome, 1984, p. 149). However, post-war reconstruction was based on a massive immigration programme in which southern European groups played a major part. About two-thirds of Melbourne's population growth in the post-war years was due to immigration (Broome, 1984, p. 202), with Italians, Greeks, Maltese and Yugoslavs making up the largest non-English speaking groups.

Mediterranean families were mainly of working-class or rural origins, and in contrast to northern and eastern Europeans, they settled in the inner areas of Melbourne in high concentrations. Comparatively low rents, cheaper housing prices, plentiful factory work and public transport all favoured this pattern as did the advantages of language and family (and indeed village) networks. Thus in the 1950s and 1960s an additional dimension of urban stratification came to be overlaid across the historical dimensions of occupational and social status.

Patterns of ethnicity have since been renewed and transformed through the arrival of new groups - Lebanese, Turks, and Indo-Chinese in particular.

With the growth of the outer suburbs of Melbourne, often at considerable distance from the central business district and from regional employment centres, population contrasts within the greater metropolitan area based on occupation, income, educational level, and ethnicity have been joined by other factors. These include the incidence of single-parent families, 'blended families' (through remarriage or cohabitation), isolation, and lack of services and facilities. The spread of the city has begun to exhaust the budgets available for new physical and social infrastructure and to divert resources needed for inner city renewal.

While Melbourne today brings together more of the state's population than ever before (about 71 per cent), the urban framework is also more evolved and the distances between groups within the space of the city are now more complex. Generalized dependence on the metropolis - for employment, for services of all kinds, for security, for personal identity - has increased the pressure for independence and for distance. In this context the education system, inherited from the pre-war years, has acquired two competing functions. On the one hand, it has been promoted and perceived as a vehicle of social advancement, on the other the inflation of credentials and the 'crowding out' of the minority space represented by academic culture has made access to selective schooling critical for maintaining status and occupational distinctions (on the notion of 'crowding out', see Boltanski, 1976). Public education was expanded in the post-war years to enhance opportunities and, in effect, to reduce the status differences between groups by facilitating movement between them. The pride of the public high school has been its openness to non-English speaking migrants and to children from working-class backgrounds. But against the unifying action of an institution upon which increasing numbers of individuals have come to depend has been the facility which formal schooling offers for enhancing status differences between individuals and for promoting or frustrating their strategies of advancement.

The schools (especially the secondary schools) do not form one system, and even those schools that are under central administrative control (the public system) enjoy enough autonomy in curriculum and policy matters and exploit such different population catchments that they function more as instruments for differentiation than unification. The ability of secondary schools to differentiate their students from others - that is, the extent to which they are able to restore and reassert distance - derives in part from their location within the social space of the city and in part from their location within the institutional geography of the education system itself. How social area favours selective schooling in Melbourne, whether of the private or the public variety, and how it disfavours non-selective schooling, is the theme of this chapter.

Social area differences in educational achievement

As more and more children have come to complete school, it is essential to measure underlying differences in access to the curriculum if final inequalities (such as entry to university) are to be understood and redressed. The upper secondary school curriculum in Melbourne schools has become increasingly diversified over the 1980s, with the emergence of subjects or full programmes that are wholly school-assessed and not recognized by universities for admissions purposes. These programmes have absorbed much of the growth in student numbers, that is, the new population staying on to complete school. The older Higher School Certificate (HSC) curriculum, while including substantial element of school assessment since the early 1980s, continues to rely on external examinations and in general its subjects alone are recognized by the universities. Access to this curriculum is therefore necessary if completing school is to be translated into university places and employment in management and the professions. However, analysis of the geographical and school origins of HSC candidates, and more particularly of their performance at the exams, shows that this access is profoundly unequal.

Children in Melbourne's working-class western suburbs, for example, have markedly weaker chances of achieving *competitive success* (honours grades) in the HSC exams than their peers in the middle-class eastern suburbs, and markedly greater chances of failing outright. For example, in the 1985 English exams, girls living in Footscray or Tottenham had 3 in 100 chances of obtaining an A grade (first class honours), while girls living in Balwyn had 16 in 100 chances.

The suburbs from which these candidates are drawn differ greatly in social status and ethnicity. Over a third of Footscray's population was born in a non-English speaking country and many more have been raised in families where English is not the main language spoken at home (in 1986 only about half of the population spoke only English at home [ABS, 1988]). Two-thirds of persons had no post-school qualifications and 57 per cent of all workers were in blue-collar occupations. By contrast, Balwyn girls come from middle and upper middle-class Anglo-Saxon families. Only 11 per cent of persons were born in non-English speaking countries, 84 per cent speak only English at home, over half have a post-school qualification (23 per cent with a university award), and only 17 per cent of workers are engaged in manual jobs.

Social area differences in competitive success also occur in mathematics. These differences are especially pronounced for girls and suggest on the one hand that social class and ethnicity involve, in many cases, a redoubling of disadvantage, and on the other that at the upper end of the social hierarchy, 'class' protects against 'gender'. In pure mathematics, 7 per cent of girls living in the lowest status suburbs of Melbourne achieved A grades at the 1985 examinations compared with 27 per cent in high status areas. In applied mathematics the figures were 7 per cent and 33 per cent respectively.

So far we have compared girls to illustrate the magnitude of social area differences in exam results. It is important to do this because the conjoint effects of occupational status and ethnicity acting through residential segregation are greater for girls than for boys. Strategies aimed at reducing gender disadvantage need to identify where, within the range of differential attainment across the urban system, they are to be targetted.

For boys, social area differences are less pronounced, but have the same general trend as for girls. In the physical sciences, for example, up to 30 per cent of male candidates in the lowest status areas of Melbourne were awarded either an A or a B grade (first or second class honours) in chemistry and physics. However, in the eastern suburbs this figure rose to as high as 45 per cent.

Failure at the exams rises as we move away from the high status and low migrant density suburbs to the east and into the low status and high migrant density suburbs to the west. In English, the failure rates for male candidates double as we cross the city. In politics, over 40 per cent in working-class districts fail, in geography 47 per cent. Large differences also occur in economics, physics, chemistry, and other subjects.

In comparing examination results across Melbourne, candidates attending both public and private schools have been included. The high concentration of private non-Catholic schools in the eastern and southern suburbs and the consistently higher success rates recorded by these establishments have a major influence on geographical differences. However, private schools are not the only form of selective secondary education in Melbourne. In the next section, we attempt to model the production of success and failure across the city by linking together features of residential segregation, institutional geography (both public and private) and school organization.

Towards a theory of differential success and failure

Patterns of success and failure at the Higher School Certificate examinations are the culmination of a process of scholastic selection reaching back into primary school. From the few studies that have been conducted in Australia into differential attainment at this level, we know that children enrolling in suburban secondary schools located in middle-class areas are likely to be more advanced in English and mathematics than their peers entering secondary schools in working-class areas (Badcock, 1977). Any theory of success and failure must start with the processes of selection at work in primary school, for example, the different levels of parental support for reading or the behavioural expectations of teachers. But it is equally crucial to explain how differences in initial attainments are converted by secondary schools into a widening social gap, characterized by early leaving on the part of working-class children, failure or poor performance at examinations, curriculum relegation, and denial of places in higher education.

Residential segregation is the basic mechanism through which the resources represented by parental education, cultural 'ethos', and attainment at primary school are concentrated in school catchments – or dispersed too thinly across them. But it is the differential provision of *selective schooling* which ensures that these resources, where they are concentrated, can be exploited. For the accumulated advantages of cultural capital depend on the continuous pooling of resources between families that occurs through schools and the ability of individual families to unite in their status strategies and to resist the erosion of their capital that occurs through socially and scholastically mixed environments.

Access to selective schooling is thus vital, and in Melbourne this is achieved in three ways: private schools, selective-entry public high schools, and district high schools which offer selective classes. The distribution of these three forms of selective schooling is unequal across Melbourne. The highest concentration of private schools occurs in the eastern and southern suburbs. These suburbs are also the main source of recruitment for the handful of prestigious selective-entry public high schools. Located close to the central business district, these establishments at the time of the study continued to recruit mainly from their zoned Central Schools.

No research has been conducted into the location of district high schools which offer selective classes through streaming, 'setting' on specific subjects (especially mathematics), and restrictive promotions policies. Streaming was common practice in Victorian schools until the late 1960s, but declined partly as the public examinations terminating Years 10 and 11 were phased out and partly as recognition of its effects became widely established. In the very nature of the case, those 'academic' schools which have retained or resuscitated the practice have a local visibility only. They rarely have a distinctive administrative status, enabling them to recruit very widely and selectively after the manner of private schools, though this does happen in the case of a few 'declared music schools'. Rather, such schools use autonomy in curriculum matters, the loose or overlapping catchment zones which have arisen through population decline, and the conservatism of their school councils to implement an 'academic' policy.

Differential access to these three forms of selective schooling helps explain the social area geography of scholastic success in Melbourne. To explore the interactions between residential segregation and selective schooling, let us consider an apparent paradox in the data on social access to the curriculum. If initial attainment is higher in the middle-class areas of Melbourne than elsewhere and if access to selective schooling is also greater, then we should expect entrolment rates in preparatory mathematics to be higher, too, in these areas. For in the eastern and southern suburbs, the organization of the school system conserves and augments individual advantages of family background through the selective pooling of achievers in the three types of selective schooling discussed above. By contrast, in working-class suburbs residential segregation tends to congregate the number of children who are scholastically or behaviourally 'at risk' into open access establishments where failure is likely to be greater, and discouragement more complete. Rates of enrolment in preparatory mathematics should, therefore, be higher in middle-class suburbs and lower in working-class areas. But they are not.

In 1985 there were three mathematics subjects which were accepted by universities for admissions purposes – pure mathematics, applied mathematics, and general mathematics (not suitable for continuing work at university). Across Melbourne, about a third of all girls attempting their HSC enrolled in general mathematics. While there is some evidence of a social trend, with enrolments ranging from 31 per cent in two low status clusters to as high as 40 per cent in one high status cluster, there was generally little variation (with a standard deviation of 2.6 per cent). In pure mathematics, one of the subjects permitting advanced university work and taken by a much smaller number of students, there was even less variation (mean 12.3 per cent, standard deviation 2.4 per cent) and even less suggestion of a social trend. On a superficial reading of this data, girls in working-class areas of Melbourne had as much chance of enrolling in preparatory mathematics as girls in middle-class areas. But such a conclusion is unjustified.

First of all, account needs to be taken of the fact that underlying equal rates of enrolment in mathematics lay large differences in survival or retention to Year 12 (when HSC is attempted). In 1985 girls in the highest status areas of Victoria as a whole were nearly twice as likely to complete school as their peers in the lowest status areas (84 per cent compared to 44 per cent) (DEET, 1987). For Melbourne, this difference was probably smaller, but still very substantial (Teese, 1989). Thus girls in working-class areas achieved a level of mathematics enrolment similar to that achieved by girls in middle-class suburbs, but based on a much lower survival rate to Year 12. Secondly, although the proportion of survivors enrolling in maths (the 'residual enrolment rate') was as high as in middle-class suburbs, this does not imply that the same absolute standard of attainment had been reached. Moreover, in both areas of Melbourne an overall poor level of enrolment in maths was recorded by comparison with male students. The real question is not the apparent paradox of working-class girls achieving the same formal access to maths as their middle-class peers, but why girls in middle-class suburbs did not achieve a *higher* level of access.

The answer would appear to lie in the policies adopted by schools. There is some evidence, though from a very small number of schools only, that in working-class suburbs, public high schools operate more liberal promotions policies. In the words of one school principal, students who want to attempt preparatory mathematics are 'given a chance'. Conversely, in the suburbs to the east and south of Melbourne, a restrictive promotions policy is often applied. Only those students who are likely to be *competitive* – to gain honours grades – are permitted to enrol. This restriction begins on entry to Year 11 as a matter of formal policy, but is really an extension of the practice of streaming or 'setting' begun at Year 8 or even Year 7 level. As a result, students surviving to enrol in preparatory mathematics in Year 12 have been exposed to a protracted process of selection.

Girls are particularly vulnerable to this process. In 1985, not more than one in two survived to study preparatory mathematics, even in the highest status areas of Melbourne. However, this heavy loss was not borne by all social groups equally. The 'weeding out' of uncompetitive pupils in these areas takes its greatest toll amongst working-class and lower-middle-class groups. As we shall see, in eastern suburban schools social selection is so severe in applied mathematics that by Year 11 a complete splitting of the school population has occurred. Children from professional and managerial families enrol in this subject in large numbers to the practical exclusion of all other groups. High academic results are achieved through this practice, but they are reserved to a scholastic and a social élite.

School organization and differential success

The problems of transition from primary to secondary school, including unequal attainment and pupil diversity, are tackled by schools in working class districts in Melbourne in a variety of ways. Some establish 'mini schools' which keep groups of pupils together for the first four years of high school. Others devise a junior school programme which preserves the 'home teacher' model derived from primary school. Still others put the stress on the 'bonding' effects of extra-curricular activities, such as excursions, the school camp, concerts, exhibitions, etc. All of these approaches are aimed at helping pupils work together as groups so that classes are productive, pupils help each other, there is a good working 'tone', and teachers can actually teach to the class as well as working with individuals and small groups. But it remains difficult for the scholastic and behavioural management strategies adopted in working-class schools to overcome differences in initial attainment and motivation, in short, to 'level the playing field' so that *competitive success* can ultimately be achieved.

Moreover, it is difficult for many working-class families directly to contribute to children's learning at secondary school level (eg, they may know little or no algebra, no French, etc.). The transition to secondary school brings with it both more *specialized* scholastic demands and more *individualized* demands. There is a much greater expectation of self-direction, which in turn presupposes effective family organization. If schools seek to moderate the effects of these demands by providing choice within the middle school curriculum, this operates at the same time as a framework of consensual streaming through which accumulated failure is registered and becomes educationally definitive.

After Year 10, when children have attained the statutory age, the rate of early leaving increases. Although the surviving student groups in local high schools are progressively 'refined' by attrition and by transfer to the refuges represented by the less 'academic' high and technical schools, they also continue to lose more able students to the private schools operationg across Melbourne and to the selective-entry high schools in the central city.

By Year 12, classes in preparatory mathematics and physical sciences are often small. But this is not necessarily an advantage. For some of the best students – the 'pilots', as French researchers call them (de Peretti, 1987) – have gone to selective schools of one type or another. Small classes mean that the focus of teaching must inevitably be on independent learning (because rote methods suitable for large, relatively homogeneous classes and for 'cramming' will not work in this context and have no meaning). But in densely working-class areas, student learning is likely to enjoy less peer and family support than in middle-class suburbs. The learners are more alone, more dependent on the individual teacher. They work in an environment much more vulnerable to the action of chance, isolated factors, such as the absence of a teacher or a sudden change in teachers or mistakes in teaching or exams preparation. Those students who compete for success in these environments are likely to fail more often (and do), while those who do succeed will be very hardy indeed (and are).

Here we can offer a brief illustration of the contrast in *access to classes* between children in working-class suburbs and those in middle-class suburbs. Figure 13.1 represents the scholastic space occupied by HSC candidates living in one postal district in the working-class west of Melbourne.

Every school attended by at least one child from this district is plotted on the chart. To locate the schools in the space of their relative attainment, two dimensions were used: the weighted mean score in HSC English and the weighted mean score in preparatory mathematics (pure maths and general maths). (The scores are standardized, with means of zero, and the scales are in units of standard deviations.)

As we ascend the line which links attainment in English with attainment in preparatory mathematics (r = .8051), we move away from the non-selective schools (both public and private) located in or adjacent to the postal district and towards selective schools (both private and public), mostly located on the other side of the city.

Only a trickle of students emigrate daily to these eastern or southern

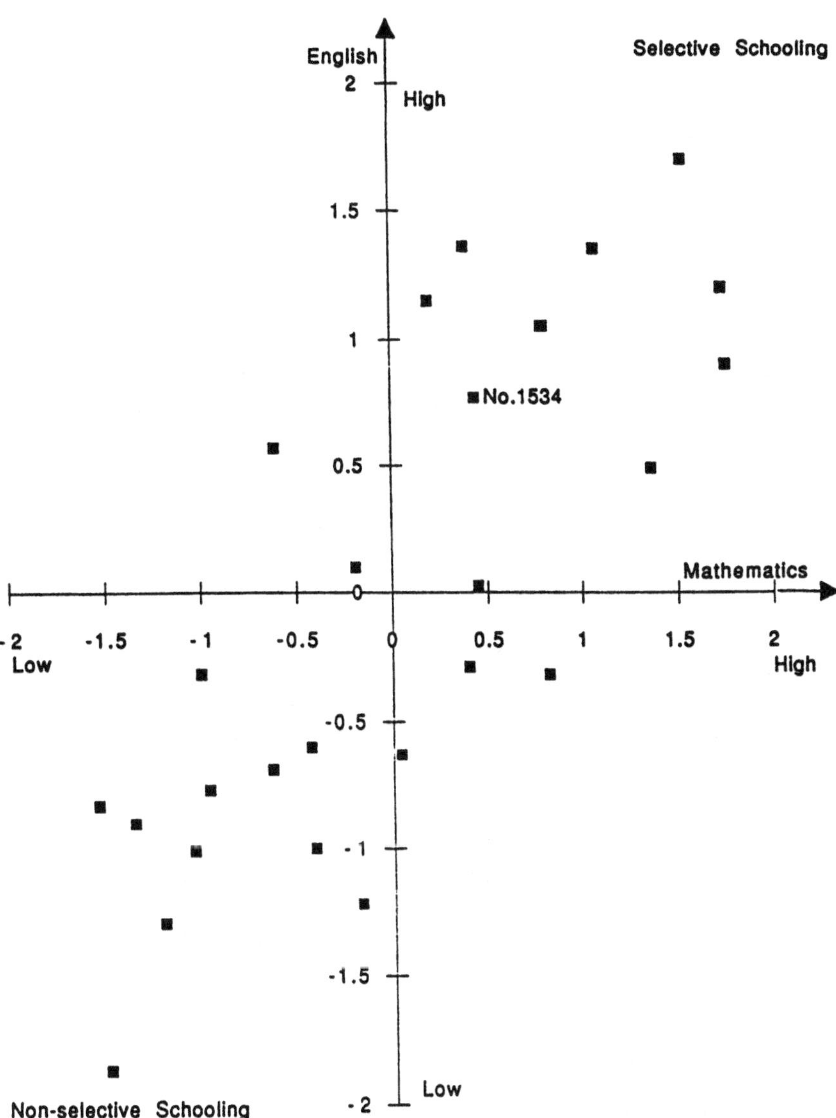

Figure 13.1 *Mean English and maths performance in schools attended by students from the working-class postal district in Melbourne*

suburban schools, but they are often the students who obtain A grades. They attend establishments which, with the exception of some of the girls' schools, are able to form at least one physics class of 20 students, usually two or three, and sometimes as many as six or seven such classes.

There is only one local school positioned on the chart near to these schools (no. 1534). This non-government school has the largest single share of all HSC students in the postal district (22 per cent), many of them able students, and its attainment profile differs drastically from the other local schools. It operates as a kind of academic refuge. Surrounded by empty paddocks in open farming country, it draws in its students by school buses.

The local public and private non-selective schools which account for a further 56 per cent of HSC candidates in the district present a very different profile. Not only are they below average both in English and in preparatory mathematics, but in physics they usually operate small or very small classes. These are often depleted of the most talented students who have either enrolled in the local 'academic refuge' or commute across the city to middle-class havens, where their chances of competitive success are much greater. Within the local non-selective schools, there remains a scattering of talented students, one, two or perhaps three at each site.

The situation in middle-class areas of Melbourne is very different, thanks to the widespread operation of selective schooling under its various forms. In our simplified model, and taking girls as an example, we argued that it is harder for those in working-class areas to complete school at all, though their final access to preparatory mathematics is in general more liberal. Conversely, while it is easier for girls in middle-class suburbs to complete school, their final access to preparatory mathematics is more restricted. A bigger and more successful pool of students can be drawn upon and filtered through the school's promotions policy. Viable and large classes can often be formed, especially in private non-Catholic schools, and these are enriched by transfers into the school, sometimes on the basis of scholarships offered by the school itself. The haemorrhage of talent that occurs in working-class schools is reversed. In the context of larger and more homogeneous classes, traditional teaching methods can be applied towards avowedly strategic ends. Routine can be built into the instructional process, based on predictability of student characteristics, continuous supervision over the long term, and the more effective functioning of the class as a group. With these differences in school organization, it is not surprising that private school students will on average do *less* well once they enter the less supervised world of the university than public high school students with the same HSC score (Dunn, 1982; West, 1985). But on the other hand they will enter this world much more often and out of proportion to their numbers in Year 12 (Anderson and Vervoorn, 1983).

Conclusion

Exploiting the social space of the city, which is relatively durable and resistent to social policy, the different types of selective schooling (private and public) depend on an institutional framework of curriculum, assessment and certification which is less stable and is exposed to more ongoing political contest. Success and failure are not the spontaneous result of urban geography – the aggregate effects of 'family background' – but depend upon the management of this framework over time. This is pre-eminently a political task, involving a variety of agencies and interest groups, and in the Victorian context the framework involves a division of functions and powers across agencies (the Victorian Curriculum and Assessment Board, the universities, various committees, etc.), rather than a concentration of roles in the one statutory authority. Despite the appearance of a dispersal of authority, a high degree of centralized curriculum control is in fact achieved, and it is thanks to this integration of secondary schooling that social and cultural differences in their particular spatial configurations can be exploited. The strategies of selection practised by private and public schools as a matter of policy (not necessity) are rewarded and the non-selective policies that some (though not all) working-class schools pursue are penalized.

Other political factors come into play which, though more visible, are secondary and depend both on the underlying pattern of urban stratification and the institutional framework of curriculum control for their effectiveness. Melbourne has the highest concentration of private schools in Australia, and the median per capita grant paid by the state government to private schools is higher than in most other states. As the most academically successful of these establishments are located in the eastern and southern suburbs, this policy of overt support for selective schooling enlarges strategic options for middle- and upper-middle-class parents and intensifies the effects of selection based on residential segregation. Given the social geography of Melbourne, the policy of expanding private school demand by subsidizing private costs has led inevitably to an undermining of educational opportunity in working-class areas, wherever these are found, and operates in effect as a policy of regional degradation.

Since 1972 federal government policy has sought to redress social area disadvantage through supplementary funding to assessed 'disadvantaged' schools. However, a fuller view of the origins of failure at upper secondary school would suggest that local improvements in the quality of teaching and learning, additional staff, and a better school environment are likely to be marginalized if the students benefiting from these improvements are forced to compete against the beneficiaries of a much more extensive programme of private school funding which enhances social area advantage. Moreover, even substantial curriculum reforms, unless they generate real choice amongst upper secondary programmes, will continue to draw all students together in an artificial 'homogenization' of abilities and achievements and into a false game of competition played out in the name of formal equality, objectivity of assessment, and administrative rationality.

References

Anderson, D S and Vervoorn, A E (1983) *Access to Privilege: Participation in Australian Post-Secondary Education*, Canberra: Australian National University.

ABS (1988) *Census 86. Profile of Legal Local Government Areas – Usual Resident Counts, Victoria*, Australian Bureau of Statistics.

Australian Schools Commission (1973) *Schools in Australia*, Report of the Inquiry of the Interim Committee, Canberra: AGPS.

Badcock, B A (1977) 'Educational achievement and participation rates in Sydney', *Australian Geographer*, 13, 325–31.

Boltanski, L (1976) 'L'encombrement et la maîtrise des "biens sans maître", *Actes de la Recherche en Sciences Sociales*, 1, 102–9.
Broome, R (1984) *The Victorians Arriving*, McMahons Point: Fairfax, Syme and Weldon.
Burnley, I H (1980) *The Australian Urban System: Growth, Change and Differentiation*, Melbourne: Longman Cheshire.
Claydon, L F (1973) *Renewing Urban Teaching*, London: Cambridge University Press.
Claydon, L F (ed) (1975) *The Urban School*, Carlton: Pitman.
DEET (1987) *Completing Secondary School in Australia: A Socio-Economic and Regional Analysis*, Canberra: DEET.
De Peretti, A (1987) *Pour une école plurielle*, Paris.
Dunn, T R (1982) 'An empirical demonstration of bias in HSC examination results', *Australian Journal of Education*, 26, 190–203.
Fisher, C H, Hagan, J S and de Lacey, P (1973) 'High school retention rates and social class', *Australian Journal of Social Issues*, 8, 221–6.
Johns, G T (1976) 'The spatial structure of educational opportunities', MA Thesis, Monash University, Melbourne.
Lamb, S (1991) 'Social selection in Australian secondary schools', unpublished Ph.D thesis, University of Melbourne.
Linke, R D (1988)) *Regional Analysis of Socioeconomic Trends in Educational Participation*, with the assistance of L M Oertel and N J M Kelsey, Canberra: ANU.
Logan, M I, Maher, C A, McKay, J and Humphreys, J S (1975) *Urban and Regional Australia: Analysis and Policy Issues*, Melbourne: Sorrett.
Maher, C A (1982) *Australian Cities in Transition*, Melbourne: Shillington House.
Neutze, M (1978) *Australian Urban Policy*, Sydney: Allen & Unwin.
Newton, P W and Johnston, R J (1981) 'Melbourne', in Pacione, M (ed) *Urban Problems and Planning in the Developed World*, London: Croom Helm.
Stilwell, F J B and Hardwick, J M (1973) 'Social inequality in Australian cities', *Australian Quarterly*, 45, 4, 18–36.
Stimson, R J (1982) *The Australian City: A Welfare Geography*, Melbourne: Longman Cheshire.
Teese, R V (1989) 'Gender and class in the transformation of the public high school in Melbourne, 1946–85', *History of Education Quarterly*, 29, 237–59.
Teese, R V (1991) 'Social Access to the Curriculum: An Overview of Four Public High Schools in Melbourne'. Unpublished report for the Schools Council of the National Board of Employment, Education and Training.
Walker, S R (1979) 'Educational service in Sydney: some spatial variations', *Australian Geographical Studies*, 17, 175–92.
West, L H T (1985) 'Differential prediction of first year university performance of students from different social backgrounds', *Australian Journal of Education*, 29, 175–87.

14. Urbanization and education in Nairobi

Kevin M Lillis

Population pressure

Like other urban centres in Kenya, Nairobi suffers extreme educational and housing problems and has done so since the early days of independence (1963). That it shares these with other Kenyan urban areas is suggested in Chapter 6. Its problems, though, are unique in tempo and degree. Not only is it the only urban concentration with city status and the political and cultural capital, it is the national communications centre by road and rail and a continental air hub, a location that encourages substantial migration. It retains a monopoly of new industrial and commercial investment and is a city of rapidly developing industrial development with considerably faster industrialization and commercialization than Mombasa or Kisumu and the other major municipalities of Nakuru, Eldoret and Thika. It is also located at a focal point within a rich agricultural hinterland of Central, Rift Valley and Eastern Provinces, characterized by plantation agricultural production, much of it marketed within or through Nairobi. It exhibits a dynamic economic vitality and a faster rate of population growth than the other top eight urban centres in the country put together. Its contemporary development continues the pre-independence colonial mode of urban development, but at an explosively and dangerously accelerated rate.

The high population growth rate of Nairobi (and Kenya) in the post-independence decades emerges from a familiar combination of declining levels of mortality, low infant mortality and high fertility rates as well as significantly improved health provision and care. A major significant issue from the educational viewpoint is the high percentage of the population under 15 years old. Although up-to-date data are not readily available at the time of writing, this is well illustrated by the 1969–79 national growth of the under-15 group from 35.97 per cent to 40.26 per cent (Opinyah, 1982), putting enormous pressures on the Nairobi City Commission to create educational opportunities.

Importantly, this population pressure emerges from both a high rate of population growth and an accelerated rate of urban migration, in which the latter has recently outweighed the former as the major cause. Inevitably, too, this impacts upon the patterns of educational provision in a resourcing context demanding community provision of educational facilities (see below). Many urban migrants exist within a context of inadequate supplies of low-income housing (and schooling). The rate of urban migration far exceeds the rate at which schools are established, resulting in outmigration of mothers in the search for educational opportunities for their children in the rural areas from which they might have originated. Nairobi, thus, has a skewed educational profile.

Population densities and spread

Inevitably, there are wide variations in population density, reflecting different land utilization patterns within what Obudho (1986) sees as six different land-use divisions: the central business areas; the industrial area; public and private open spaces; public and government land; residential areas; underdeveloped land. Such land utilization and population density patterns are reflected in the availability of schools and in the differential opportunities of access to education. Nairobi's 162 primary schools (1989 total) are spread throughout the city's 693 square kilometres but clearly not mapped out in an equitable way. There are obvious shortages in the central business and industrial areas (despite the popular practice of working parents driving their children to school in these areas). Equally, in areas of high population density in specific residential areas, there are many shortages. Obudho (1986) also suggests six residential areas of varying population density and social mix and these also appear to reflect particular patterns of educational advantage and disadvantage, as well as differential enrolment and achievement rates.

Many areas of the city have witnessed both uncontrolled expansion of 'housing' and the evolution of low-income residential zones and estates. It cannot be overstressed that it is within these areas that urban poverty and deprivation is at its starkest. Here there are densities of population of over 2,000 people per square hectare (UNICEF, 1989), often 40–60 per cent higher than the city average and living in unplanned settlements. Sixty-six per cent of this population live in rental accommodation, often spending 40 per cent of their disposable income on rents alone. The substantial research in these areas (see UNICEF, 1989) reports low nutritional levels and expensive food and cooking fuel, including charcoal. Changes of cooking habits affect the protein intake of the children, which itself affects learning. Some estimates are that in some squatter settlements, 50–60 per cent of children are malnourished, with many below average height and weight. The slums and squatter areas reveal the highest levels of disease, the lowest levels of immunization and the highest levels of infant mortality. Here the women retain high levels of fertility (an average of 8+ per woman in squatter settlements, in contrast to decreasing average levels in Kenya). Not surprisingly, educational enrolments are lowest in such areas. Up to 60 per cent of children in squatter areas do not attend pre-school: nursery schools are available in middle and high income areas but are expensive and, even where the Nairboi City Commission operates nursery schools, eg, in Mathare Valley, they are beyond the affordability (or comprehension) of most squatter families. Even where local committees or NGOs do provide pre-schools, they are devoid of learning materials. Such groups are under-represented in primary education in Nairobi (where, in any case, the gross enrolment ratio is below the national average). When pupils from these areas do go to school, they represent the highest drop-out rates before Standard.

Financing education and the pressures on communities

Since 1985, Kenya's educational policy has focused upon a major structural and curricular reform - the '8-4-4' system of education - which has sought to change the structures of the system from 7-6-3, which, amongst other major shifts now causing major nation-wide implementation headaches, added a year to the primary school cycle. In addition, it sought to add a vocational bias into what was seen as an excessively academic curriculum. Hitherto, in the face of enormous social demand for education, the Kenyan educational budget had absorbed up to 40 per cent of annual recurrent expenditure. Given a 1976 government moratorium on capital expenditures at primary level, the burden for financing much of the reform fell upon already overtaxed parents. 'Standard 8' classrooms as well as domestic science, woodwork and metalwork shops were to be provided by parents and communities. In many parts of the country, the well-known community mobilization phenomenon of 'harambee' (Bray and Lillis, 1988) was able to satisfy the resourcing and building demands of providing such facilities for over 13,500 schools.

Harambee has many origins, dynamics and motivations. However, essentially, 'harambee' is a peer group, kinship group, community force. It is not in essence a mobilization force that has taken root in urban situations, where the notion of community is much harder to define and the notions of a tight-knit series of relationships within homogeneous groups is much more difficult to identify and mobilize. In Nairobi, as in other cities, there is often a deep sense of isolation, even alienation from neighbours and in the new cosmopolitan housing estates, people frequently do not know their neighbours' names, in contrast with communal practices in rural areas. Consequently, there is no tradition of 'harambee' within the City (although parental gifts to schools are common, and an easier option). Many City dwellers have two allegiances, a house in Nairobi and a home elsewhere and those inclined to participate in 'harambee' activities do so in the rural areas from which they originate. The consequence for education is that many facilities demanded for 8-4-4 from the non-existent financing partnership have not accrued. Schools, already under-resourced, have become relatively more deprived, and hard-pressed head teachers and school managers have not been able to compensate for the resourcing shortfalls in the way that many schools in the rich areas of Central Province surrounding Nairobi have been able to do so. Equally importantly, in rural areas, many communities build whole schools, though there is no evidence of such community provision of a school in the City of Nairobi.

Although there is widespread clamour to revise these elements of cost-sharing, they continue in existence, militating against attempts to provide universal qualitative education throughout the City. Also, the limited City Commission Budget for Education is targeted at the provision of learning materials rather than towards capital developmen. Nor is there any surplus purchasing power in the bulk of the population (especially in the slums of Kibera and Mathare Valley) to enable compensatory parental beneficence, as exists, by contrast, in the high-income areas of Muthaiga and Karen, for example, to add to the existing head start in educational privilege already enjoyed within such areas. It is interesting to note an official response to this situation. The Permanent Secretary to the Ministry for Energy is quoted in the *Daily Nation* of 10 September 1990 as telling the residents of Nairobi that 'more school facilities are a must' since 167 primary schools and 83 secondary schools were insufficient to cater for the one million children making up Nairobi's one and a half million population. Since Nairobi's examination results 'lagged behind the rural districts ... residents must change the mentality that they were sojourning in the city and were, therefore, not required to participate in its development. People spend most of their working life in the city and unless they put up more schools, they will be in trouble.'

District primary school enrolments

Kenya has long espoused the principle and right of universal primary education and claims a 1987 94 per cent gross enrolment rate (GRE) ie 5.03 million of 5.36 million school-age children. Certain districts can boast 100+ per cent GREs (eg, Kisumu, Siaya, Kericho, Bungoma and Nandi). Elgeyo Marakwet in 1987 could boast 62,805 primary school children enrolled in its schools, although it only had 44,735 school-age children in the district, ie a 140 per cent GRE, explained through in-migration in search of educational opportunity as well as by enrolment of 'over-age' pupils and underestimation of population projections.

By contrast, the arid and semi-arid districts, Wajir (14 per cent), Garissa (20 per cent) and Mandera (26 per cent), with a high concentration of nomads with no deep tradition of formal education, evidence the lowest enrolment ratios. If the harshness of certain parts of the urban context were overlooked, Nairobi's 1987 GRE might prove surprising. Can it be anticipated that the capital would enrol 100 per cent of its primary age population? 'Why City Education is lagging behind' was the enraged headline of the *Kenya Times* on 6 June 1990. 'Nairobi – believe it or not – is among 9 of Kenya's 43 districts with the lowest enrolment rates in primary schools in recent years'. Its 63 per cent GRE in 1987 was 31 per cent behind the national average of 94 per cent. The *Kenya Times*, essentially a KANU Party mouthpiece accused Nairobi (and Mombasa, the second largest urban area where 57,816 out of 89,781 children were enrolled) of being 'lackadaisacal' and of 'unsatisfactory' provision of schools, classes and teacher:pupil ratios. 'The cities are ranked 30th', it complained, 'far below the rural districts... The urban poor, living in squatter and slum areas, who constitute about 30 per cent of the urban poor of Nairobi are particularly afflicted by a problem of the shortage of places'. However, enrolment data (Mwangi, 1988) reveal a number of paradoxes, including unfilled places in schools.

As elsewhere in Kenya, there are high drop-out rates in Nairobi. For example, 63.2 per cent of the 1974 Standard 1 intake did not reach Standard 7 (then the last year of primary education) in 1980. Of the 1979 Standard 1 intake, 64.7 per cent did not reach Standard 8 in 1986. Between 1985 and 1986, 19.2 per cent of boys and 30.2 per cent of girls dropped out of primary schools in the City between Standards 1 and 8.

Inevitably, the majority of the drop-outs are from already disadvantaged groups. Those from poor urban areas who manage to enter school often drop out either before or after Standard 8 either for lack of money or lack of motivation (or for familiar city-related problems of alcohol and drugs) or for failure in their examinations. Mothers in such areas work in the informal sectors, hawking, kiosking and in prostitution. Older children are often required to take care of their younger siblings and to take charge of home-based businesses such as selling changaa, charcoal or paraffin, meaning that there is an over-riding impetus in poor urban areas towards dropping out of school.

Importantly, the Nairobi City Commission, now (despite earlier initiatives linked with NGO support) appears to disregard these urban drop-outs, 'push-outs' and 'left-outs'. As with other local councils, the Commission encourages enrolments in tune with the government policy of universal primary education. Its own management problems focus upon maintaining and slightly expanding and improving its existing educational infrastructures and shows little concern for the disadvantaged by-passed by the mainstream. There are, though, a limited number of successful initiatives targetted at solving the educational problems of these marginalized outsiders. One of the most visible and successful (amongst others promoted by a variety of NGOs) is the Undugu Basic Education Programme which seeks to provide both care and shelter for these disadvantaged youth and a meaningful education programme to enable future survival and employment opportunity for them in the full awareness that they are unlikely to proceed far within the formal educational and employment structures. One important feature of the programme is the telescope curriculum so that the normal eight-year primary school syllabus may be covered in three, after which the children may become apprenticed within youth polytechnic programmes. Undugu also provides a flexible approach to accommodating children who can attend only intermittently for reasons suggested above, namely that schools compete with necessary family and personal basic survival activities. Equally, Undugu seeks a real-life approach to the process of education, attempting to draw upon children's very experience and skills in these survival processes and hence to reach, not alienate, the youth who are by-passed by the City Commission formal mainstream.

KCPE: the pressure cooker

The Kenya Certificate of Primary Education (KCPE), the primary school leaving certificate, is a notorious trauma for Kenyan Standard 8 pupils as the yardstick through which they pass into the highly prized secondary school places. The *Sunday Nation*, 14 May 1989, graphically captures the nature of the struggle: 'The driving force . . . is the cut-throat competition in our examination system which is used as a criterion for selecting those who continue for further education'. '"The pressure to excel in school is driving kids crazy" – expert. Parents' dreams have turned pupils' lives into nightmares' (*Daily Nation*, 9 August 1990).

Each year the publication of the KCPE results leads to a widespread orgy of recrimination within those districts not ranked within the 'league table' published by the Kenya National Examinations Council as a proxy for the top-achieving districts. This includes the majority of the municipalities, those urban councils and commissions responsible for managing their own education subsystems. The declining quality of standards in urban areas has been a debating point in primary education since the poor performance of Nairobi District subsequent to the 1983 Certificate of Primary Education (CPE) results. This was the first time since districts had been used as units of analysis in the publication of primary school leaving results that Nairobi District had not topped the league table. (It was 2nd!)

The results are normally greeted by the establishment of an official enquiry to determine the reasons for the unexpectedly poor and unacceptable results with the determination of the culprits and scapegoats: indolent/truant pupils; inefficient/absentee teachers, and clamours for their arrest; illiterate school committees; scarce and decrepit facilities; high class sizes. The urban areas now complain of 'rural bias' in the 8-4-4 curriculum (and it is true that, subsequent to the 1985 8-4-4 reform, the KCPE curricula and examination items have sought to eliminate the perceived erstwhile urban bias [Somerset, 1988]). They complain of specific phenomena that militate against achievement in town schools, in addition to the above: the lack of agricultural facilities (since agriculture is now given a premium in the examinations); the lack of adequate community support for capital infrastructure; the pressures of co-curricular activities; the disadvantaged nature of the vast majority of the urban schools' intake; cheating; transport problems; TV; the problems of social discipline in the face of drinking, discos, prostitution, drugs, etc.

The individual, community and parental pressures for success result in a number of phenomena which are dramatically portrayed within the City.

Pressures to enter primary schools

The pressure to *enter* schools is enormous. In the UK context, Ball (1990) demonstrates that proximity, congeniality, affordability and achievement of the school are criteria influencing parental choice of the schools they prefer for their children in the growing free-market in the UK. In Nairobi, parents equally have the right of choice over their preferred school for their children, although the City Education Office officially seeks to encourage parents to use their neighbourhood primary school. However, the reputation and environmental location of the school almost invariably override proximity, especially for those parents who have the understanding as well as the mobility and finances to seek better alternatives, even within the limited number of Nairobi City Commission schools. There are numerous examples of parents camping out all night (or more than one night) to be early in the queue to obtain Standard 1 admission application forms (application forms, note!). Government policy is to enable a maximum of 50 pupils per class and schools may issue application forms for the anticipated intake, plus 10 per cent. About 20 successful schools are subject to 'queuing pressure' and there is often heated reaction from parents resentful of 'outsiders' seeking admission to specific schools. For example, parents who had unsuccessfully sought their children's admission to Standard 1 in the highly acclaimed Hospital Hill School in 1988 appealed to the government to declare admissions into the school to be null and void on the argument that priority should be given to parents living within the school vicinity. As it was, of the 180 places available, 93 were filled by pupils with siblings already there; 87 were filled by new pupils as a result of queuing and the notion of the neighbourhood school did not exist.

That capacity to pay is a criterion for survival after access is well illustrated below. Many of the magnet schools are located within the affluent residential areas and, in the case of Nairobi Primary School for example, close to the heart of the city, enabling politicians, civil servants and business people to drop their children off en route to and from work (or get their drivers to do so).

By contrast, there are many illustrations that location militates against a school's appeal. Parents choose only as a last resort many of the schools in the overcrowded, disadvantaged environments in residential districts, provided alternative possibilities present themselves. Equally, the educated upwardly-mobile bourgeoisie choose to neglect their neighbourhood school in favour of those known to process their offspring through higher levels of the system. Teachers at Lenana School, Nairobi, one of Kenya's most successful national secondary schools situated on the edge of the forest to the west of the city, choose not the local Ngong Forest School but the more successful private or high-cost City Commission schools within the affluent residential areas. The clientele of Ngong Forest School are largely workers from the City Commission Forest Nursery and cooks from Lenana School, etc. Clearly, this then militates against the school achieving high success.

Preconditions for entry

The pressure to enter the schools most perceived as successful in the KCPE has resulted in many of them using pre-primary education as a criterion for admission. This, of course, is an illustration of the law of supply and demand and the apparent shortage of places in the 'best' schools. More importantly, this process favours the well-off. Fees for the private pre-schools and for the City Commission pre-schools are beyond the means of most poor people, even if they possessed the aspirations to send their children to them. The pre-school criterion inevitably militates against the poor, although some estimate that 30 per cent of Nairobi's three- to five-year-olds attend pre-school classes.

Affordability

The above scenario illustrates the fear that 'good education' may end up by being the preserve of those who can afford it. Already those who can and do take advantage of the flourishing group of high-cost, high-achieving private schools in Nairobi (about 20 in number) reinforce the head-start gained by their children learning in small classes that enable individual tuition. (These classically withhold slow learners from the KCPE, thus reinforcing the image of their success.) There is also a fear that capacity and ability to pay determines access to and continuation in the best City Commission schools, despite the official Ministry of Education post-1979 national policy of free primary education. Whilst there are no fees *per se* in City Commission schools, there are numerous levies and/or school development funds and 'user-charges' for stationery, uniforms, text-books, etc., all in the name of 'cost-sharing' at all levels (including post-1990, at tertiary level) – the official policy enunciated in Sessional Paper No 6, 1989, 'Education and Manpower Training for the next decade and beyond'.

In 1989 over K Shs 1,000 was required on average to purchase for Standard 8 pupils all the essential text-books recommended by the Ministry of Education. The costs of uniforms ranged from Shs 500–1,000; PTA funds ranged from Shs 1,000–3,000. Other levies included those for examinations, stationery and swimming. To this, parents need to add costs of food and bus fares where relevant. However, in a country and city in which average fertility rates have exceeded 8.0 and large families are the norm, parents would be paying for a large number of children. The statutory fee for government-maintained day secondary schools in 1989 was Shs 450, for boarding schools Shs 1,350 with fees, costs of books and levies 300 per cent more. Parents might pay Shs 7,000–8,000 for a coveted place in a government-maintained secondary school. Private school costs range from Shs 6,000–20,000 and are accessible only to the affluent. *Average* per capita income in Nairobi in 1989 was Shs 6,000, all of which could be spent on educating one child for one year in a public secondary school.

Private tuition

Despite official opposition from the City Education Department there are flourishing practices of private tuition and commercial coaching, often conducted by moonlighting City Commission teachers. The *Sunday Nation*, 14 May 1989, condemns those who charge for private tuition and 'scramble for the quick shilling by cashing in on parents' anxieties to have their children do well in the KCPE'. The cost-efficacy has yet to be demonstrated, for parents can clearly pay out exhorbitant sums and their children register poor results, just as high-cost schools can register poor results.

Repeaters

There is a widespread practice of schools holding back certain candidates to repeat either Standards 6 or 7 to gain adequate grounding in the pre-examination classes. It is a widely held view that such 'repeaters' are more likely to succeed in the primary school leaving examination first time and schools (especially fee-paying private schools) can present an image of success if they can reveal a high percentage of passes in the KCPE. This is common practice within 'successful' rural districts, argue Nairobi City Commission officials, but not within the city. The press, though, declaims otherwise:

> Some schools want good results and present the best candidates . . . weak pupils are sacrificed at the altar of prestige . . . notorious high-cost schools register good results through dubious means . . . they don't present average candidates and force others to repeat or to register as private candidates (*Sunday Nation*, 14 May 1989).

Effective schools

Despite the scenarios above indicating the advantages enjoyed by the affluent and by high-cost schools, they are not of necessity always the best, although the top performing schools have tended to sustain their image of quality as a result of teacher, parental and pupil pressure which establishes a self-fulfilling prophecy. The image of 'bad schools' is also the converse self-fulfilling prophecy. In the worst-performing districts in Nairobi (the neighbouring peri-urban districts of Dagoretti and Waithaka, only 'annexed' to the City after the 1963 boundary reforms) there is no tradition of high attainment and little evidence of the psychological effects of competition evidenced in the affluent suburbs like Langata and Lavington. Nevertheless, there are obviously many illustrations of schools that overcome the disadvantages of their immediate urban environments to act as models for other aspirants. When, for example, Olympic Primary School in Kibera became the top school in Nairobi (and the only low-cost primary school in the ten best City Commission schools) and the 33rd school in the country in the 1987 KCPE, it was greeted with press acclaim:

> Primary Olympic stuns the best.... The little Davids from Olympic Primary School gave the Nairobi Goliaths a technical knock-out in academic gymnastics. They studied under trees and in the evenings they used paraffin lamps in their mud houses. [It is a school of] crowded families with no lighting and no furniture ... study takes place in makeshift wooden classes where there is a lack of text-books ... which shows that any school can do well regardless of its locality (*Daily Nation*, 8 October 1987).

The teachers apparently attributed their success to a 'rigorous system of fortnightly tests'. There was a good deal of romanticizing of this case, for, in fact, many of the parents of Olympic pupils were owner-occupiers, educated, middle-class and relatively affluent. The real 'little Davids' from the low-income families with informal sector employment living in the Laini slums of Kibera estate attended the nearby Kibera Primary School, a much lower-ranked school (103rd in 1986, 108th in 1988). A significant issue is not only the success of the Olympic pupils but their potential impact, by contagion, upon their less-fortunate cousins from Kibera, for in 1989 it was placed 76th!

Conclusion

The commentary within this chapter on the qualitative differences between districts and environments in Nairobi and between Nairobi and elsewhere confirms the findings of the limited earlier Kenyan based research (Kathuri, 1986; Kinyanjui, 1981; Gakuru, 1977; Somerset, 1977) – namely that whilst many variables influence the performance of pupils in the primary school leaving examinations, the combined influence of head-start and socio-economic environment are hard to overcome for the poorest of the urban disadvantaged. These are part of the bulk of the 227,564 primary school leavers out of 345,108 KCPE candidates nationally in 1987 (65 per cent) and 216,213 out of 389,334 in 1988 destined to terminate their formal education as a result of failing to secure a secondary school place. By contrast, the cream, processed by the private schools, the high-cost primary schools and other 'little Davids', are amongst those fortunate few gaining entry to the national schools par excellence as well as to other government-maintained, grant-aided and public schools that are the gateways to higher education and hence into the urban-based modern sector economy that is likely to spawn the next self-propagating cycles of advantage and disadvantage.

References

Ball, S J (1990) 'Values in Crisis' inaugural lecture, Kings College, London, October.

Bray, M and Lillis, K M (1988) *Community Financing of Education in Developing Countries*, London: Pergamon.

Gakuru, O N (1977) *Pre-School Education and Access to Educational Opportunities in Nairobi*, University of Nairobi Institute of Development Studies, Working Paper 321.

Kathuri, N (1986) *Factors Influencing the Performance of Pupils in CPE*, Kenyatta University, Bureau of Education, Research Paper 1.10.

Kinyanjui, K (1981) *Education and Inequality in Kenya: Some Research Experience and Issues*, University of Nairobi Institute of Development Studies, Working Paper 373.

Mwangi, J J (1988) 'Pressure for Entry into City Council Schools at the Onset of Education: a Demographic Interpretation', M.A. thesis, University of Nairobi Population Studies and Research Institute.

Obudho, R A (1986) 'Urbanisation and Spatial Planning in Kenya: A Case for Bottom Up Approach to Planning', presented at Silver Springs Seminar, Nairobi, 24–27 April 1986.

Opinyah, N (1982) 'Population Pressure on Urban Housing: the Case of Nairobi', M.A. thesis, University of Nairobi Department of Urban Planning.

Somerset, H C A (1977) *Who Goes to Secondary Schools: Efficiency, Equality and Relevance in Secondary School Selection*, University of Nairobi Institute of Development Studies: mimeo.

Somerset H C A (1988) 'Examinations as an instrument to improve pedagogy', in Heyneman, S P and Fagerlind, I (eds) *University Examinations and Standardised Testing – Principles, Experience and Policy Options*, World Bank Technical Paper 78, Washington, DC: World Bank.

UNICEF (1989) *Situation Analysis of Children and Women in Kenya*, Nairobi: UNICEF.

15. Urban decline and educational opportunities in secondary schools of Pittsburgh, Pennsylvania, 1950-79

William B Thomas and Kevin J Moran

Introduction

Between 1950 and 1980 there were dramatic changes in economic and social relations in Pittsburgh, Pennsylvania, USA. During these three decades, this city, like some urban, industrial communities in the United Kingdom, France, Germany, Poland, and the Northeastern section of the United States, experienced incremental, but major transformations in its economy (See Academy of Economics in Cracow and University of Pittsburgh, 1981). This was a time of economic decline in Pittsburgh, characterized by its ageing infrastructures, eroding tax bases, and the increasing competition for fewer resources. Economic conditions accelerated the pace of social change in this city. Typically, these changes influenced demographic patterns in such a way as to have important consequences for the racial character and social class composition of its neighbourhoods and public institutions.

In 1950, Pittsburgh had a population of 671,659. As the eighth largest city in the United States, it had an undisputed international reputation as a steel producing capital. At this time, 32.3 per cent of the city's workforce was employed in skilled and semi-skilled occupations in production industries. However, between 1954 and 1977, the demand for steel production fell, resulting in the elimination of 25,000 jobs in steel manufacturing alone, and having a geometric effect upon employment in those businesses which had serviced the retrenching steel industry. In addition to unemployment, the exodus of 247,721 (36.9 per cent) of the city's residents by 1980 placed further burdens upon its tax coffers. This population decrease may be attributed in some measure to the attraction of expanding suburban communities. Others sought new opportunities in parts of the United States experiencing economic growth.

There was a compelling combination of factors which contributed to economic decline and outward migration. These included competition from expanded world markets in steel manufacturing; trends toward diversification in other industries by US steel producers; a reluctance of local manufacturers to keep pace with modern technological changes in steel production; and bureaucratization of labour unions, discouraging the relocation of new businesses in the area. Consequently, steel production, as the predominant employer of blue-collar craftsmen, semi-skilled workers, and labourers in Pittsburgh, relinquished its undisputed position in the international marketplace to a white collar, high-tech and service economy. In fact, by 1980, 33.4 per cent of the city's workforce comprised part of an economy involved in sales and service alone. In this economy, universities and hospitals replaced steel mills as the largest employers of the city's labour force.

These economic changes had a dramatic effect upon demographic patterns in the city. As its total population decreased by over one-third within three decades, there was a concomitant rise in its black population. In 1950, there were 62,423 (9.3 per cent of the total population) African-Americans living in Pittsburgh; in 1980, this group constituted 24.0 per cent of the city's population. With the emigration of whites to suburban communities, and as the numbers of African-Americans increased to replace them, there were discernible changes in the social composition of some city neighbourhoods.

In the 1950s, major slum clearance and urban renewal projects displaced members of an urban underclass. For example, city planning surveys show that 312 white families and 1,239 black families were removed in the redevelopment of the central city. Most of these displaced families remained with the city. Some moved into those neighbourhoods formerly inhabited by upwardly-mobile whites. When African-Americans resettled, larger numbers of their group tended to cluster in those areas experiencing increased population density, and consisting of multiple-occupancy dwellings. In addition, and as a contributor to *de facto* racial segregation in the city, they gravitated toward those communities whose black populations in 1960 were either rapidly approaching or had already exceeded 50 per cent of the neighbourhood.

Larger numbers of African-Americans, whose economic mobility was stunted by prejudice and fewer opportunities in a shifting job market, contributed to the expansion of urban poverty in this city. Characteristically, as neighbourhoods became progressively black, the gap widened between the city's median family income and the median family income for African-Americans who clustered in these neighbourhoods.

These economic and demographic changes in Pittsburgh, in turn, had far-reaching consequences for the city's schools. As the economy declined, there were challenges to traditional social values, which eroded beliefs in the school as an equitable institution. Youth began to question authority. Militant African-Americans, who now composed the majority racial group in many urban schools, insisted on curricula and activities that reflected their history and life experiences. Some even demanded the dismissal of their teachers, whom they charged with racial prejudice. Their demands, coupled with parental pressure for more community control over predominantly black schools, intensified the social conflicts between school groups. They also led to activities highlighting racial and ethnic identities, such as black awareness clubs. In response to increased racial and class conflict in schools, the board of education mandated the organization of human relations extracurricular activities in the schools. The content of programmes fostering racial pride and harmony, however, was probably aimed more toward political activism than toward the academic school achievement, which a revitalizing high-tech economy would require of blacks and whites entering the work force.

Amid this turbulence, teacher demands also posed problems for urban school administrators. As a special interest group, teachers demanded more responsiveness to their particular concerns for job security, higher salaries, and pupils' waning respect for their authority. With the ever-present threat of legal action against school personnel, and violence directed at school authorities, some teachers retreated into their protective unions and school bureaucracies. Focusing their attention upon political issues of the day, such as appeasing constituents over school desegregation, school authorities did little to strengthen the articulation between the demands of a high-tech economy and the academic needs of lower- and working-class youths.

These and other economic, social, and political events occurring over a 30-year period permit us to illustrate their impact upon the schools in this city. As a contribution to the growing body of research by sociologists and social theorists on social class, race, and schooling (Young, 1971; Keddie, 1971; Apple, 1977; Bernstein, 1977; Bourdieu and Passeron, 1977; Anyon, 1981; Apple and Weiss, 1983; Thomas, 1988; Thomas and Moran, 1988), this study examines the knowledge-transmission process embedded in the extracurricular activities offered in four Pittsburgh high schools. In this chapter, we illustrate how schools responded to changes in their student body composition, occurring as a function of economically-driven population shifts. We contend that they differentiated by school the knowledge transmitted so as to reflect the social class and racial composition of the respective school populations. They then stratified the knowledge they disseminated to their pupils and retrenched academic educational opportunities that had once been available in these schools prior to the enrolment of larger percentages of African-Americans from the lower classes.

Social class and racial characteristics of school neighbourhoods

In this study, we collected data from the *Standard Metropolitan Statistical Areas of the United States Census* (1950–80), neighbourhood inventories of the Department of City Planning of Pittsburgh, Pennsylvania, and school attendance boundary maps to identify four urban high schools representing varied pupil populations over a 30-year period. Our analysis of these data indicated that by 1979, students in these high schools were drawn from communities comprising distinctively different social class and racial groups (see Tables 15.1 and 15.2). One high school student body (School A) consisted primarily of upper- and lower-middle-class whites. Another (School B) comprised African-Americans drawn primarily from the lower-middle- and upper-working-classes. A third high school (School C) drew heavily from a white ethnic, upper-working-class population. The fourth (School D) drew from a predominantly black, lower-working-class population.

From 1950–79, School A, located near three major universities, consistently served a predominantly white upper- and lower-middle-class pupil population. Most of these students were Jewish. In 1950, the highest median incomes in one feeder neighbourhood (North Squirrel Hill) to this school were $4,958; $11,284 in 1960; $16,140 in 1970; and $25,012 in 1980. The changing economy of the city was reflected in this school's feeder neighbourhoods. The predominant occupations of the parents shifted from professional and skilled workers in 1950 to professional and commercial employees by 1980. Parental education attainment was high. In 1950, 28.4 per cent of the residents in North Squirrel Hill were college graduates; 60.3 per cent were college graduates by 1980. Not only was School A predominantly white throughout the years of this study, but its black student population remained under 10 per cent until 1976, when the city school board accelerated its efforts to racially desegregate this school. So, by 1979, 22.8 per cent of the pupil population was black, but drawing mostly from the professional and clerical occupational classes.

Similarly, School B is situated in close proximity to three of the city's universities, but over the years it drew from a more ethnically-diverse pupil population than did School A. The predominant ethnic groups included Italians, Poles, and African-Americans. Although there were fewer pupils from professional homes represented in School B than in School A, this school served

Table 15.1 *Socio-economic indicators for school neighbourhoods by race, 1950*

School neighbourhoods	*Median income*	*Predominant occupation*	*College attendance*	*% of African-Americans*
School A				
Greenfield	3,605	S (32.6%)	6.0%	0.8%
Regent Square	4,958	P (42.9%)	20.7%	0.3%
N Squirrel Hill	2,801	P (46.6%)	28.4%	1.4%
S Squirrel Hill	3,921	P (43.7%)	15.3%	0.6%
Swisshelm Park	NA	S (44.3%)	6.5%	0.1%
Point Breeze	4,026	S (35.1%)	16.3%	17.5%
31st Ward	3,643	S (48.1%)	3.5%	3.8%
East Hills	2,784	S (33.6%)	5.7%	27.9%
School B				
Bloomfield	2,836	C (28.8%)	7.7%	1.7%
Lower Oakland	2,787	C (30.6%)	6.8%	0.2%
N Oakland	2,530	P (44.2%)	24.8%	1.3%
S Oakland	2,921	S (32.0%)	4.2%	8.2%
Lower Lawrenceville	2,615	S (40.9%)	2.1%	7.9%
Strip District	NA	L (49.2%)	1.4%	43.3%
Polish Hill	2,488	S (50.7%)	0.9%	9.5%
Bedford Dwellings	NA	L (63.3%)	1.8%	92.3%
Terrace Village	2,131	L (46.7%)	2.3%	44.7%
Upper Hill	2,393	L (44.6%)	5.8%	72.9%
Middle Hill	1,892	L (63.2%)	2.1%	94.8%
School C				
Southside Slopes	3,033	S (45.8%)	1.4%	0.9%
Southside Flats	NA	S (38.2%)	1.9%	1.9%
School D				
N Homewood	3,059	S (36.0%)	4.4%	32.8%
S Homewood	2,708	S (37.5%)	2.9%	20.4%
W Homewood	2,577	S (37.8%)	2.3%	11.2%

P – professional C – clerical S – skilled L – labourer NA – not available

Source: *1950 Standard Metropolitan Statistical Area, Pittsburgh, PA*, GPO: Washington, DC, 1953.

Table 15.2 *Socio-economic indicators for school neighbourhoods by race, 1980*

School neighbourhoods	*Median income*	*Predominant occupation*	*College attendance*	*% of African-Americans*
School A				
Greenfield	14,202	C (35%)	15.5%	0.9%
Regent Square	18,520	C (42%)	34.8%	0.1%
N Squirrel Hill	25,012	P (51%)	60.3%	4.3%
S Squirrel Hill	18,021	P (49%)	40.2%	2.0%
Swisshelm Park	21,250	C (35%)	12.9%	0.4%
Point Breeze	22,707	P (52%)	48.0%	3.3%
Point Breeze North	15,806	P (39%)	31.6%	53.3%
Lincoln Place	19,889	C (39%)	7.2%	0.1%
Hays	15,170	C (46%)	0.0%	0.0%
New Homestead	20,799	C (35%)	14.8%	15.7%
East Hills	13,318	C (34%)	7.3%	93.0%
School B				
Bloomfield	12,860	C (35%)	15.0%	3.1%
W Oakland	7,859	L (33%)	17.0%	68.3%
Central Oakland	8,223	P (35%)	30.6%	8.3%
N Oakland	12,597	P (48%)	51.0%	9.2%
S Oakland	10,808	C (35%)	14.4%	33.8%
Lower Lawrenceville	9,097	C (30%)	5.6%	12.3%
Strip District	9,948	L (40%)	2.1%	55.9%
Polish Hill	13,400	C (42%)	8.8%	8.5%
Bedford Dwellings	5,669	L (44%)	1.9%	95.1%
Terrace Village	4,573	C (36%)	2.4%	97.9%
Upper Hill	13,617	C (34%)	15.5%	86.1%
Middle Hill	9,146	L (39%)	2.6%	98.3%
School C				
Southside Slopes	13,299	C (31%)	2.1%	1.8%
Southside Flats	9,582	C (31%)	5.3%	1.9%
Arlington Heights	4,070	L (29%)	1.1%	94.0%
School D				
N Homewood	11,409	L (33%)	6.4%	97.4%
S Homewood	7,811	L (32%)	3.9%	96.9%
W Homewood	8,387	C (34%)	3.0%	93.4%

Source: *1980 Standard Metropolitan Statistical Area, Pittsburgh, PA*, Washington, DC: GPO, 1983.

neighbourhoods dominated by employees drawn from the skilled, clerical, and labouring occupations. In one of these neighbourhoods (North Oakland), 24.8 per cent of the residents were college graduates by 1950, and by 1980, 51.0 per cent had graduated from college. These residents earned a median income of $2,530 in 1950; $8,125 in 1960; $11,983 in 1970; but only £12,597 in 1980.

In 1950, the black pupil population at School B was 37.0 per cent. Some of these pupils were from a small, stable neighbourhood (Upper Hill) of African-Americans, whose ancestors had been part of the pre-World War I migration from southern states. Some had worked as servants in the homes of the city's élites. Initially, the median income of this neighbourhood was $2,393, with 5.8 per cent of these residents holding college degrees. In 1960, 7.5 per cent of the residents were college graduates and earned a median income of $5,433. Although 38.8 per cent of the workers in this neighbourhood were labourers in 1970, 9.9 per cent of the residents were college graduates, and the median income at that time was $8,822. By 1980, the predominant occupation of the residents had shifted upward from labourer to clerical, with a median income of $13,617. In striking contrast with residents in this predominantly black neighbourhood, there were also those black student cohorts attending School B in the 1970s from families at the lowest end of the income scale (Middle Hill). Some of these families had been victims of the slum clearance projects of the late 1950s. At this time, the differential between the median incomes of the higher social class and the lower social class African-Americans in these two neighbourhoods was $5,266. However, by 1980, the differential had nearly doubled to $9,044. In these later years, only 2.4 per cent of the residents in the lower social class neighbourhood were college graduates, in contrast with the 15.5 per cent of residents in the higher social class neighbourhood who had graduated from college. Unlike enrolment at School A, black enrolment at School B drifted steadily from 37.0 per cent in 1950 to 50.6 per cent in 1960, and to 72.5 per cent in 1970. By 1979, black enrolment had peaked at 89.9 per cent.

In contrast with Schools A and B, and as a school consistently serving predominantly white ethnic, working-class neighbourhoods over the 30-year period, School C is farthest removed from a university setting. It is situated in the shadows of the once-thriving steel mills of the city. Similar to School A, and prior to 1968, its black student population remained less than 10.0 per cent. African-Americans gradually increased to 23.7 per cent by 1979 as a consequence of the pupil influx from a labour-class neighbourhood (Arlington Heights) that was 94.0 per cent black. Some of these African-Americans had relocated there in the wake of the city's slum clearance projects. The highest median income for residents of the neighbourhoods populating this school was $3,033 in 1950; $5,237 in 1960; $8,228 in 1970; and $13,299 in 1980. By this time, only 5.3 per cent of the residents were college graduates. Between 1950 and 1970, the predominant occupation in this area was skilled worker, until this changed to clerical in 1980. This change also reflected the general shifts which were occurring in the economy of the city.

For over 30 years, the most dramatic changes in neighbourhoods serving the four high schools occurred in those serving School D. Much like patterns in School B, its black student enrolment stood at 38.0 per cent in 1950. However, by 1960, 86.2 per cent of the students were African-Americans; by 1970, 99.3 per cent were so; and by 1975, African-Americans comprised 100 per cent of this school's population. There were also discernible changes in the characteristics of the school's feeder neighbourhoods. The predominant occupation in School D's three communities was skilled worker in 1950, when the largest concentration of African-Americans comprised only 32.8 per cent of one neighbourhood's (North Homewood) population. By 1960, the predominant occupational status declined to that of labourer, as the percentage of African-Americans in this neighbourhood rose to 82.5 per cent. Over the next two decades, the primary occupation remained labourer, as the percentage of black residents increased to

97.4 per cent. In 1950, the neighbourhood having the highest median income ($3,059) in this school community had been comparable with that of residents in the attendance boundaries of School C. Moreover, their 1950 incomes had been commensurate with the city's median income of $2,858. But, as this neighbourhood became progressively black, the median income level did not keep pace with that of residents living in School C attendance zone. In addition, by 1980, median incomes in this black community lagged far behind that of the city's median. College completion levels for this neighbourhood remained consistently low, rising from 2.8 per cent in 1960 to no more than 6.4 per cent in 1980.

Discontinuity between school and the new economy

We contend that extracurricular activities play an important role in the teaching, learning, and credentialing processes of high schools in the United States. The availability of and pupil participation in some of these activities may contribute immeasurably to a rich school experience, enhancing the employability and life chances of those pupils who either volunteer or are selected to take part in the activities. There may be standardization in the city-wide goals and purposes of extracurricular activities; however, as Keddie (1971, p.143) claims, there may be differences by school in this undifferentiated curriculum. Differentiated opportunities for pupils to participate in school activities give pause for concern, especially since the selection and organization of school knowledge may influence the pupils' internalization of social norms (Oakes, 1982), their aspirations, and ultimately their placement in the occupational structure. When the social class and racial backgrounds of the students are taken into account, the differentiated outcomes of this process are all the more invidious.

In the context of a changeover in the Pittsburgh economy, there were new demands placed upon schools for preparing those who aspired to higher status, technological and service-oriented occupations. In the past, access to production and manufacturing occupations had required minimal academic preparation and a greater emphasis upon technical and social skills related to on-the-job efficiency, conformity, discipline, team effort, following directions, and punctuality. In the new society, academics and their related activities would play a much greater role in the economy than they had under former economic arrangements. In the Pittsburgh schools, academic extracurricular activities, as an integral part of schools' formal curricula, afforded some pupils greater involvement in the learning process and promoted positive informal interactions with teachers of academic subjects. These organizations included foreign language, maths, history, journalism, and science clubs, honour and debate societies, and activities in the performing arts.

In addition, occupation-oriented extracurricular activities took on a new and greater significance. They hold the potential to complement programmes preparing youth to meet the requirementsof a transforming economy. They are aids in the early socialization of youth into the occupational world, providing knowledge and guidance about entry requirements, while establishing useful contacts with successful adults as role models in the field. For example, these organizations in Pittsburgh schools included the Future Teachers of America, with its linkages to all academic subjects, and the pre-medical club, organized in conjunction with the maths and science curriculum.

Conversely, there were those clubs which served less academic and occupation-preparation functions. Instead, they stressed social and physical development. The goals of these activities, ie, to foster school spirit through athletic competition, may have been transitory. They also served more immediate ends, ostensibly to enhance the personal and social characteristics of pupils. To be sure, they helped perpetuate the organizational goals of the school. For reasons which are not always apparent, the Pittsburgh schools serving lower- and working-class students tended to overemphasize the activities aimed at social and physical development. What is more, they did so at the expense of academics.

Whether it was athletics, social clubs, or any activity devoted primarily to peer status attainment or school order, non-academic activities proliferated in the lower- and working-class schools. They did so despite the possibility that high school graduates might later hold aspirations for educational levels or for occupations requiring a quite different orientation from that once required in the thriving steel production economy. For example, pupils whose high school careers consisted of large doses of sports and social activities and little academically-oriented club affiliation, possibly realized deficits in their high school preparation upon entering college on athletic scholarships. Unable to compete in an academic environment, they were forced to drop out. In effect, this pattern by which schools stratified knowledge validates McLaren's (1989, p.224) contention that 'the educational system is really a loaded social lottery, in which each student gets as many chances as his or her parents have dollars'.

Stratifying school knowledge by social class and race

The greatest quantitative differences in extracurricular activity offerings at these schools are in the emphases they placed upon the academic and the athletic opportunities they afforded their students (see Figure 15.1).

School A

Throughout the 30 years, School A overshadowed the remaining three schools in its academically-oriented extracurricular offerings. Academic clubs spanned the entire spectrum of this school's formal curriculum. Its foreign language offerings included the French, Latin, Spanish, German, Russian, and Hebrew clubs. In the areas of science and mathematics, there were the slide rule, the microscope, the physics, the botany, the mathematics, and the biology clubs. A decided advantage which students at School A enjoyed was its science test club to tutor them in preparation for highly competitive national examinations. In the 1960s, advanced placement courses, with opportunities for university credit, supplanted many of these informal school programmes. In the 1970s, School A then enriched its science and maths extracurricular programmes with an advanced aerodynamics club, a science explorers club, and the computer laboratory assistants, whose responsibilities were to work closely with their faculty mentors. In the areas of social studies and the humanities, School A

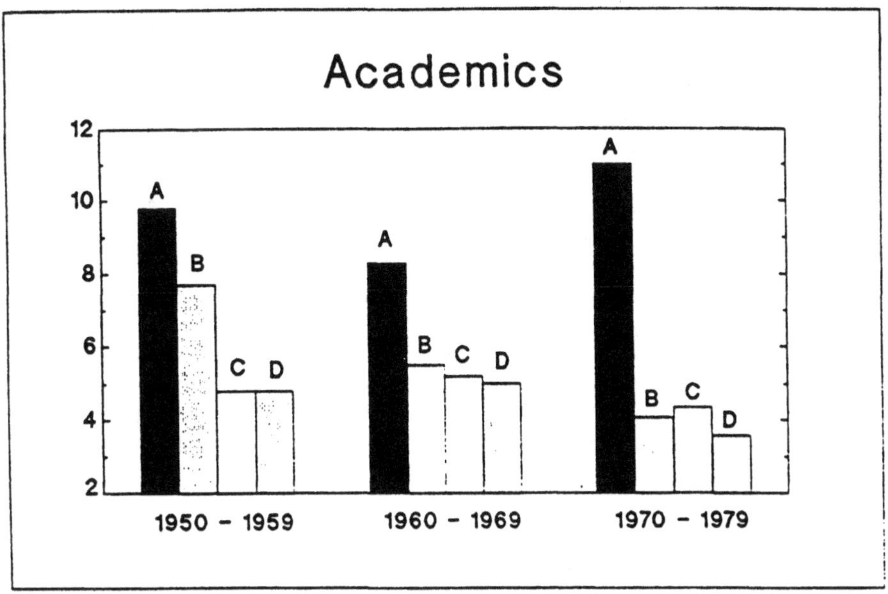

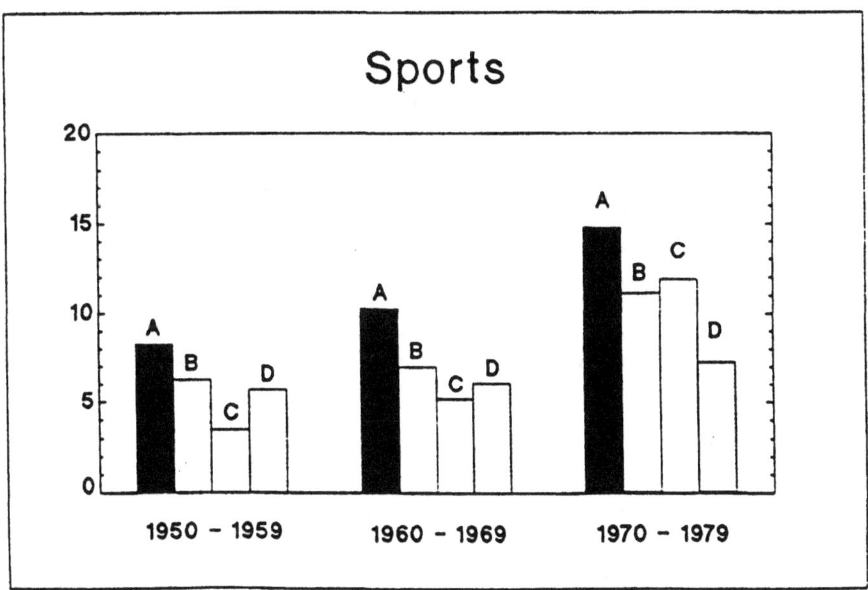

Figure 15.1 *Average number of extracurricular activities by category at four urban high schools*

provided a rich variety of opportunities to enhance its students' knowledge of local, national, and international affairs and of the arts. These organizations included a debate society, junior town meeting, the United Nations Club, discussion groups, Oriental studies, literary and creative writing societies, psychology and philosophy clubs, and the art club.

Over the three decades, there was an increase in the numbers of athletic extracurricular activities at School A. Although all schools offered football, basketball, baseball, and track for males, athletic activities at School A increased at a greater rate than they did in any of the other three high schools. Moreover, opportunities to participate in unique athletic activities in this school surpassed those offered at any other high school. Gymnastics, volleyball, rhythmic swimming, field hockey and soccer were options for female students in the 1950s, long before these activities were available in the other high schools. Even more striking were the options of co-educational types of activities including skiing, fencing, archery, bowling, cross crountry (running), golf, and tennis.

School B

In the 1950s, there were more similarities between academic opportunities at School A and at School B than there were between School B and the remaining two high schools. At this time, School B served a lower-middle and an upper-working-class pupil population. In the 1950s, academic opportunities ran the gamut from debate and the National Honour societies, journalism, and history and book clubs to more specialized activities, such as the microscope, the slide rule, the psychology, and the nature study clubs. Visiting professors from nearby universities augmented this school's academic curriculum by teaching challenging courses in subjects such as biology, English, French, geometry, and the social sciences. As this school drew increasingly from among the lower-working-class of African-Americans and ethnic-Americans, academic extracurricular activity opportunities diminished to a level on a par with those in other schools which were predominantly black and white working-class. In fact, by the 1970s, School B lagged far behind School A in the characteristics of its academic extracurricular activities.

As these academic options decreased, the number of athletic activities took a noticeable upswing from seven in 1973 to 17 by 1979. In this decade, girls' athletics thrived with offerings in nearly every sport available to boys, except for football. By comparison, the number of academic opportunities in this school dwindled, fluctuating throughout the 1970s between three and five activities.

School C

In contrast with Schools A and B, academic extracurricular offerings at School C were noticeably fewer over the 30-year period. Sparse offerings in the 1950s were limited to a French and maths club, a junior town meeting club, the newspaper, and the National Honour Society. Later in the decade, its offerings included the Spanish, Latin, reading, and a junior historian club. Interestingly, in the wake of McCarthyism in the United States, these young historians discussed politically-sensitive topics such as communism and Marxism. Not until 1970 were there debate, mathematics, and science clubs, which then lasted only two years. As the school approached the latter-half of the 1970s, there was a further decline in its academically-oriented club offerings. Pupil choices were now limited to the newspaper and the National Honour Society. In effect, over a 30-year period, School C came full circle in its academic extracurricular offerings. Moreover, career-oriented opportunities at this school continued to be circumscribed by the traditional working-class female roles of nursing, secretary, and homemaking.

As in the case of School B, some of the most telling shifts in extracurricular activities at School C occurred in athletics. With the rise in this school's emphasis on sports also came a decline in its emphasis on academic activities. It experimented with golf for a single year. Interestingly as well, School C organized a girls' football team (the Powder Puff League) in 1971 and sustained this activity throughout the entire decade.

School D

In 1950, there were seven academic extracurricular activities in School D. These included the National Honour Society, a college, a reading, and two discussion clubs, the physics laboratory assistants, and the school newspaper. As was the case in School A, a college club, lasting from 1950–63, prepared pupils to take standardized national examinations for college entrance, while counselling them in academic fields to which the students seemed best suited. In the early 1950s, this school served primarily an Italian student population. Yearbooks show that there was an Italian language club in 1955, the year when the student population reached a black majority of 53.4 per cent. To strengthen waning academic activity offerings in this decade, the school added a current events and a junior historian club, an organization which by now had become well-entrenched in School C. The 1961 school year saw a revitalization of these kinds of academic clubs, which now included French, poetry, speech, and creative writing clubs, and the laboratory assistants. The primary duties of these young scientists were checking pupils' homework, correcting tests, setting up laboratory equipment, and learning laboratory techniques, such as conducting blood tests.

However, from mid-decade to 1969, most of the academic extracurricular activities at School D declined to the extent that there were only the Honour Society, student newespaper, the student United Nations club, and a short lived 'Quiz Club'. New academic opportunities emerged in 1969 with the addition of the horticulture, art, and the jazz (music appreciation) clubs. With the exception of a Latin and a biology club, added in 1973 and 1975, respectively, none of the earlier academic extracurricular activities at School D, save the National Honour Society and the student newspaper, survived the decade of the 1970s. In fact, the number of academic options fluctuated between two and five.

In the early 1950s, the availability of extracurricular activities in sports at School D remained relatively high. Students chose from a wide variety of athletic activities, including gymnastics and recreational swimming. As the social class and racial composition of the school changed, the range of choices constricted. In a pattern which continued to 1974, opportunities for boys were limited to the basic offerings of football, basketball, baseball, swimming, and track. From 1974 to 1979, the number and variety of athletic extracurricular activities increased by a small margin. In these years, there were tennis, volleyball, and cross country, in addition to weightlifting, bowling, and karate, most of which were short-lived.

Discussion

Despite the increasing turmoil and bureaucratization in school and society, a disturbing fact remains. These conditions seemed not to have affected educational opportunities at the public school serving pupils from the highest social class in this study. Rather, academic extracurricular activities in this school continued to flourish. As they did so, differences between offerings in the higher and the lower social class schools became even more apparent than was the case prior to student unrest. These facts raise questions about possible linkages between school and economy.

In this case, we find that in urban societies, such as Pittsburgh, change in the means of production prefaced changes in social relations. As the steel manufacturing economy in this city declined, the social class composition of some of its neighbourhoods and the schools serving them also declined. There was also a concomitant decline in the educational opportunities offered in those schools which served lower- and working-class pupils. The effect demonstrates a direct relationship between the social class of the pupils and the schools' emphases upon academic school knowledge, and that as economic conditions worsen in urban societies, we may expect a corresponding increase in activities, such as sports, for social control.

Much like the students in School A, lower-middle and upper-working-class students at School B in the 1950s were the beneficiaries of an enriched extracurricular programme. This was the case despite its rising enrolment of African-Americans. The predominantly white ethnic, solidly upper-working-class School C, with a black enrolment not exceeding 11.1 per cent in the 1950s, afforded its students fewer academic opportunities than did School B. Academic offerings at School C were commensurate with those available at School D, which also served a solidly upper-working-class community at this time.

Over the 30 years, the black enrolment in School B increased to 89.9 per cent. However, as the number of African-Americans increased, there was also a corresponding shift in the social class make-up of this school. In the 1960s, it drew progressively from a lower-working-class community. It is impossible to know what would have occurred in extracurricular activity offerings had School B continued to draw upon a lower-middle and upper-working-class student population. It is certain, though, that School B eventually resembled the social class composition of School C, whose pupil population had remained predominantly white. As School B changed, there was a recognizable retrenchment of academic opportunities once afforded its pupils.

The arrival of larger numbers of pupils drawn from the lower-working-class may account for a greater emphasis upon athletics as a traditional mechanism of social control. Aimed, no doubt, at encouraging alienated pupils to remain in school and at building the self-esteem of pupils from economically deprived backgrounds, these schools inflated their athletic activity offerings. As these activities proliferated at all schools, activities differed in their orientation. Discernible differences in the types of athletic activities illustrate how schools stratified the knowledge-transmission process so as to reflect the social characteristics of their students while reproducing social class relations.

All schools offered some forms of team sports. Yet School A supplemented its athletic programme with options which allowed its pupils to perform and excel on an individual basis. These opportunities included archery, fencing, golf, gymnastics, and tennis, which tend to encourage individuals to strive beyond the performance levels of team members. Unlike the others, School A had instituted a ski club in 1969, and it remained intact throughout the next decade. Clubs such as these reproduced middle-class values, since participation often requires membership in private clubs that are inaccessible to members of the working and lower classes.

In contrast, increases in athletic opportunities at Schools C and D were limited to team sports. In these activities, coaches stress group solidarity, coordinated effort, and most importantly, obedience to authority. In addition, team sports required the subordination of the individual will to that of the group. Similarly, drill teams in working-class schools complemented the work of athletics in particular ways. Working-class, more so than middle-class youth, probably would volunteer or be drafted by the military upon leaving school. It is not surprising, therefore, that Schools C and D initiated the drill team, with its emphasis on regimentation and discipline, to prepare school leavers for their future places in the social order.

The possible functions of these differentiated opportunities were to reinforce middle-class norms of individual achievement and meritocracy in the higher-class schools, while perpetuating working-class values of group cohesiveness, patriotism, and obedience to authority in working-class schools. Paradoxically, these social controls for subordinating the self in working-class schools may have suppressed students' individual initiative, which was needed for white-collar positions in the new service economy of the city.

Popular belief holds that children of the poor aspire to careers in professional sports, primarily as escape routes out of their poverty. Be that as it may, the odds of mobility for many youth were greatly curtailed by the reality that large numbers of prospective professional athletes competed for limited numbers of team positions. Having devoted an inordinate amount of after-school time to athletics, therefore, these urban students were left with even fewer options to improve their economic condition. Unsuccessful high school athletes, if rejected by colleges and professional ball clubs, no longer had the safety net of high-paying, heavy industrial jobs upon which their parents at one time relied.

Conclusion

Some students at School B were sensitive to this over-emphasis on sports in their schools and its implications for their life-chances. Illustratively, the 1978 senior class president chided her school for neglecting its responsibilities for providing more academic opportunities for its college-bound students. She asserted in her school newspaper:

> [School B] is the kind of high school that is more concerned with athletics, than the academic work of a person. [It] is not a bad school if you like sports; if you are college bound, [it] is what you make it.

As a student leader, she laid much of the responsibility for the decline in the school's academic emphasis on the teachers and her schoolmates. She wrote:

> There are some teachers who could not care less whether you learn anything in their class or not. They feel it is on the individual because they get paid whether they teach or not. There are others who are really concerned about whether you attend their class or not. The worst problem is loafing in the halls at [School B].

Other students sensed a demise in their school's commitment to mathematics and science. They astutely perceived the discontinuity between increasing demands of a technological/service economy and the educational provisions offered by their school. They called, instead, for a greater emphasis upon mathematics and science, in view of the fact that black youth were overlooking engineering as a career option. They charged that 'most of them are not aware of the opportunities. Too few develop maths and science skills. This emphasizes the need for students to prepare for their careers in the ninth grade, even earlier'.

The stratification of school knowledge severely limits the possibilities of discovering and developing the full range of potential talent needed for a reviving economy. In this case, the results were a diminished productivity of talents, not only for the black population of Pittsburgh at that time, but also for the overall development of any youth from the lower- and working-class homes of the city.

Acknowledgements

The authors gratefully acknowledge the generous support of the Buhl Foundation (Pittsburgh, PA), the National Research Council (Ford Foundation), and the Spencer Foundation for this research.

References

Academy of Economics in Cracow and University of Pittsburgh (1981) *Seminar on Urban Concentrations: Pittsburgh and Cracow*, Cracow: Cracow Academy of Economics.

Anyon, J (1981) 'Social class and school knowledge', *Curriculum Inquiry*, 11, 3–42.

Apple, M (1977) 'Power and social knowledge', *Review of Education*, 3, 26–49.

Apple, M and Weiss, L (1983) *Ideology and Practice in Schooling*, Philadelphia: Temple University Press.

Bernstein, B (1977) *Class, Codes, and Control, Vol. 3*, Boston: Routledge and Kegan Paul.

Bourdieu, P and Passeron, J C (1977) *Reproduction in Education, Society, and Culture*, London: Sage.

Keddie, N (1971) 'Classroom knowledge', in Young, M (ed), *Knowledge and Control*, London: Collier-Macmillan.

Mclaren, P (1989) *Life in Schools*, New York: Longman.

Oakes, J (1982) 'Classroom social relationships: exploring the Bowles and Gintis hypothesis', *Sociology of Education*, 55, 197–212.

Thomas, W B (1988) 'A quantitative study of differentiated school knowledge transmission in Buffalo, 1918–1931', *Journal of Negro Education*, 57, 1, 66–80.

Thomas, W B and Moran, K J (1988) 'Social stratification of school knowledge in character training programs of South Buffalo, New York, 1918–1932', *Journal of Education*, 170(1), 77–94.

Young, M (1971) *Knowledge and Control*, London: Collier-Macmillan.

16. Rotterdam: combatting educational disadvantage

Ton Peters

Introduction

This chapter looks at developments in education in Rotterdam in the last 20 years. Rotterdam used to be a typical blue-collar city, the majority of whose population worked in the port. Generally speaking, the work was fairly unsophisticated and meant that the majority of the work force required little or no training. This situation changed after the recession and the subsequent economic recovery, since when Rotterdam has been transformed into a city where business and service centres play a key role alongside the intense level of activity in the port. This has naturally made considerable demands on the education system and on training facilities.

Table 16.1 shows the level of education of the work force of Rotterdam, the other major Dutch cities and the Netherlands as a whole.

Table 16.1 *Average level of education in four cities in the Netherlands in percentages on 1 January 1988*

	Primary	*Junior sec.*	*Higher sec.*	*Higher*	*Not known*
Amsterdam	15.8	22.9	30.2	23.7	4.9
Rotterdam	25.1	28.2	29.3	13	2.6
The Hague	19.6	29.8	29.3	18.5	1
Utrecht	21.8	23.8	26.8	21.4	6.1
Netherlands	15.6	28.0	35.7	16.6	2.1

All the cities have larger than average groups of people who have only had primary education (and junior secondary vocational education). The same applies to higher education in three of the four cities. The exception is Rotterdam where the percentage of people with a low level of educational qualifications is highest and the percentage of people who have had higher education is below the national average.

The 1970s

In the late 1960s, sociological research into school careers showed that pupils from working-class families lagged far behind the national average in terms of their educational achievements and level of enrolment in general secondary schools. Influenced by the American compensatory education programmes, small-scale projects were set up to develop compensatory education programmes for day-care centres and kindergartens with the aim of creating more educational opportunities for these pupils. In the early 1970s, compensatory education and family involvement projects were initiated by the local authorities in Amsterdam, Rotterdam and Utrecht. One of them was the Education and the Social Environment Project which was originally a local innovation project. In 1974, the Dutch Minister of Education presented a plan for a national compensatory education policy which he called an 'educational development policy'. Kindergartens and primary schools (which at that stage had not been integrated into the new-style primary schools for pupils aged four to 12) with high percentages of children from lower income families were given extra facilities (ie, more money and teachers) and cooperation between schools and social and cultural institutions was stimulated. The three local projects which had been started in the early 1970s were subsidized by the Ministry under the terms of the new educational development policy. The aims and design of the Education and Social Environment Project were redeemed in the light of the supplementary source of finance and the project was upgraded from a local innovation project into a national curriculum development and evaluation project.

The Education and Social Environment Project (OSM)

The Education and the Social Environment Project (Onderwijs en Sociaal Milieu: OSM) was started in 1969 with the aim of creating better educational opportunities for children from deprived neighbourhoods. It was based on the dissertation by Jan Grandia and its development was closely associated with his work. The aims of the project were to be achieved by developing special curriculum teacher-training courses, parent involvement programmes, adult education and cooperation with other educational and cultural institutions. From the outset, attempts were made to secure grants from central government. The applications were consistently refused largely because it was felt that the project did not have a proper scientific basis. This situation changed when a research team was appointed and three advisors were taken on. This marked the beginning of the second phase of the OSM project (1971–86) when its aims were redefined in the following terms: *to develop, evaluate and promote the dissemination of programmes aimed at producing at least the national average figures for the transfer of pupils from lower social groups to general secondary schools.* Development refers to the fact that the OSM project was to draw up empirical programmes aimed at stimulating target figures. Evaluation was to consist of determining whether the target figures were the result of programmes which had been implemented or, if not, the other causes. Promotion means that the programmes must be suitable for implementation on a wider scale outside the confines of the OSM Project (in cooperation with institutions from the Dutch educational support structure or otherwise). It also means that information must be provided about the programmes and how to use them.

The programmes for development fall into three categories:

a. compensatory education to affect pupil behaviour;
b. family involvement programmes to affect parental behaviour; and
c. educational guidance programmes to stimulate the introduction of implementation of educational advancement and family involvement programmes.

The plan of action can be divided into six parts:

1. analysis of the causes of specific environmental factors which affect the transfer to secondary education;
2. analysis of proven means of affecting these causes;
3. a list of the compensatory education and family involvement programmes to be developed on the basis of (1) and (2) and the subsequent implementation programmes;
4. a curriculum development strategy to help develop and evaluate these programmes;
5. a rough indication of the phasing and criteria for evaluation of the programmes; and
6. a plan for the dissemination of the programmes.

Field of action

The OSM project covered 23 primary schools. They carried out the stimulation and family involvement programmes which had been developed as part of the project with the help of OSM counsellors. The counsellors worked in accordance with educational counselling or implementation programmes. The evaluation of the three types of programmes took place at the schools and was directed by the pupils. All of the schools had secondary school pupil transfer figures below the national average and were mainly populated by working-class pupils.

The number of schools participating in the project was originally 17. However, there was a marked rise in the number of pupils from ethnic minorities attending these schools, from slightly below 11 per cent in 1974 to over 50 per cent in 1979, and a corresponding drop in the Dutch target population. The idea was to establish the effects of the OSM programmes by following one generation longitudinally. The evaluation was to cover pupils from grades 1 and 2 of primary school up to grade 8. However, given the change in ethnic profile, the project was extended to include 23 schools so as to ensure a sufficiently large number of Dutch pupils in the longitudinal target group. The main selection criteria were clearly negative secondary education transfer figures and a low number of pupils from ethnic minorities.

Of course attention was also paid to the problems of the pupils from ethnic groups. The OSM project, major Dutch cities other than Rotterdam, the National Educational Advisory Centre and the National Institute of Curriculum Development (SLO) worked together on a large-scale teaching-materials project which was presented to the Minister of Education. Rotterdam also set up its own Educational Priority Project Group to develop educational programmes to ethnic minority pupils (see below). Each year a counselling plan was drawn up in consultation with the schools involved in the OSM project, incorporating decisions about the programmes which are to be carried out and the frequency of counselling. Some programmes in the counselling plan were identical for all schools, especially the programmes to be evaluated in the generation of pupils to be followed longitudinally. The OSM project was financed by the city of Rotterdam, the Ministry of Education and Science and the SVO (Institute for Educational Research). The total cost for the period from 1974 was Dfl. 47,500,000. Forty-six full-time posts were created and shared by 100 members of staff.

Results of the OSM project

The limited space in this Yearbook means we can only give a general indication of the results. Full details have been published in Slavenburg and Peters (1989) and Scheerens (1987). Five major conclusions can be drawn about the overall results of the OSM programmes:

1. Three compensatory education programmes were implemented satisfactorily.
2. Four compensatory education programmes were goal-effective or almost goal-effective (measured by criterion-referenced tests); these included the three programmes which were implemented satisfactorily.
3. None of the family involvement programmes were implemented satisfactorily; nor were they effective in terms of criterion-referenced tests.
4. The national averages on the standard referenced tests were not achieved; on the contrary, in the eighth grade, the group followed longitudinally scored in the lowest 5 per cent of the test standard group.
5. The number of pupils who repeated a year or were placed in special schools went down to below the national averages; intake levels to general secondary schools increased but were still below the national average.

Overall this means that the aims of the OSM project have not been achieved. The OSM programmes were not effective but, on the other hand, the evaluation provides detailed information and recommendations for educational priority policy.

Educational priority policy

In 1982, the Dutch Government announced its educational priority policy which was designed to raise the level of educational achievement of Dutch and migrant children from working-class families. The policy placed more emphasis on concentrating and integrating activities in disadvantaged areas for which additional funds were also made available. The areas were defined as containing sets of at least ten primary schools that meet the eligibility criteria for extra funding, a welfare organization and three types of secondary schools. Nine areas in Rotterdam were approved and given grants in 1986. Educational priority policy differs considerably from previous development policy by virtue of the attention it devotes to migrant children. The strong influx of children from migrant families in the last decade has led to a marked increase in the magnitude of this educational problem area (Scheerens, 1987).

In addition to the funds available for individual schools in deprived areas, extra money was made available for areas in which schools and welfare institutions work together. The funds were provided as soon as a plan of activities was submitted and approved. Nine areas in Rotterdam were included, consisting of 127 primary schools, 21 special education schools and 36 secondary schools, as well as institutions such as public libraries and day-care centres. The nine priority areas received a combined total of 8.3 million guilders. The areas were designated as priority areas for periods of four years. At the time of writing, the first plans are being implemented. The objective of the Rotterdam educational priority policy can be summarized as follows: to improve the quality of education and to harmonize the measures taken in separate policy areas such as social policy and welfare policy for the benefit of education.

As has already been noted, priority policy focuses on migrant children and Dutch children from deprived areas. The number of migrant children is increasing steadily in Rotterdam as a result of the unification of families (children who come from other countries to join their parents who are working in the city) and because migrants tend to have larger families. The total population of Rotterdam (576,000 on 1 January 1990) will increase because of this and other factors to a total of 610,000 by the year 2000. Migrants now make up 17.8 per cent of Rotterdam's population; in the year 2000 the figure will be 25 per cent. Turks (15,000), Moroccans (15,000) and Surinamese (36,000) are the largest groups. The growth in the population is most marked among young people.

Table 16.2 *Number of pupils in the main categories of education in Rotterdam (1989)*

	Primary education	*Special education*	*Secondary education*	*Total*
Public schools	20,000	1,750	9,200	30,950
Private schools	27,000	2,800	29,500	59,300
Total	47,000	4,550	38,700	90,250

Table 16.3 *Percentage of Dutch and migrant pupils in primary education (1985, 1989)*

	Dutch	*Moroccans*	*Turks*	*Others*
1985	77.4	6.1	10.0	6.5
1989	70.0	7.1	10.4	12.5

Table 6.4 *Percentage of Dutch and migrant pupils in special education (1985, 1989)*

	Dutch	*Moroccans*	*Turks*	*Others*
1985	89.3	3.0	4.2	3.5
1989	81.4	4.2	4.9	9.5

Table 16.5 *Percentage of Dutch and migrant pupils in secondary education (1985, 1989)*

	Dutch	*Moroccans*	*Turks*	*Others*
1985	92.1	1.7	3.2	3.0
1989	83.7	3.4	4.6	8.3

Tables 16.2–16.5 show that the rise in the number of children from migrant families was already apparent in the period from 1985 to 1989. On 1 January 1989, 64 per cent of migrants were under the age of 30, whereas the figure for the population of Rotterdam as a whole was only 40 per cent. These figures naturally have consequences for various areas of policy, particularly education.

Points of emphasis in educational priority policy

In the Dutch education system, it is virtually impossible to make stringent demands on the substance of education. Freedom of education is guaranteed by law which means that no further demands are made as regards the content of education and virtually none regarding its form. Nevertheless, attempts have been made in Rotterdam to influence schools which are taking part by means of a centrally-directed educational priority plan. The writers have based their approach on the results of the effective schools research. There were four main elements:

- emphasis on basic skills;
- strong administrative leadership;
- frequent evaluation of student progress; and
- high expectations of student learning.

The main emphasis regarding activities which fall under welfare policy was on:

- pre-school activities (learning by playing);
- reducing the level of truancy and drop-outs from secondary school; and
- parental involvement.

The plans which were drawn up in the nine areas were evaluated in the light of elements from the above priorities before they were submitted. During the four-year period of the plan, evaluation took place at both city and area levels. The results of the evaluations are not yet available although we do have a number of educated guesses which will shortly result in amendments to the priority policy.

Schools and educational priority areas have taken up the policy in highly effective terms and numerous activities relating to the priorities have been undertaken. The first evaluation results again confirm that better student performance cannot be achieved in a short time. The choice in Rotterdam of pre-school activities was universally regarded as a basic necessity to tackle the problem of educational disadvantages. The idea that smaller classes have a positive effect on the performance of pupils (the official figure in the Netherlands is 32 pupils per teacher but additional facilities mean there are usually no more than 25) has also more or less been laid to rest. Even so, reducing the size of classes was the most common method used in the priority areas. This is a great pity. In November 1989, an interim report was published concerning the Rotterdam evaluation. It related to 61 schools, 39 per cent of whose pupils were Dutch, 22 per cent Turkish, 13 per cent Moroccan and 15 per cent Surinamese on average. In interviews, one in four teachers said they were unhappy with the facilities available in their schools (staff and materials) and also said that motivation was a problem. More than 35 per cent of teachers feel that their colleagues do less than they do (De Groot, 1989). As far as the emphasis on basic skills is concerned, it became apparent that much more attention needs to be devoted to mathematics. The interviews also revealed that teachers support the objectives of the educational priority policy but 22 per cent feel that the policy is not being given sufficient practical form and that financial resources are channelled into too many different areas.

The study by De Groot (1989) produced the following more general conclusions:

- Mathematics must receive more attention as part of the emphasis on basic skills. As earlier evaluation results have shown, specific groups lag behind in developing effective skills in this particular subject.
- Information policy must be extended and intensified. A considerable proportion of teachers are unaware or not sufficiently aware of the substance and objectives of educational priority policy.
- Teachers must have opportunities to take goal-oriented in-service training courses geared to the educational problems of their own schools. Skills in teaching children from working-class families and migrant children can be improved considerably. This would help alleviate some of the extra pressures on teachers.
- The education world must obtain more information on the advantages of using the expertise of welfare establishments. This applies particularly to contracts and ways of influencing the behaviour of parents in supporting education. Teachers feel that it is an important factor in the existence of educational disadvantages.

Towards an amended educational priority policy

Educational priority policy in Rotterdam was amended in the light of the first evaluation results. In addition to the Rotterdam findings, the results of national research into the effects of educational priority policy were deliberately included in the process. This shows that the achievement level of schools can vary. The 20 per cent of schools which performed worst were only one year behind the schools which performed best in terms of dealing with the syllabus (Bosker and Scheerens, 1989). Children largely learn mathematics at school, but they learn language at home and through reading magazines and books. Meijnen (1984) says that 20 per cent of the achievement in mathematics at the end of primary school is attributable to differences between schools but the figure is less than 10 per cent for language.

Ultimately this means that more and more information becomes available about measures which can have a positive influence on education. Slowly but surely, the belief is growing that an effective school can create conditions to improve student performance in key areas by optimizing the effect of teaching.

The aims of the Rotterdam educational priority policy were amended slightly in 1990 when they were redefined as seeking to reduce differences in student performance in basic skills and school careers which can be specifically attributed to the environment. The reformulated priorities are:

- to create structured education in the basic skills;
- to promote effective teacher behaviour;
- to create effective educational management; and
- to create effective relationships between schools and parents.

The pre-school period occupies an important place in all of this. We can expect a statement from Rotterdam which will tell schools the measures they can take to improve the pupil performance at schools. It can therefore be concluded that attempts will continue to be made to improve the effectiveness of education in Rotterdam by adopting the recommendations of the evaluation of the OSM project and using the results of the effective school research as guidelines for new educational measures.

Despite the fact that efforts in the past 25 years to improve opportunities for educationally disadvantaged children have met with little success, this will remain one of the priorities in Rotterdam and will continue to be a central theme of its education policy.

References

Bosker, R and Scheerens, J (1989) 'Criterion definition, effect size and stability, three fundamental questions in school effectiveness research' in Creemers, B, Peters, T and Reynolds, D (eds) (1989) *School Effectiveness and School Improvement*, Amsterdam: Swets & Zeitlinger.

Creemers, B, Peters, T and Reynolds, D (eds) (1989) *School Effectiveness and School Improvement*, Amsterdam: Swets & Zeitlinger.

De Groot, H (1989) *Stedelijk effectevaluatle van het onderwijsvoorrangibeleid te Rotterdam* (Evaluation of the effects of educational priority policy in Rotterdam) Rotterdam: Projektburo OVB/RISBO.

Kloprogge, J (1989) *Naar beter voorrangsonderwijs* (Towards better priority education), The Hague, SVO.

Meijnen, G W (1984) *Van zes tot twaal* (From six to twelve), Harlingen: Flevodruk.

Scheerens, J (1987) *Enhancing Educational Opportunities for Disadvantaged Learners*, Amsterdam, North Holland Publishing Company.

Slavenburg, J and Peters, T (1989) *Het projekt Onderwijs en Sociaal Milieu: een eindtalans* (The Education and the Social Environment Projects: a Final Balance), Rotterdam: School Advics Dienst (Schools Advisory Service).

17. Soweto: urban educational issues

Miranda Bell

Introduction

Soweto defies the whole range of theoretical dispositions which have grown up around the concept and definition of the word 'city'. Formed from an amalgamation of urban labour settlements, the name Soweto is the unromantic acronym for South Western Townships. It is the last word which is of interest here, as Soweto is neither a city nor a suburb. It falls somewhere in between the two and is most usually referred to as a 'township'. The township is a familiar sight at the outer edges of white designated South African cities. It is an artificial construct with few of the aspects of that organic growth which characterizes even the most well planned cities in the third world. The only reason for which Soweto existed in the first place was as a labour reservoir for the white city of Johannesburg. Its 1.5 million black residents serve the city's factories, offices, shops, parks, hospitals and white domestic dwellings.

What makes Soweto, and Sowetan education in particular, a difficult subject for study at the start of the 1990s is the rapid speed with which things are changing, and while there is plenty of research into South African education as a whole, there are relatively few studies which focus on Soweto. Yet developments in the education sector in Soweto, from the inception of 'Bantu Education' in the 1950s to the equally definitive Soweto Declaration on Peoples' Education at the end of 1985, provide a fascinating study of the way in which black urban schools in South Africa became, in microcosm, the battlegrounds on which the apartheid regime fought to preserve its dominant role against, first, students, then students and parents, and finally an entirely new strategic alliance of parents, students, teachers and representatives of other sectors within the oppressed black majority.

Writing after the 1976 explosion in Soweto schools, Kane-Berman (1978, p.ix) said

> Urban Africans in South Africa are probably subject to more regulation and restriction than any other race or class on earth. To many of them the business of daily living must seem like a pilgrim's progress through a world invented by Kafka. Nevertheless ... George Orwell would have understood it perfectly.

It is within the extraordinary world which the policies of transience and influx control have created for blacks at the edges of the 'peculiarly rigid apartheid city structure' (Simon, 1989, p.13) that Sowetan schools go about their business.

The development of black education

It is not possible here to provide more than a brief overview of the development of black education in South Africa since 1949 but it is essential to do so since South Africa is the only regime in the world which has overtly articulated what theorists have diagnosed as the covert ideology in numerous other capitalist states: the deliberate exercise of control over social reproduction through the systematic manipulation of various aspects of schooling. Dr Hendrik Verwoerd, apartheid's architect and later South African Prime Minister, bluntly outlined the role of black schooling while he was Minister of Native Affairs:

> The school must equip him to meet the demands which the economic life will impose on him. . . . There is no place for him above the levels of certain forms of labour. . . . For that reason it is of no avail for him to receive a training which has as its main aim absorption in the European community (Hirson, 1979).

Verwoerd also underlined the explicitly socially reproductive role which 'Bantu Education' was to play within the grand apartheid framework:

> My department's policy is that education should stand with both feet in the Reserve and have its roots in the spirit and being of Bantu society. . . . The basis of the provision and organization of education in a Bantu community should, where possible, be the tribal organization (ibid).

These statements were incorporated into policy in 1959 when it was announced that 'as far as higher primary and post-primary schools are concerned, it is the intention to give preference to Bantu areas (ie the bantustans)' (Horrell, 1968 p.42–3). Already grossly inadequate, capital investment in education (both in the form of the construction of schools and teacher training) was concentrated in rural areas of the country set aside for black occupation, then known as 'bantustans'. While doing little to meet the needs of these areas, this bias added to the existing crisis in the supply of education to urban black South Africans. It has had the lasting and deepening effect of separating the educational experience of urban blacks in white designated areas more profoundly and definitely from that of the 'homeland' dwellers than the gulf which is experienced between rural and urban schools around the world. The Soweto experience, which illustrates this urban separation over a 40-year period, is also the focus around which opposition to the state's education policies first emerged in 1976 and then developed its political clarity over the following ten years.

By examining the structure and provision of schooling in Soweto in the context of the apartheid state, it is possible to see how the schools have emerged from their original role as the reproductive core within an education system which was one of the main pillars of apartheid to their new focus as the seedbeds of power. In the 1970s and early 1980s, education was regarded as expendable by young black South Africans in the struggle against apartheid. By the end of

1985 Soweto parents' and students' organizations had led the way to standing this policy on its head. Instead, the schools, in their new regional operating structures within the National Education Crisis Committee, formed in 1986, were invested with the task of shifting the decade of struggle in urban black education onto entirely new strategic ground.

In this chapter, after briefly outlining some of the features which characterize the ugly peri-urban sprawl of Soweto and the development of urbanization in South Africa, the system of apartheid schooling and its accompanying structures are examined in the context of the township's schools and of urban policy. The combined deprivations in all aspects of education in Soweto, from the lack of classrooms and other basic resources to the impoverished and deliberately biased curricula, are explored and located within the overall control mechanisms employed by the apartheid state.

Township schools and urban policy

There are well over a million people living in Soweto, which is situated about ten miles north of Johannesburg. Nobody knows what the true population figure is though Mashabela (1988, p.147) reckons the highest official figure of 1987 of 1,474,000 an underestimate. Certainly, while the Group Areas Act and the numerous restrictions on freedom of movement for black South Africans remained in place, there were limited possibilities for an accurate census because of the high penalties incurred by admitting to being in an urban area illegally. Because one of the only ways in which it was legal to live in Soweto was to work for an employer in Johannesburg or to be the offspring of someone who did, the vast majority of people in Soweto either worked in Johannesburg, South Africa's largest and most prosperous 'white' city, or were unemployed.

Soweto is by far the biggest urban residential area designated by black occupation under the Group Areas Acts (1950 and 1966) which apportioned various areas for occupation by the various legal racial categories in South Africa, viz. black, white, Indian and coloured.

It was not until the Black Local Authorities Act of 1982 that the presence of urban black people in white designated South Africa was finally recognized as permanent. Prior to this Act, which was based on the recommendations of the Riekert Commission of 1979, the long history of legislation relating to urban blacks had been based on the fundamental premise of impermanence. The 1980s, by contrast, saw the introduction of a rather different urban programme by the apartheid regime, backed by the major private concerns which shared its desire for the creation of a strong middle-class buffer against the upheavals which had characterized urban life in the years since 1976.

In 1988 there were 178 primary schools in Soweto and 72 high schools. The population was served by four libraries, ten clinics and 39 creches (Mashabela, 1988, p.150). There were also four technical schools, a teacher training college and a campus of Vista University (ibid., p.149). However only 30 per cent of the houses had running water, and there were substantial problems with services such as water-borne sewerage (ibid p.149) A number of shanty settlements have grown up in the township, none of which had any water-borne sewerage in 1988. Communications in the township were by then hampered even more by the hostility of the Council towards the community groups which had sprung up in the wake of the state of emergency and which were the real focus of popular power in the township. The chronic shortage of housing meant that existing dwellings were massively overcrowded with the average number of residents per house at nine or ten persons. Conditions could hardly be less conducive to sustaining progress through school, particularly under the examination and knowledge-based curriculum which characterizes Soweto schools.

In a briefing paper on urban policy prepared for the South African Institute of Race Relations by Franks and Morris in 1986, a whole series of measures were cited as evidence of the South African regime's new policies in regard to urban Africans in the 1980s: these include the introduction of property rights and the almost simultaneous promotion of home ownership; the promotion of black businesses (which had previously been hedged about by crippling restrictions); the upgrading of urban infrastructure (for example, by 1988 nearly all of Soweto had been electrified); the establishment of service industrial sites in urban townships; creating access to higher education in the urban townships, and increasing local government powers for urban blacks.

Interestingly, the regime's *education* reform programme, which involved a stated intention to increase spending on black schools over a period of several years and to establish (separately) parity with white schools, was not included in the list. Yet if the deliberate impoverishment of black schooling had been part of the strategy of grand apartheid, then the education reform programme initiated by the regime in 1985 was clearly part of an equally deliberate attempt to contain the revolutionay opposition. This was to be achieved by taking away the most obvious and immediate roots of dissent whilst at the same time making it increasingly difficult to organize around the revolutionary alternatives. In this sense, the educational 'reform' initiatives were an integral part of the attempt to establish an urban 'buffer' in the form of a strong middle class in the township. It is essential to note here that the vital underlying principle of segregation in education was at no stage part of the regime's reform agenda in the 1980s – and even schools in the 'open' residential areas which were first mooted in 1987 were to remain separate.

In order to understand the fundamental nature of the struggle in Soweto schools during the period between 1976 and 1990, a struggle in which the nature of power and the means of control and social reproduction were at issue, it is necessary to trace the roots of the conflict to the establishment of the system of 'Bantu Education' in the 1950s. Verwoerd's many speeches (see above) had spelt out the principle on which the system of schooling for black South Africans (then referred to as 'bantus') was based. Almost immediately, the limited tactics available to opponents of this 'bare-faced' policy revealed themselves: for boycott to work, alternatives would have to be provided, a costly and impossible strategy. Hence, as Troup (1976, p.22) explains, parents were left with an unhappy choice of exposing their children to 'Bantu education' or giving them no education at all. Since, in the 1950s, only one African child in every two of school age was actually attending school, it was understandable that parents were unwilling to give up an opportunity to get even some inferior education for those lucky enough to gain access to it.

The system of 'Bantu education', one of the fundamental props of structural apartheid, transferred all responsibility for black education to central government. Of the three types of school established under the system, community schools, voluntary or state aided schools, and government schools, it was the latter which dominated urban schooling and which comprised by far the majority of schools in Soweto as state policy gradually squeezed out most of the quasi-independent and mission schools.

As far as the administration of the schools was concerned, a committee system was set up with provision for directly elected parent representatives. The majority of committee members were direct nominees. The (limited) parental involvement in the running of individual schools was invariably a conservative force rather than a force for resistance or change. This was to change radically in the next 30 years as state policy towards control of schooling created a situation where it became almost impossible for parents to remain outside the education struggle which was being waged by their children in township schools. Areas such as the curriculum and the training of teachers, however, remained firmly under central control.

Resourcing education

One of the major differences between state provision of education for whites and blacks was in the level of resourcing. This is particularly significant in the context of urban schooling in Soweto, which, as we have seen, was nothing more than a labour reservoir for the city of Johannesburg, with consistently high levels of unemployment. The underfunding of black education by the state meant a heavy burden on parents who had to pay fees and for books, stationery and uniforms. Demand was therefore depressed far below the levels which even conservative population estimates would have predicted had parents been able to take advantage of a free state education system. Nevertheless, overcrowding was endemic in Soweto schools.

In 1953, according to Kane-Berman (1978, p.187), the State spent an average of R17 per capita on black education compared with R128 on each white pupil. In 1971–2, the figures were R25 and R461 and in 1975–6, R42 and R644. By 1986, the Department of Education and Training (which replaced the Department of Bantu Education in 1979) gave the figures for per capita expenditure on African education in the white designated areas as R387.02 compared with the white per capita figure of R2746.00 (SARS 1986, p.417). In 1970, the proportion of the white age cohort at school in South Africa, was 97.6 per cent. The school enrolment ratio for black children, however, was only 54 per cent. At high school level, the figures for 1970 were 87.7 per cent and 8 per cent respectively (Auerbach, 1979, p.39).

Two methods adopted to cope with demand without increasing expenditure were the 'hot seat' system and the 'platoon' system. In the former, schools were used in shifts, shorter than the normal school day, so that teachers and classrooms could serve double the number of pupils per day. In the platoon system, the classrooms were used by different teachers and pupils in two daily sessions. Troup (1976, p.32) cites 1971 figures which show that these doubling-up devices enabled 35 African schools to cater for 35,000 pupils: 20,700 in the mornings and 14,400 in the afternoons. Both systems remained a feature of township education in the 1980s.

'Bantu education'

One of the most distinctive features of the system of 'Bantu education' was the insistence on mother tongue education throughout the primary years. In practice, of course, this would have the effect of isolating different groups of pupils according to the language spoken and of cutting them off from access to the languages of power. Criticism at the time was voiced thus:

> mother tongue instruction would have the effect of reducing the horizons of Africans, cramping them intellectually within the narrow bounds of tribal society, and diminishing the opportunity of inter-communication between the African groups themselves and also with the wider world in general of which they formed part (Horrell, 1968, p.60).

Prior to the Soweto explosion in 1976, secondary school students were expected to learn through three language media: English, Afrikaans and mother tongue. Troup describes the apartheid regime's policy of mother tongue eduction as 'part of its general concern to foster ethnic consciousness in the African population' (1976, p.36). In this way, in large urban conglomerations such as Soweto, the regime attempted to reproduce the national ethnic pattern and the artificial division of the country into 'homelands' via the schooling system: thus in 1972 Troup identifies 18 Xhosa schools, 13 North Sotho, 11 Shangaan and seven Venda. An attitude survey among Soweto residents, on the other hand, could not have provided much comfort to the architects of this policy: 75 per cent of those surveyed regarded Soweto as their permanent home; 66 per cent 'declined to consider the homelands as their real home and 75 per cent thought that tribal affiliations were becoming less important (ibid, p.37). Certainly the numerous community and youth organizations which formed (and repeatedly regrouped as the state attempted to eradicate organized opposition) owed nothing whatsoever to ethnic affiliations. The divisions between many of these organizations were ideological and summarized thus by Mashabela:

> The community of Soweto was thus divided into two sections – the majority rejecting black local authorities and a minority willing to co-operate with them. In addition, the organizations opposed to participation were ideologically divided between those affiliated to the nonracial UDF and those operating under the banner of the black consciousness National Forum Committee (1988, p.142).

Another major characteristic of urban black schooling in the years of 'Bantu education' prior to 1976 was the age profile of black school students. The lack of compulsory education, economic circumstances and lack of schools meant that the average black urban school student was seven or eight before starting school and tended to leave the system before the end of primary schooling. Added to this is the devastating effect of user charge (school fees). Given the late start and the effects of a system which required annual accreditation in order to pass from year to year, it was not uncommon to find students in their mid-teens in primary school. Given also the shortage of space, the complete lack of amenities and the need for older children to look after younger ones whilst parents worked, it is hardly surprising that only a small proportion of the schoolgoing population survives its multi-lingual introductory years and makes its way to secondary school.

The revolt in Soweto schools in 1976 marked the end of the era of 'Bantu education' and the beginning of the 'reform' era in education as well as in other areas of the regime's operations (such as urban and industrial policy). It was no surprise to learn from the Commission of Inquiry set up to investigate the causes of the 1976 explosion, (which reported only in 1980), that political deprivation was as much a cause of the uprising as the immediate spark, which was the enforced teaching of Afrikaans in black schools. The year 1976 also marked the start of organized opposition on a number of fronts, most notably schools and workplaces. By 1979 a new national students' organization has been formed, the Congress of South African Students (COSAS) which differed radically from its predecessors in that it eschewed black consciousness. This, as will be seen, was a vital element in the formation of the alliances with organized labour, mass popular movements such as the United Democratic Front and with grassroots community organizations in the township itself.

The 1980s: 'people's education'

The 1980s in South Africa were characterized by national conflict as the apartheid regime adopted a broadly reformist strategy to cope with the effects of severe economic recession and increased black militancy. In Soweto, schools were affected by what one commentator has described as 'equal parts ofreform and repression' (Chisholm, 1986, p.18). This in turn has channelled the course of the ongoing education struggle into one of repression and revival. The most significant shift which the state strategy and the student response achieved was in the level of participation of the two groups without which 'people's education' would never succeed: parents and teachers. The former, particularly, had, since the early days of 'Bantu education', been a conservative force in township education both for economic reasons and because of the effective system of central control of all the significant aspects of schooling such as curricula and resourcing. Rightly suspicious as parents were of the education offered to their children in the township's schools, it was still perceived as the only means of economic betterment. Similarly, although there were of course exceptions, the majority of black teachers, poorly trained and badly paid, were subject to a stringent system of regulations and controls and belonged to the largely apolitical union, ATASA. Indeed, it was only in the early 1980s that political grouping among teachers took place with any real effect.

When the Soweto Parents Crisis Committee (SPCC) was established in October 1985, it was against a background of several years of turmoil in the township's schools. The Congress of South African Students had focused its opposition for some time on the management of the schools themselves, demanding a greater democratic role for student representatives, among other things. The regime's post-1976 reform platform, however, although it eventually included 'parity' with white schools in terms of resourcing, better training for teachers and a long-term capital investment programme, retained central (and separate) control of township schools, including a largely nominated committee structure with no provision for democratic participation by the students. Hence the focus of the students' opposition reflected the national focus of opposition to the apartheid regime: participation and control.

By July 1985, when the State of Emergency was imposed in the Transvaal, black education had endured nearly three years of prolonged disruption with increasingly repressive measures on the part of the regime strengthening rather than diminishing organized opposition. The deployment of police and army units in Soweto had done nothing to prevent school boycotts or to damage the new series of alliances, despite the fact that over 500 members of COSAS had been either banned or detained by the time the organization itself was banned in August 1985. The intensely repressive measures adopted by the state at the same time as it attempted to implement its reform programme in the schools, had the effect of heightening opposition rather than defusing it. It was clear by the end of 1985, when student action had resulted in the closure of most Soweto schools, that boycotts were counter-productive for a number of reasons. They denied access to meeting places in schools and created strategic planning problems as well as problems in maintaining student unity. Also and more importantly for the purposes of this study, they continued to foster divisions between parents and students and hence to obscure the common cause between them. The concern was to establish links with parents and with the wider liberation movement.

In October 1985 this concern turned to reality as the Soweto Parents Crisis Committee (SPCC) was established and lost no time in calling a conference in Johannesburg to discuss the education crisis. The conference, held in December at the University of the Witwatersrand and attended by representatives of a very large number of organized groups, moved the organization forward to the establishment of the National Education Crisis Committee (NECC). At the same time the SPCC conference articulated for the first time what the various student organizations had been groping towards for some time: 'people's education for people's power'. The strategy of boycott, spurred by messages from the exiled leadership of the African National Congress, was dropped in favour of a return to school, provided a number of demands were met within a defined timespan: the unbanning of the Congress of South African Students, the effective recognition of the SRCs (student representative councils); the release of detainees; the rescheduling of the examinations to give students and teachers time to meet the curricular requirements; the refurbishment of damaged school buildings and the immediate reinstatement of sacked teachers.

There has been a good deal written about people's education since 1986, and a good deal of argument as to the exact nature of the concept. There is no doubt at all though that the adoption of the new slogan at the end of 1985 and subsequent developments in conferences the following year mark the beginning of a major change in South Africa. Muller sums it up thus: 'With the advent of people's education, the educational struggle in South Africa moved from protest to challenge' (1987, p.18).

In practice, however, and while new national alliances and tactics were evolved from the SPCC initiative, 1986 did not see any radical improvements in the schooling situation in Soweto. Continuing boycotts, as large numbers of students failed to return, were followed by state retaliation in the form of closing schools: by the end of 1986, ten Soweto secondary schools had been closed. National NECC leaders were detained all over the country and the planned third

National Consultative Conference was banned in November 1986. However, these developments had been accompanied by increasing involvement in the struggle of the hitherto quiescent and moderate African Teachers Association of South Africa (ATASA) which had been 'forced to confront its isolation from the education struggle' (Chisholm, 1986, p.14). Together with the burgeoning growth of 'alternative' teacher organizations which supported people's education within the structural framework created by the NECC, this development was an essential part of the progress of people's education. The principles of people's education revolve around the democratic control of schooling and it is the Parent Teacher Associations which are charged with the development of alternative curricula and their delivery. The continued and increased involvement of teacher organizations is a vital ingredient in this fundamental aspect of people's education – as it is in the other basic element of the new approach: local and regional control structures.

A significant factor in the development of people's education in Soweto is the role of the Youth Congresses. Muller points out that the townships include a massive constituency for whom 'education for liberation' (the middle-ground view of people's education) may not necessarily represent an appropriate strategy. They are the vast urban army of unemployed who are educational casualties of the 'liberation before education' strategy. Their numbers were increasing every year even as the organizers of people's education moved slowly forward under the repressive tactics adopted by the regime.

In 1989, prominent South African educationist Dr Ken Hartshorne conducted his seventh annual review of black matriculation results. The pass rate in Soweto was lower than for nearly every other urban area, overall results which he termed 'disastrous' (Hartshorne, 1990, p.70). Challenging the argument that the results are statistically manipulated as a mechanism of social control, he argues that a 'manipulation theory' is unnecessary 'when neglect, inefficiency and indifference over a long period of time have served equally well to limit the progress of black youngsters. Because of this and its ideological purpose and content, black education has indeed operated as a mechanism of social control'. Referring to the numerous calls for students to return to school from the various political groupings, Hartshorne questions whether this will achieve an improvement in the quality indicators: '. . . the years since 1987 have shown that the 'return to school' has been fragile and vulnerable in a situation where so little of a fundamental nature in the school system has changed' (p.74).

There can be no doubt that the Soweto experience bears out the more general contention that urban black education is degenerating. Research published in August 1989 by the University of the Witwatersrand Educational Policy Unit describes the continuing crisis in Soweto's schools as 'an amalgamation of crises in . . . the schooling structure and functioning. We can conceptualize this crisis firstly in terms of the provision and administration of schooling and secondly in terms of schooling. These factors are obviously influenced by the crisis of apartheid itself'. Boycotts notwithstanding, the researchers point out that demand is still outstripping provision: 'every major urban area has experienced a crisis in terms of access to schools, especially those pupils wanting to matriculate' (Narsing, 1989, p.1). The research report, which focuses squarely on the provision and administration of schooling in Soweto, is worthy of attention as it uses information gathered directly from students and teachers in the township. It concludes that the real demand for schooling in the township is far higher than official government estimates (p.33) and that large numbers have been deliberately excluded from schools, for spurious reasons. Despite the regime's reform commitments, schools were still operating with a 'significant number of severely damaged classrooms' (p.34). Ludicrously heavy teacher workloads, which include teaching 42 periods a week, administrative responsibilities and an expectation of self-development in terms of further training have led to a real dilution of quality and quantity of teaching. The researchers claim that the most serious qualitative problem in Soweto schooling is the pervasive decay of authority of any kind. Clearly, in the absence of the kind of pedagogic reform envisaged by the architects of people's education, the teachers lack even the authority conferred by a respectable curriculum. The situation is further complicated by the continual harassment of the SRCs. Official organizations such as the school management councils, which replaced the PTSAs in 1988, have little support.

The 1990s

January 1990 opened with reports of overcrowding in Sowetan schools following the worst matriculation results on record. Student and community leaders once again joined with parents to campaign for those who had failed to be readmitted. High school enrolment in Soweto had increased from 60,000 in 1985 to 70,000 in 1990 at a time when the Department of Education and Training was retrenching unqualified teachers and when large numbers of teachers had been detained under the ongoing state of emergency. Those remaining in classrooms were shouldering average weekly loads of between 46 and 60 periods. By mid-January, the ever-present crisis in Soweto's schools once again occupied centre stage in newspapers serving the township's residents.

As the political programme in South Africa shifted dramatically towards real change and the end of apartheid began to seem possible, students were identifying unused white schools which, they suggested, could be put to use to help resolve the supply crisis. Soweto teachers began industrial action in March 1990 but with no prior support from the parents, students and community groups without which no popular movement could hope to survive. Coordinated through the Soweto branch of NEUSA (National Education Union of South Africa), the strike involved all teachers from the 350 schools in Soweto, Alexandra and Tembisa. Although the strike ended on the advice of the newly released Mandela, the UDF and other community organizations, five weeks after it started, there may have been some gains for teachers from their action, most notably in the increase in unity and political purpose which the action engendered. In terms of the prospects for people's education, teachers have made progress towards democratic school control. And in terms of the process and content of schooling, teachers and students have agreed to shun Department of Education and Training extramural activities in favour of alternative cultural and sporting activities. This, if it can be sustained and if the Soweto thrust can be structurally transmitted to other townships and regions, represents a small but highly significant step on the township's road to people's education.

The start of the 1990s saw a major shift in battlegrounds as the schools ceased to be the focus of struggle in the national arena. Participation and democratic control are now on the national agenda in South Africa and people's education has taken on a new meaning as the possibility of effective people's power edges closer. As a result, new alliances are forming between teachers' unions and between teachers and students. There is no doubt that desegregated schools are on the political agenda for the first time in over 40 years; nor that provision and administration will be high on the reform programme of a new state authority in South Africa. The momentum which people's education, despite the severity of the repression which it encountered in the 1980s, has begun to achieve, will inform the pedagogic changes introduced by a new, post-apartheid South African state.

But, as Simon (1989, p.13) points out, the urban experience of 'decolonization' in Africa, including Zimbabwe and Namibia, has been one of slow and often symbolic rather than substantial change. 'Africans have filtered into former white or Asian suburbs . . . but only seldom have the *class* characteristics of particular suburbs changed'. The converse is also applicable. In Harare, Zimbabwe, for example, the 'township' has effectively been replaced with the 'high-density area'. Different housing strategies have undoubtedly resulted in a gradual penetration by higher income groups into home ownership (Amis and Lloyd, 1990), but this remains relative to the middle-class affluence of the former white suburbs. With the end of the racially based laws governing the movement of people, squatting is also likely to become a much larger feature of Sowetan life and the problems of urban housing will escalate. The effect on the township's schools will be severe as demand multiplies. Unless post-apartheid South Africa effects a radical urban transformation, it is unlikely that Soweto will escape this depressing pattern. However effective a new state will be in meeting the supply deficit and however dramatic the improvement in provision, whatever democratic changes are made in administration and curriculum, Soweto schools will still be in Soweto. The transformational thrust of people's education, therefore, will not be able to overturn the socially reproductive role of schooling in the township without an accompanying radical set of urban policies.

References

Amis, P and Lloyd, P (eds) (1990) *Housing Africa's Urban Poor*, Manchester: Manchester University Press.

Auerbach, F E (1979) *Measuring Educational Development in South Africa*, Johannesburg: South African Institute of Race Relations (SAIRR).

Chisholm, Linda (1986) 'From revolt to a search for alternatives', *Work in Progress*, 42, 14–18.

Franks, P and Morris, P (1986) *Urban Black Government and Policy*, Johannesburg: SAIRR.

Hartshorne, K (1990) 'Look back in anger: African Matric Results 1988–89', *Indicator SA*, 7, 2.

Hirson, B (1979) *Year of Fire, Year of Ash. The Soweto Revolt: Roots of a Revolution?*, London: Zed Press.

Horrell, M (1968) *Bantu Education to 1968*, Johannesburg: SAIRR.

Kane-Berman, J (1978) *Soweto: Black Revolt White Reaction*, Johannesburg: Ravan Press.

Mashabela, H (1988) *Townships of the PWV*, Johannesburg: SAIRR.

Muller, J (1987) 'People's Education and the National Crisis Committee', in *South African Review 4*, Johannesburg: Ravan Press.

Narsing, Y P (1989) *Learning in Limbo. Experience of Schooling in Soweto*, Johannesburg: Educational Policy Unit, University of the Witwatersrand.
SARS (South African Research Service) (1986) *South African Review 3*, Johannesburg: Ravan Press.
Simon, D (1989) *Crisis and Change in South Africa: Implications for the Apartheid City*, London: Discussion paper, Institute of Commonwealth Studies.
Sikekane, J (1976) *Window on Soweto*, London: International Defence and Aid Fund.
Troup, F (1976) *Forbidden Pastures. Education Under Apartheid*, London: International Defence and Aid Fund.

18. Tokyo: urbanization and education

Hiroshi Kimura, Haruo Sato and Asahiro Arai

Tokyo

Tokyo is the capital of Japan, known worldwide as a gigantic city, with a population of over 12 million. It is the political and economic centre of Japan, where the main central government agencies, foreign embassies and legations as well as the offices of large companies and financial agencies such as banks are concentrated. In addition, there are many cultural services and institutions such as schools, universities, research institutions, museums, libraries, theatres, large newspaper offices, and broadcasting stations. They are mostly located in the borough area, composed of 23 boroughs, of Tokyo.

Tokyo is divided into a borough area and a municipal area. The borough area can be divided into three central boroughs, ten rim boroughs and ten surrounding boroughs. The municipal area consists of the Tama district which is mostly a new residential area, the Okutama district which is covered with mountains, and an offshore islands area called Izu comprising seven islands. What is called the metropolis is the borough area, having 70 per cent of the population of all Tokyo. Therefore, the Tokyo Metropolitan area is not directly equivalent to a conventional great city. However, the image that Tokyo equals a great city is a powerful one since the priority of the borough area in terms of population, industry, economics, and culture is so strong compared with Tokyo as a whole.

Education in Tokyo

There are many schools in Tokyo because of its large population. The number of kindergartens totals 1,317 which is 8.7 per cent of the total for the whole country. While the number of public kindergartens is larger than that of private ones in the borough area, the number of private kindergartens is larger in the municipal area, illustrating the high degrees of dependence on private institutions in that area. As the birth rate decreases, the number of entrants to kindergartens is dropping year by year. As for the percentage of kindergarten attendance, the figures in May 1989 for the borough area of 55.1 per cent and that of the municipal area at 55.2 per cent are almost the same.

The number of elementary schools in Tokyo totals 1,479, including six national, 1,422 public, and 51 private. This number is 5.9 per cent of those in the whole country. In the case of lower secondary schools, the number in Tokyo as a whole is 858, including eight national, 665 public, and 185 private, 7.6 per cent of those in the whole country. As for upper secondary schools, the number in all of Tokyo is 467, including seven national, 215 public, and 245 private. The proportion of private schools in the total is high compared with other preferences. As the birth rate decreases, the number of students in elementary and lower secondary schools is decreasing, and problems such as the reorganization of schools are arising. Also, enrolment in private schools has tended to increase; this issue is referred to later.

Table 18.1 *Number of schools in Tokyo metropolis*

	National	*Public*	*Private*	*Total*
Kindergartens	2	300	1,015	1,317
Elementary schools	6	1,422	51	1,479
Junior high schools	8	665	185	858
Senior high schools	7	215	245	467

Source: Tokyo Metropolitan Board of Education, 1990a.

The educational administration

Tokyo has the Tokyo Metropolitan Office of Education functioning as the secretariat of the Tokyo Metropolitan Board of Education to administer public schools and social education. Private schools and metropolitan universities are under the jurisdiction of the Governor.

Each borough and municipality has a board of education and its secretariat. Regarding public schools, while upper secondary schools are established and managed by the metropolis, elementary schools and lower secondary schools are established by the borough or municipality. Although the status of a teacher in an elementary school or a lower secondary school is that of a municipal employee of the area in question, the metropolis makes initial appointments and pays salaries. While elementary and lower secondary school teachers work under the municipal boards of education, they are employed by the Metropolitan Board of Education. The metropolis and municipality organize curriculum and guidance sections dealing with the curriculum and content of education in addition to facilities sections taking care of the planning, administration and construction of school facilities.

Issues for education in Tokyo

The educational problems and issues facing Tokyo as a great city are briefly illustrated below.

The decrease in the number of students in the central areas of Tokyo

First of all, there is the issue of the reorganization and scaling down of schools as a result of the decrease in the numbers of students in the area of the central and rim boroughs of Tokyo.

Most government and business offices are concentrated in these areas. As a result of the concentration of the office worker population in Tokyo accompanied with the centralization of governmental as well as commercial and financial administrative functions, land values rose enormously. This resulted in a severe housing shortage, causing many office workers to locate their residences outside the city. The increase in day time and decrease at night in the population of Tokyo cause a severe hollowing-out effect in the population of these areas.

In some elementary schools in the central area of Tokyo, the number of students in each class (grade) is less than ten, causing sluggishness in educational activities, including school events. In some cases, schools are reorganized (abolished and unified with some other schools) in the same way as in rural isolated areas. As for the change in the class size of public schools, the average number of students per class dropped from 33.5 in 1987 to 32.2 in 1989. As for the average in terms of school scale, the average number of classes in one school decreased from 16 in 1987 to 15.3 in 1989.

The increase in the number of students in the surrounding areas of Tokyo

The second issue is overcrowded schools as a result of the population increase in the surrounding boroughs and Tama district caused by the outflow of population from the central boroughs. In particular, the population increase in the municipal areas is outstanding and some schools have over one thousand students. In such a large school, there is an increasing incidence of problem behaviour, as well as a lessening of the sense of belonging to the school, leading to a decline in the quality of educational activities. When school violence became recognized as a social problem, indications of it emerged notably in these areas.

In Tokyo, the maximum number of students per class is set at 45 by law, and there is a strong demand to reduce this number to 40 in the outlying areas. While the reorganization of schools is proceeding and the average number of students per class is less than 40 in the central areas, new schools are being established to cope with overcrowded schools in the outlying areas.

Separation between school and community

The third issue is the problem of weak communication between a school and its community. The reasons for this are threefold. First, the breakdown of the traditional community. This is a matter of the school catchment area. In a city, a school catchment area often coincides with a traditional community; however this may be divided by a construction of a principal road. As a result, the link between a school and a community becomes weaker.

Second, students wanting admission to a school in another district. Because of the depopulation of catchment areas of traditionally prestigious public schools, many students from other districts come to this kind of school. Although students are not allowed to go to school in another district in principle, the actual number of those who do is not small. This brings about a separation between the area where children have their homes and the area where they go to school.

Third, a weakening of the connection between teachers and the community. As a result of increasing separation between a teacher's residence and his or her school, teachers have come to live in areas having no relation to their school. Especially in recent years, the situation has developed where acquiring a residence in the city area is quite difficult, so many teachers are compelled to live far from their own schools. In Tokyo, the principle of 'necessary reshuffling', according to which new teachers have to be posted in all of the three areas (Tokyo is divided into three areas, called A, B and C for placing teachers in schools), is applied with the aim of improving teacher quality. The consequence is that teachers have to leave one school after a certain period, which also makes for the separation between a teacher's residence and his or her school, and becomes another cause of weakening the connection between teachers and the community.

Inclination to choose private schools

The fourth issue is a noticeable inclination to choose a private school for elementary and secondary education. Although the number of students as a whole is decreasing in both elementary and lower secondary schools, the number of students in private schools is increasing.

For example, at lower secondary school level, the number of students in private schools increased by 2,009 as against the number of students in public schools which decreased by 68,312 compared to two years before (TMBE, 1990b).

In the case of upper secondary schools, the number of schools remains the same, but there is a change in the number of students. Unlike elementary schools or lower secondary schools, the number of students in upper secondary schools in 1989 increased by 6,000 compared with 1987 (ibid.). Of this number, about 4,500 or 80 per cent were the enrolment increase in private schools. Here again, the phenomenon of an increasing inclination to choose private schools can be seen in the same way as in the case of elementary and lower secondary schools.

The reasons for this strengthening inclination to choose private schools are threefold. Firstly, there is the issue of the decline of public schools and the upgrading of private schools. Given the present emphasis on school background, many students or their parents try as hard as possible to get into better schools. In such circumstances, a preference for private schools attached to upper-stage schools or private six-year secondary schools has become noticeable, for public schools themselves cannot now cope with these expectations. The tendency to choose private schools is getting stronger and stronger at a time when education geared to entrance examinations is extending to elementary schools and even to kindergartens.

The second issue is the perception of corruption in the public school system. School violence, which reached its peak in 1982, gave an opportunity to reconsider current school education. Subsequently, some educational problems such as bullying and truancy emerged. Since these problems became more and more conspicuous, especially in the public schools, the mistrust of public schools increased. Furthermore the increase in violence inflicted on students by teachers, under the guise of pastoral care, is another reason for the growing mistrust of public schools. In such circumstances, the advantages of private school education become more evident.

The third issue is the residual influence of the upper secondary schools' group-schools-system on the current system. There used to be some notable public upper secondary schools with a high percentage of their graduates going on to good national universities, including Tokyo University. Many of those schools have a long history under the former school system of the present post-war 6-3-3 single-track education system. Too many students favoured these prestigious schools, so the difference between schools became more notable and the competition through entrance examinations for these schools became extreme. Hence, the group-school-system for upper secondary school entrance examinations was introduced. It started in 1967, and aimed at reducing the difference between schools by restricting students' choice of schools. For example, even if a student wanted to enter a notable traditional upper secondary school, they were not permitted to take the entrance examination for that school if they lived in another area. Moreover, students were placed in schools mechanically without considering their own preferences. As a result, the individual features of each school became weak, students' feeling of attachment toward their own schools plunged, the attainment of students in public upper secondary schools declined, and former notable schools existed in name only. A tendency emerged among students to favour private upper secondary schools, resulting in a move away from the public schools. As these problems were realized, a modified group-schools-system was introduced in 1982, relaxing these restrictions. However, there is still a residual influence from the above-mentioned system, and private schools are still popular.

Academic excellence depending upon Juku

The fifth issue is a tendency to depend on private study institutions outside the school system, such as Juku. Juku can be divided into two types, one the 'academic school' and the other the 'culture school'. The 'academic school' is a private institution outside the ordinary school system with the purpose of supplementing or improving children's academic study, mostly in relation to elementary and lower secondary schools. On the other hand, the 'culture school' is an institution for fostering children's interest and individuality and enriching their cultivation. As children get older, the percentage of students going to the academic type increases, while the percentage of pupils attending the cultural school declines. It is important to look at these types of Juku in more detail.

The founders of academic Juku could be either an individual or a corporation. One type of Juku is the 'cramming Juku' for preparation for the entrance examination of notable schools; another is the 'supplemental Juku' for supplementing study at an ordinary school; the third is the 'comprehensive Juku', combining the aims of the above two. In recent years, a ranking among academic Juku has emerged and it is said to be difficult to enter a notable academic Juku. In such a notable Juku, a more advanced level of content is taught compared to ordinary schools, thus offering an advantage to children when taking entrance examinations.

Because of this, the academic Juku industry has prospered and the percentage of students going to academic Juku has become high. According to a survey by the Tokyo Metropolis, the percentage of children of the third grade in elementary school going to academic Juku is about 20 per cent, in the fifth grade of elementary school about 40 per cent, and in the second grade of lower secondary school, 60 per cent.

Significant numbers of students and parents trust teachers in academic Juku more than teachers in ordinary schools. It has been noted that there are some parents who consider ordinary school as a place for pastoral care and academic Juku as a place for academic study.

Table 18.2 *Percentage of children going to Juku*

	Boys				*Girls*			
	Year				Year			
	3	5	8	Total	3	5	8	Total
Music	16.1	9.3	4.2	9.3	58.2	46.1	26.2	43.1
Calligraphy, abacus	33.2	27.4	5.7	20.7	49.0	45.0	12.2	35.0
Academic	19.1	39.5	59.7	41.3	21.5	34.9	53.3	37.0
Sports	73.1	52.4	16.8	44.8	39.1	19.8	5.5	21.0
Total	89.8	90.1	80.9	86.4	92.8	96.1	84.0	90.9

Notes: Music includes piano, electric organ and violin. Academic means English, mathematics, Japanese, science and social study. Sports includes swimming, Kendo, Judo, baseball and soccer.

Year 3 shows the third grade in elementary school and Year 8 shows the second grade in lower secondary school.

Source: Tokyo Metropolis, 1990a, page 120.

In Tokyo, many children go to cultural Juku. Many students of elementary schools go to study calligraphy, abacus, ballet, English conversation, or Kendo after school. These practices are good for fostering children's individuality and developing their ability. However, the point cannot be overlooked that they deprive children of free time. As against academic Juku, the number of children going to cultural Juku declines as their age goes up. In relation to gender, the percentage of boys is high in sports, and the percentage of girls is high in art and practical skill, such as music, calligraphy, and abacus.

Truancy

The sixth issue is the increase in students' truancy. The 1989 number has doubled compared with the figure for 1984. Amongst the causes of truancy are dislike of school as a result of laziness, physical causes, emotional disorders, intellectual disorders, and family background issues. In addition, the number of cases of dislike of school and emotional disorders as a result of bullying is increasing. In elementary school, the percentage of dislike of school rose to 38 per cent in 1989, the percentage in 1984 being 26 per cent. In the case of lower secondary school, the figures for 1989 increased to 78 per cent from 64 per cent in 1984. A significant number of cases of dislike of school relate to bullying.

Foreign students from South East Asia

The seventh issue concerns foreign students from South East Asia. People come to Tokyo not only from all the prefectures but also from many countries in the world. In recent years especially, the number of students from South East Asia has increased.

The main purpose for coming to Japan for some foreign students, who are students in name only, is to work in Japan. In many cases, such students register in Japanese language schools and work in the evening. Many schools have been founded in response to these demands, some of which just aim to get entrance fees and tuition fees, causing trouble for such foreign students.

Students staying in and coming back from overseas

There are many Japanese students living in foreign countries who return home to Tokyo, since many international companies are concentrated there. The number has increased in the centre of the Metropolis and was three times greater in 1988 than in 1975. Education for these students is a major issue, especially in Tokyo.

When students who have stayed in foreign countries come back to Tokyo, they normally enter Japanese schools. However, there are many cases where such students find it hard to adjust to their new schools because of differences of language, manners and customs. To help solve these problems, reception classes have been opened in some designated schools. At the same time, there are some students who have entered international schools in Tokyo after coming back from foreign countries.

International schools are regarded as miscellaneous schools in law, so their students are not eligible to have an official diploma for each of their formal education stages even if they completed the course of primary and secondary education in these schools. In principle, students who have Japanese nationality cannot enter these schools, but returned students who stay in a foreign country for a long time are exceptions. However, Japanese nationals graduating from international schools are not considered as having the same qualification provided by Article 1 of the School Education Law.

Centralization and change of location of universities

More than 20 per cent of all four-year universities or colleges are located in Tokyo; in the case of two-year junior colleges, 13.5 per cent are in Tokyo. In particular, the centralization of private institutions of this kind is remarkable. As for the scale of universities, Tokyo has many large-scale institutions: in the case of four-year universities, the average number of students in universities located in Tokyo is 5,602, while the average for the whole country is 4,142. In the case of junior colleges, the average number of students in junior colleges located in Tokyo is 1,109 while the average for the whole country is 790. Tokyo

Metropolis has two four-year metropolitan universities and three metropolitan junior colleges. This centralization of universities within Tokyo is a major cause of population inflow.

Table 18.3 *Number of universities in Japan*

	Four-year university				*Junior college*			
	Total	National	Public	Private	Total	National	Public	Private
Whole country	499	96	39	364	584	41	53	490
Tokyo	106	12	2	92	79	1	3	75

Source: TMBE, 1990a.

In recent years, there has been a tendency for the relocation of universities. Previously located in the central area, they are now being shifted to so-called 'dormitory towns' (residential areas) or have built new branches there. This is to escape from the aggravation of the educational environment in the central city area and to allow them room for expansion to cope with the increase in the number of students. For example, Hachioji-city has become a campus city, with over 16 universities and junior colleges. This outflow of universities from the central city area is expected to increase, but this causes problems for working students on evening courses at some of those universities.

Conclusion

Among all these educational issues facing Tokyo, the intensification of education geared to entrance examinations coupled to the increase in private schools is the most significant. This issue affects and distorts many of the other educational issues.

For example, the issue of children going to school in another district derives from their wanting a better school in terms of preparation for the entrance examination for the upper stage, as does the increased desire for private schools. Now, education geared towards entrance examinations exists even at the infant stage. There is a new structure, a notable upper secondary school for going on to a notable university, a notable lower secondary school for going on to a notable upper secondary school, a notable elementary school for going on to a notable lower secondary school, and an appropriate kindergarten for going on to a notable elementary school. Many good schools in Tokyo are private schools. At the same time, academic Juku exist in addition to the ordinary school system for facilitating this competition over entrance examinations. There is even an academic Juku for getting in a notable kindergarten.

Under this intensification of education geared to entrance examinations, problems such as truancy and bullying emerge. We cannot say that there is no relation between the intensification of education geared to entrance examinations and these problems. The increase can be considered to be a result of a loss of humanity in schools geared too much to entrance examinations.

There is said to be a so-called 'academic career based society' as a background for this intensification of an education geared to entrance examinations. An academic career-based society is one that esteems one's academic career when selection or evaluation occur in a social context.

Tokyo is a city where many educational functions are concentrated, so the Tokyo way of education has an influence on the entire country. Fortunately, a tendency exists to decrease the numbers of students in the central area of Tokyo. Examining the intensification of education geared to entrance examinations, the conditions to make it possible to have a delicate, comfortable, and humanistic education in both public and private schools are slowly being set. Now, humanizing schools by encouraging a more flexible administration is strongly expected of schools in Tokyo.

References

Iwasaki, S *et al.* (1986) 'The reason for amending the attending school area requirement and the actual research conducted to justify amending the regulations', *Journal of Japanese Society of Educational Administration*, 12.

Tokyo Metropolis (1990) *School Basic Survey in 1989*, Tokyo: The General Bureau of the Tokyo Metropolis.

Tokyo Metropolis (1984–90) *Youth in Tokyo Metropolis: the Outline of the Policy* Tokyo: Life and Cultural Affairs Bureau of the Tokyo Metropolis [Annual Reports].

Tokyo Metropolitan Board of Education (TMBE) (1985) *Education in Tokyo*, Tokyo: TMBE.

Tokyo Metropolitan Board of Education (TMBE) (1986) *Education in Tokyo*, Tokyo: TMBE.

Tokyo Metropolitan Board of Education (TMBE) (1987) *Education in tokyo*, Tokyo: TMBE.

Tokyo Metropolitan Board of Education (TMBE) (1990a) *Education in Tokyo*, Tokyo, TMBE.

Tokyo Metropolitan Board of Education (TMBE) (1990b) *Newsletter of the Tokyo Metropolitan Office of Education*, Tokyo: TMBE.

Tokyo Metropolitan Board of Education (TMBE) (1990c) *Public Education of Tokyo*, Tokyo: TMBE.

Part 4: Developing patterns in urban education

19. Cities, diversity and education

Crispin Jones

Introduction

Cities do not exist in isolation. They are integral parts of the state within which they are located, and, just as states are diverse societies, so are cities. However, cities represent more than a quantitatively superior expression of such general diversity; their diversity poses serious questions as to how a state perceives itself, and in that perception, the role of schooling takes an important part. As a consequence, the way in which city education systems perceive and deal with issues of diversity is an essential element in understanding, not just the education system, but also the way in which state social policy generally is constructed. This chapter, therefore, is an attempt to set out some of the major issues that arise from an analysis of state and urban diversity and the consequences of such an analysis for urban education.

Little educational analysis of this area has so far been attempted (Bash, 1987; Coulby and Jones, 1990), and the consequences for urban education of such a dearth of analysis in this area are profound. For example, much of the work in relation to education in and for a culturally diverse society is confused, contains internal contradictions, and, most importantly of all, is ineffective in either reducing the discriminatory and prejudiced behaviour of many majority pupils and students or in improving the educational attainments of many groups of minority students.

In an attempt to demonstrate both the importance and value of this aspect of urban analysis, namely the significance of diversity within the urban environment, this chapter will examine four related areas. First, the debate about definitional terms in relation to concepts of the state, the nation and diversity. This conceptual area has not been adequately considered by educationists over the last two decades in relation to education generally, and urban education in particular. Second, the nature of diversity, concentrating on the concept of multiculturalism. This discussion is based on an investigation of social group discrimination within state contexts, initially using a model derived from the comparative education work of Nicholas Hans (1949). Third, a taxonomic arrangement by which state responses to diversity and in particular, urban diversity, can be analysed. Fourth, some critical themes within contemporary urban educational policy and practice in the light of the preceding analysis.

Definitional issues. *Civus Romanus sum*, or, are you really British?

The starting point seems, on the surface, somewhat trivial. But how you define a citizen, a member of the state, is a crucial starting point. Through much of the English speaking world, the suggestion is made that 'when in Rome, do as the Romans do'. The implication of the saying is that migrants who settle must abandon their own culture and adopt wholesale the culture of the state in which they have settled. They must become 'Romans'. The problem is that it is seldom clear in any state who the Romans actually are. Usually they are a set of representational stereotypes of the dominant group within a particular state masquerading as a representation of all the citizenry. Worse, the many nationalities contained within the modern state are submerged in this stereotype, which is considered the sole nationality that resides within the state. This view is maintained when the term 'nation state' is used, as that term supports the assertion that the state contains but one nationality, with state nationalism being its embodiment in international relations. This wayward view is one often strongly supported by education, for example, in relation to state language policies for education (Fishman, 1975).

But at the earlier stage of state *description* there is a similar, potentially dangerous confusion between the concept of the national and the concept of the state. A good example of this confusion occurs in England, a part of Britain, over the use of the terms Briton, Britain and British. To many English people, English/British, England/Britain are synonyms. They subsume the part/nation (England) with the whole/state (Britain). The Scots, the Welsh and other British nationalities rarely make the same mistake, despite the constant reiteration of the error throughout the English-dominated media and education systems. Indeed, many English, when this error is made and drawn to their attention, are more usually mystified as to why the issue is of any importance.

This issue is important however, as the example illustrates that many of the issues relating to diversity in urban education reflect not merely ignorance but also certain inequalities that are part of the institutional texture and structure of many states. As such, it makes a useful starting point for analysis and the re-examination of concepts like the nation, nationality(ies), nationalism and the state.

The above starting point is also chosen in preference to the more usual examination and discussion of terms such as intercultural, multicultural, multiracial and multiethnic in relation to education, because it is only through an earlier discussion of concepts of nationalities, the state and so forth that these more educationally related terms achieve their full resonance.

There is, of course, an extensive literature on the concept of the nation and nationalism (eg Breuilly, 1985; Edwards, 1985; Gellner, 1985). In the context of this chapter, it is argued that because of the absence of complementarity between the state and its contributing nationalities and ethnicities, many states, through their institutions, and in particular through the provision of education, construct a fallacious ideal typical model of a nation state which is, in fact, a small scale society somehow writ large. By this process many modern unitary states attempt to disguise their fractured and often predatory origins. Although Soviet leaders such as Lenin (1914) and Stalin (1946) asserted that this was the characteristic feature of a bourgeois nation designed to preserve class domination, actual practice within the Soviet Union itself showed that similar structural processes were at work there. In a sense, such views parallel similar statements about the nature of a socialist city, where the view was expressed that by virtue of their location in a socialist society, the cities were by definition socialist, ignoring the spatial inequalities that lingered on from pre-revolutionary times as well as new inequalities created under communism (Bater, 1980; Morton and Stuart, 1985; Coulby and Jones, 1990). Indeed, recent events within the Soviet Union (discussed elsewhere in this book), reveal that despite considerable educational and other social policy efforts to maintain hegemonic unity, the unitary fiction of the Soviet Motherland has been largely rejected and the reality of urban inequalities openly accepted.

Such myths of national state unity are, in fact, a codification of the dominant group(s)' social and economic arrangements, a legitimation of an unequal set of socio-economic arrangements. Thus, the model of the so called nation that has emerged through this process is one that asserts that its citizens share some or all of the following:

- a common state language or languages;
- an agreed set of economic arrangements;
- a common state history, sometimes with agreed regional variation;
- if religion is present, it should be one accepted, if not believed in, by all.

Such a listing helps to understand the critical role of the educational system, particularly its curriculum content, in reproducing a citizenry that accepts such criteria. It further helps to define groups that fail to meet these and similar criteria so that they can be seen as 'alien' to the state and potentially divisive. However, within the urban areas of the state, this marginalization is less easy, though it can be made visibly manifest in the formation of shanty towns or ghettoes, recurrent features of many major cities where internationalization of migration has occurred. Within such cities, these groups, including their school-age children, come to be seen as problems for the state, their children the recipients of often inappropriate educational provision.

This marginalization process has a long history. Amongst its social consequences are prejudice, discrimination, racism and xenophobia. A spatial manifestation of this in urban areas is segregation. Thus, cultural and/or racial segregation is on the increase in many world cities despite seemingly contrary trends such as minority embourgeoisement and spatial relocation along North American lines.

At one level, it is not surprising that immigrant groups (using the term in its correct sense) in urban areas are often placed into this marginal position. Their socio-spatial marginalization is often reinforced by legislation concerning their status as citizens or residents. As an example, linking up with the earlier idea of 'Britishness', successive UK governments have tied themselves up in the knots of ever more complex immigration and nationality laws, the purpose of which is to preserve the state from being 'swamped' by 'alien' (ie, black) cultures. That this legislative framework is as it is, is a serious issue, and one which few other states either wish or are able to resolve in a satisfactory manner. Indeed, if the fictitious unitary nation state is partly defined in terms of the 'other', it is difficult to see how such exclusive states can do otherwise.

However, the issue does not stop there. What is perhaps surprising, and is most certainly a cause of equally serious concern, is the marginalization of certain groups within many states who are *not* immigrant. As an example, many black EC citizens remain as marginalized as their immigrant ancestors, unlike many other EC citizens with similar immigrant origins, such as those whose white forebears migrated from Eastern Europe. A clear demonstration of this continued marginalization for one such community is revealed in recent prison statistics released by the British Home Office (Pienaar, 1990). Pienaar's account of these statistics shows that the black population of Britain, about 5 per cent of the total, make up about 16 per cent of the prison population. Yet black prisoners have fewer previous offences and are less likely to receive bail after arrest. In other words, the evidence shows that black people follow a negative discriminatory 'fast track' through the justice system. One has to stress that black communities in the EC are not alone in this general marginalization, as equally discriminatory practices against minority groups can be found in most states.

The consequent urban stratification, particularly in its racist manifestations, sustains and creates societal divisions that result in advantaged and disadvantaged groups having unequal access to urban power and resources. Such institutionalized discrimination is usually most apparent in urban areas in the spatial segregation discussed earlier. It is the reproduction of this unequal social positioning through the education system that helps to ensure its intergenerational continuation.

As an example of this, the failure in both imagination and policy by governments in the EC that has led to an increasing ethnic and racial socio-spatial differentiation in many cities, has particularly serious implications for inner city school populations. One consequence has been an increasing tendency in many European cities towards a segregated schooling system. This is partly due to housing segregation but is also a consequence of white/majority group parents wishing to avoid sending their children to schools with a high percentage of minority/mainly black group pupils. And, like the argument that took place some decades ago in the USA, separate schools for black and white children are very likely to be inherently unequal (Spring, 1982).

The consequence of this is that within the urban areas of metropolitan democratic societies, peripheral groups, however defined, seldom have access to significant institutions in a manner sufficient to bring about a reallocation of power and resources, including those relating to education. Such groups consequently remain unrepresented, under represented or tokenistically represented in the dominant social institutions. This lack of adequate representation usually implies an equal lack of power, although the exceptions to this are important areas for study (Castells, 1983).

What follows from this is the issue of the epistemological stance that is taken in relation to an individual's, or more problematically, a group's perception of its objective interests (Habermas, 1976; Lukes, 1974). Illustrative of this problematic is the nature and purpose of group responses to unequal access and resource provision. For example, if a minority group makes no comment about an educational policy that affects its members, does this mean acquiescence, approval or realistic resignation, the 'it makes no difference what we say anyway' stance? Only detailed empirical studies have given any useful pointers (eg, Saunders, 1980).

Such studies usually emphasize the complexity of the issues involved when groups and/or individuals seek to speak for 'their' community. A key issue for minority groups therefore, in urban areas as elsewhere, in attempting to make their voice heard in education, is one of constructing an anti-hegemonic ideology that offers the possibility of successful intervention and/or protest. Unfortunately, much of what passes for multiculturalism, in education as elsewhere, does not attempt this.

This multicultural, plural nature of many states' populations, in particular the urban population, has to be acknowledged as a crucial political issue, not merely a theoretical scholarly problem. Current events in the Soviet Union are not to be regarded as some sort of exotic ethnic and national flowering of little concern to other states, save in terms of political and economic advantage. Around the world, subordinated national minorities regard events in Lithuania and the Ukraine with more than a passing interest. Equally, such national groupings within the Soviet Union and elsewhere, such as in Eastern Europe, look towards the EC, where national aspirations within a supranational organization appear to be growing.

Such events raise the question as to whether modern states can survive in their contemporary form. More to the point of this chapter, the question should be one of how state, and often nationalistic state education systems, can deal with this issue within urban classrooms, whose populations so often reflect many different forms of cultural and national identity, forms that are often overtly or covertly rejected by the education that is being provided. One way of examining this is to look at ways in which diversity itself might be construed, the concern of the next section of this chapter.

Axes of diversity

For supporters of the unitary, monocultural conceptualization of the nation, the criteria used are similar to those put forward for a more pluralistic version, namely:

> language, religion, custom, associations and traditions of political order – in short, all those forces that generate nations (Scruton, 1982, p.14).

However, it is the use of the singular rather than the plural for language, religion and custom that is significant in Scruton's assertion. Used, however, as a plurality, the terms may be developed in a way that helps rather than hinders an understanding of the reality of the modern state. The terms also help in understanding some of the educational debates about the content of a centralized curriculum that are of concern in many educational systems, particularly in their urban manifestations.

Such an awareness of state plurality is, of course, not new. Shortly after the end of World War II, Nicholas Hans identified religious, linguistic, geographical, racial and political 'factors' as ones of significance in understanding the range of issues that face national educational systems (Hans, 1949).

Hans' framework has often been the unacknowledged basis for much analysis of multiculturalism by educationalists. It forms a useful starting point from which a wider range of significant categories can be put forward that help to define the range of groups that make up the population of a state. Thus, a particular state's diversity may be defined in terms of axes of diversity such as nationality, class, status, gender, sexual orientation, race, language, religion, disability and spatial location or territoriality.

Although such axes of diversity help to clarify a complex social reality, they are also used, in part, to describe groups in negative and stereotypical ways. In particular, some teachers in dynamically pluralistic urban schools may use versions of these categorizations to make negative and stereotypical judgements about the unfamiliar and complex classroom environment that they are facing. A particularly important aspect of this process would be the way in which concepts of intelligence and educability are differentially ascribed to groups within the school (and indeed, the state) on the basis of these stereotypes. Such teacher perceptions are significant in the learning of the children concerned. As Green's work on classroom interactions demonstrated (DES, 1985), the stereotypes that teachers had of minority students were a significant factor in their interactions with such students, usually, but not always, to the student's detriment.

The consequences of such stereotyped perceptions and their associated behaviours may lead, in some circumstances, to a seeming but illusory confirmation of the stereotype, and as such, this is likely to make a significant contribution to the poor educational attainments of many minority group children in urban schools. However, it is important not to see the poor educational attainment levels of many such subordinated urban groups as merely due to discrimination. Such simplistic neo-Althussarian explanations ignore the realities of school practice and its consequences for pupil performance. The state's aims for education, school organization, the curriculum, teaching styles, indeed the whole pedagogic economy of the school, seldom challenges the dominant assertions about the diversity within a state. Indeed, it is sometimes surprising how far apart the diverse reality of an inner city school can be from the educational expectations of those in control of the educational system. Even if the diversity is acknowledged, it is all too frequently in terms of the stereotypes discussed earlier. Thus working-class children are often regarded as stupid and their parents perceived as uncaring about their children's education. Stereotypical gender roles for both boys and girls are reinforced and seldom challenged. Obviously, a wide range of other factors is at work here, particularly out-of-school factors over which the school has little control, but the fact remains that such negative teacher expectations do affect educational attainment.

What such examples help to reveal, however, is the potential value of such a taxonomic framework for the effective analysis of the racism, xenophobia, prejudice and discrimination that is often a feature of practice in urban schooling systems. It also demonstrates that struggles over gender and class/status oppression within states are connected, in quite subtle ways, with those over race, religion and language. Furthermore, at the level of practical intervention in the educational process, such taxonomic frameworks enable a more systematic and effective analysis of the issues to be made, so that intervention is based upon a more accurate understanding of them and the context within which they occur. As many of the contributions to this book describe, such systematic and effective analysis is seldom made by those managing or working within urban education systems characterized by high levels of diversity.

Social and educational policy in multicultural states

If much of the conceptualization of multiculturalism in its individual state context has been over-simplified, as has been asserted in this chapter, it is not surprising that effective social, and as part of that, educational policy and practice in relation to societal diversity has been equally over-simplified. It has also been, partly as a consequence of this failure in adequate conceptualization, often ineffective. This ineffectiveness is visible whatever the political stance that has been taken; in other words, incompetence is not the preserve of any part of the political spectrum.

Furthermore, taxonomic frameworks for analysis such as those put forward by Street-Porter (1976), although useful in their time, need revision, both in terms of current circumstances and in terms of rescuing them from simplistic utilization such as their extension within the British literature to include anti-racism (eg, ILEA, 1983). Put briefly, such taxonomies evoke a range of societal responses to diversity which range from assimilation, through integration to (cultural) pluralism. Where it has been used in the simplistic manner referred to, anti-racism has been used as either a strategy for operationalizing a preferred but unclear societal response, or as the societal response itself, where its logical distinction from other categories remains obscure (ibid., pp. 5–7). Revision is also needed for three further reasons. First, too often such taxonomies are used as if states had suddenly and recently become multicultural; this clearly is not the case, as even a cursory examination of the evidence reveals. It is even more unrealistic in cities, which partly develop through pluralistic in-migration.

Second, too frequently, they also ignore broader debates within education about educational disadvantage generally. This has meant that the taxonomies tend to be used as stages towards a state of spiritual and social grace, in this case, racial justice, with education tagging along behind in a well-intentioned vacuity.

Finally, taxonomies such as this can be used in a unilinear way, as if there is a progression from one mode of social response to another in a sort of inexorable manner. Thus assimilation is often seen as the starting point and pluralism as the end point.

However, such taxonomies do contain valuable elements, most noticeably the recognition of the range of potential societal responses to diversity, and their potential to help unpick and understand the seeming confusion that often attends any analysis of policy in this area.

One way in which such taxonomies can be given greater clarity is by looking again at their internal dynamics. What is needed is a taxonomy that addresses the permanent but ever changing nature of the issue of a state's diversity, its contested nature and its relation with other substantive contested areas of social policy generally and educational policy in particular. This may be done by developing the taxonomy into a series of *oscillating polarities*, between separation/segregation and assimilation, between efficiency and just distribution in relation to resource allocation, and between competition and cooperation. Such a model is one on which urban social policy and practice, and urban educational policy and practice in particular, can be better located, as it allows for the backwards and forwards nature of such policy and practice in this area. This is the concern of the next section.

Diversity in urban educational systems: the politics of nationalism

The taxonomy developed in the previous section is used here to explore briefly the way in which the various interested educational parties might change and renegotiate their roles in the light of changing urban circumstances. Although the motive force for such changes often originate outside the educational debate, an attempt will be made to interweave the two themes. To focus the discussion, it will concentrate on debates concerning the political 'New Right' that dominated much educational discourse within the EC states and North America during the 1980s.

Up until the 1980s, urban educational policy in relation to societal diversity within many European and North American urban education systems did, in the main, follow the Street-Porter model. There appeared to be a slow move in both general social policy, and in educational policy in particular, towards an acceptance of cultural pluralism and an acknowledgement of the racism and xenophobia in the wider society that schooling was doing all too little to prevent. It was not a steady movement towards a more favourable educational climate, of course. Indeed, much educational policy has remained stubbornly assimilationist in most urban schooling systems. Thus, policy responses to diversity fit more comfortably within a model based upon oscillation rather than the more linear progression of models like that of Street-Porter.

A specific national example of this oscillation may be found in the genesis and response to the major British government enquiry into this area of education [DES, 1985]. This particular report, the Swann Report, charted the moves from assimilation to pluralism within British education, using examples mainly from the urban schooling system. However, its main recommendations, in particular its advocacy of an 'education for all' which was pluralistic in conception, were ignored by a government that was increasingly becoming assimilationist in its attitude towards diversity and hostile to what it claimed were fallacious views in relation to equality within a modern society. With hindsight, this rejection of the report can be seen as unsurprising, given the ideological shifts that were taking place in political thinking within the ruling Conservative party at that time. Such shifts were not purely national in character but were, in fact, part of a more complex set of realignments and repositionings on the part of many Western right wing political parties that continue to have significant consequences for the education of underprivileged groups within urban schooling systems.

There are at least four elements in this right wing ideological restructuring of the 1980s and early 1990s. The first is market libertarianism, often associated with the monetarist economic writings of Hayek. At its most extreme, it has an almost messianic belief in the power of the market to regulate not just inefficiency but also injustice. Not, however, inequality, which is seen as a necessary part of the market's efforts to reduce inefficiency and injustice. A British Conservative politician, Sir Keith Joseph, at one time Secretary of State for Education and Science in the Conservative administration claimed,

> The blind, unplanned, uncoordinated wisdom of the market . . . is overwhelmingly superior to the well researched, rational, systematic, well meaning, co-operative, science based, forward looking, statistically respectable plans of governments . . . (quoted in Jones, K, 1989, p.46).

The opposition to most aspects of the Western post-war social consensus is clear. From this perspective, if there were problems with educational underattainment, untrammelled market forces, a form of rampant social Darwinism, would quickly bring justice into the system.

The second element in this right wing restructuring was less new. In this element, there is a desire to interface with the market, but only in a manner beneficial to business, on the grounds that a booming economy benefited everybody. Thus, for example, this strand of opinion supported and encouraged temporary in-migration in order to keep wages down or to provide adequate labour at a time of labour shortage, a common feature of the labour markets of many Western economies in the post-war period. This strand does, however, recognize some of the social issues that arise out of this labour supply policy and are thus interventionist in other areas of social policy as well, arguing that social dereliction can lead to potential breakdowns in the social order. Such a perspective is perhaps best exemplified in the often hostile relationships between the minority groups and the police and certain types of governmental responses to such breakdowns.

The third strand of right wing thought more directly addresses itself to the issue of national diversity. During the 1960s and 70s, the changes in the demographic and cultural profiles of many major urban areas caused such people to fear, erroneously, for the stability of their society. Although usually shy of being called racist, they advocated racist social policies. They sought and continue to seek for ever stronger immigration controls to keep further 'visible' minorities from entering 'their' country. Many go even further, encouraging the 'repatriation' of those already settled, whether they be citizens or not; indeed, they make little or no distinction between the two groups. If this element of right wing thought has an education policy, it is one that is centred around the reaffirmation of a mythic national culture and the need for an education policy that supports the assimilation of all children into such a culture.

Such views are not new. What was new, in the 1980s, was their expression within mainstream political parties, rather than in merely the extreme right wing fringe. Indeed, in some countries, electoral support for extreme right wing parties slumped as it was perceived that some of their policies had been espoused by such mainstream parties.

The consequences of such views for inner city education are profound, as they seek to deny the validity of the presence of many of the pupils in the schools. However, many of the teachers and administrators of urban schooling systems hold oppositional views and thus the debate about an appropriate education for minority group pupils often becomes polarized.

On religious matters, surprisingly, some of these right wing forces are slightly more tolerant, perhaps because they recognize similar reactionary tendencies in certain elements within the range of religious faiths which are now such a feature of urban schools. However, religious tolerance goes against the spirit of assimilation, and their tolerance is seldom more than provisional, with many systems of education still maintaining an explicit religious foundation.

The fourth strand of this new right wing ideology is, in many ways, in conflict with this traditional right wing element of conservative thinking. This final strand is also interesting in that its proponents are not only to be found in right wing groups. This strand is meritocratic, and is based on the assumption that if the competition is fair, the losers deserve to lose and the winners deserve all the prizes. To this group, tradition is worthless unless it supports efficiency, modernization and the development of a meritocracy. Such a meritocracy is not egalitarian but within it, people, and by implication, school children, get their just deserts.

Clearly, there is much in common with the market-led strand of thinking. In education, it means that nothing is to be left unquestioned if it cannot demonstrate its contribution to the economic growth of the society. Schools are seen as institutions that should attempt to give all children an equal chance, which, on the surface, seems a worthy objective. Indeed, if inner city schools serving minority group children could be resourced equally, some progress might be made. The issue is as to what constitutes equal resourcing. It is not simply about money, but is also about how money and other scarce resources, such as skilled personnel, are distributed. More money might ensure a steady stream of high quality teachers into the multicultural inner city schools, and it is certainly worth a try, but the sums involved are probably too high to be politically acceptable. Elections are seldom won by promising to spend more money on the poor.

If the rise of a range of right wing ideologies, in education and elsewhere, mark much of the 1980s and early 1990s, they also mark a decline in confidence among the more progressive elements within education. The taxonomies to understand societal and educational responses to issues of diversity that were evolved in the 1970s appeared to rest on a consensual view that a form of linear progression from assimilation to pluralism was taking place. More specifically, there was a consensus that the inadequacies to be found in inner city schools where minority pupils were concentrated had been reasonably accurately identified and that the will and the expertise to remedy them were potentially available. The true oscillating nature of the response was still disguised, even as the civil rights movement in the United States began to lose impetus and the post-war liberal consensus in many European societies finally began to break down.

With forms of right wing ideology in the ascendant, it is not surprising that the response to it took many forms. One was an atavistic return to the purity of earlier dogmas, often best summed up by left wing politicians explaining away electoral defeat by asserting that they had not been radical enough during the campaign. Another was to accept the failure of the liberal educational consensus and attempt to take on board the conservative critique – a reactive response.

However, as many Western government policies move towards a narrow assimilationist definition of the state, events within the Soviet Union, Eastern Europe and the European Community appear to be moving in an opposite direction. Yet, it is clearly not so simple. What might be called European decolonization clearly has boundaries in relation to what is acceptable and what is not. The moves within Britain and other EC states towards greater unity, *pace* 1992, for example, pose further questions to add to those raised earlier in this chapter and indeed act as a counter to those aspects of current British educational policy that appear to encourage a flattening assimilationist perspective and practice. This is because issues of nationality and nationalism, which pose very real questions for all shades of political and educational opinion within the Community and elsewhere within Europe, are increasingly being seen as best resolved by a much greater plurality within as well as between the states that make it up. However, the caveat must be entered that this issue is currently being bitterly contested within the Soviet Union, and that the practical reality is that the solution to such issues within that federation has consequences that go far beyond that nation's boundaries.

Moreover, it has been an across-Europe concern with the educational fate of migrants and other minorities that has frequently kept the educational debate within the EC alive and flourishing, even if the debate has to be conducted without too much overt reference to formal schooling.

As an example of the value of such a debate, the concern about language within the Community has meant a series of legally binding European Community Directives about language and the language rights (including educational entitlements) of minorities that move in a counter direction to the forces of assimilation. Indeed, much of the blame for current educational inadequacies in relation to these groups is seen as being caused by inadequate individual governmental responses. These national inadequacies have been documented over a long period, and this has helped to ensure that a counterbalancing debate is held in opposition to that espoused within the UK state. As the policy oscillation towards assimilation seemingly gains power within British education as the new Education Act is implemented, such a policy is widely described by Britain's Community partners as being outmoded and unrealistic.

Some consequences of this change are already apparent. The 'Eurospeak' for pluralistic initiatives in relation to education – 'intercultural education' (Batelaan, 1983; Jones and Kimberley, 1991) – has enabled educationists across the Community and within that wider European context that is supported by the Council of Europe, to exchange concepts, contexts and practice in a manner which is excitingly new. This potential for development and change extends beyond educationists. Minorities, for example the Romany, have made new groupings that transcend national boundaries, giving them the potential to make more effective interventions both at the national and the European levels. A consequence is that minorities have the potential to gain a platform in their own right, avoiding, if they wish, the device of using the state of origin as their sponsor.

Thus, a new world is called into being, as it were, to counter the old. For example, as educational policy in the UK moves in the direction of assimilation, other parts of Europe help provide a support to those forces within British education who desire a more pluralistic perspective. To predict the outcome of this debate is beyond the scope of this chapter, and indeed, is not its purpose. Its prospect does, however, provide an opportunity to end on a modestly optimistic note.

References

Bash, L (ed) (1987) *Comparative Urban Education: Towards an Agenda*, London: DICE.
Bater, J (1980) *The Soviet City*, London: Arnold.
Batelaan, P (1983) *The Practice of Intercultural Education*, London: Commission for Racial Equality.
Breuilly, J (1985) *Nationalism and the State*, Manchester: Manchester University Press.
Castells, M (1983) *The City and the Grassroots*, London: Arnold.

Coulby, D and Jones, C (1990) 'Urban education in Soviet cities', in Cowen, R and Jones, C (eds) (1990) *Essays in Honour of J J Tomiak*, London: DICE.
Council of the European Communities (1970) *Council Directive of 25 July 1977 on the education of the children of migrant workers. [77/486/EEC]*, Brussels: CEC.
Department of Education and Science (DES) (1985) *Education For All* [The Swann Report], London: HMSO.
Edwards, J (1985) *Language, Society and Identity*, Oxford: Blackwell.
Fishman, J (1975) *Language and Nationalism*, Roweley, Massachusetts: Newbury House.
Foot, P (1965) *Immigration and Race in British Politics*, Harmondsworth: Penguin.
Gellner, E (1985) *Nations and Nationalism*, Oxford: Blackwell.
Hans, N (1949) *Comparative Education*, London: Routledge.
Habermas, J (1976) *Legitimation Crisis*, London: Heinemann.
Hechter, M (1975) *Internal Colonialism: The Celtic Fringe in British National Development*, Berkeley, University of California Press.
Home Office (1981) *The Brixton Disorders* (The Scarman Report), Cmnd 8427, London: HMSO.
Inner London Education Authority (ILEA) (1983) *Race, Sex, and Class. 3. A Policy for Equality: Race*, London: ILEA.
Jones, C and Kimberley, K (1991) *Intercultural Perspectives on the National Curriculum for England and Wales*, London: Centre for Multicultural Education.
Jones, K (1989) *Right Turn: The Conservative Revolution in Education*, London: Hutchinson.
Lenin, V (1914) 'The right of nations to self determination', in *Collected Works*. Volume 20 (1964) Moscow: State Publishing House.
Lukes, S (1974) *Power: a Radical View*, London: Macmillan.
Morton, H and Stuart, R (eds) (1985) *The Contemporary Soviet City*, London: Macmillan.
Pienaar, J (1990) 'Review of racial bias in sentencing' *The Independent*, 11 December.
Saunders, P (1980) *Urban Politics*, Harmondsworth: Penguin.
Scruton (1982) 'Thinkers of the left: E P Thompson', in *Salisbury Review*, autumn, 1, p.14.
Spring, J (1982) *American Education*, Second edn, London: Longman.
Stalin, J (1946) 'The national question and Leninism', in *Collected Works*, Volume 11, Moscow: State Publishing House.
Street-Porter, R (1976) *Race, Children and Cities*, Milton Keynes: Open University Press.
Tower Hamlets, London Borough of (1988) *Tower Hamlets Education: Getting it Right, Draft Development Plan*, London: London Borough of Tower Hamlets.

20. Urban civic culture and education

David Coulby

Introduction

This chapter attempts to establish, particularly for education, a notion of urban civic culture as a conceptual area where a fruitful polar dichotomy can appropriately be recognized. It emphasizes the role of educational institutions in the selection and reproduction of urban civic culture from the two identified forms of epistemological organization to be available within heterogeneous urban areas, which are referred to as traditional and international urban civic culture. These two notions of civic culture are examined using Europe as a case study. The suggested polarity, in this particular case, is thus between traditional European civic culture and international European civic culture. However, this concern with cultural selection within Europe should not be seen as an aspect of the ethnocentricity which has so often characterized that continent. Indeed, it is in the choice between traditionalist Eurocentrism and a more international conceptualization of what it is to be a European citizen that the dichotomies of this chapter operate. For this reason it begins with a brief consideration of global variations and patterns in urbanization before focusing on European civic culture and its educational dimensions. The argument centres on the cities and states of the European Community (EC) although, as is made clear later, this concentration is both arbitrary and historically defined. Since the intention of this chapter is to broaden the conception of what it is to be a European citizen, it would be unfortunate if it were to be seen to be confusing Europe with the EC.

Changing patterns of international urbanization

Urban educational issues are differentially perceived according to which state is being examined. The concern with improving access to higher education which is apparent in Pittsburgh and Rotterdam may seem something of an irrelevance when faced with the difficulties which many children and young people encounter in the cities of Kenya. It may seem that the comparative study of urban education in such differing contexts offers little mutual illumination. In fact this is not the case; as is shown below, there are common themes even between such apparently differing cities as Tokyo and Soweto.

Another difficulty which besets international studies of urban education is that of the unit of analysis. Are cities themselves the right unit of generalization? (Saunders, 1981). There are huge economic, social and cultural differences between people who live in various areas of cities. These differences are not always rigidly geographically segregated, as they are in New York or Cape Town; they can sometimes be found on the same street, as is the case in many European cities. Of course these differences are the challenge of urban studies and of urban policy areas such as education. To point to such differences is only to open the debate, it is not to abandon it. Furthermore, cities are embedded in states to differing degrees. Some, like Singapore, are effectively city states. Others, like Soweto or Riga, sit uneasily within the political frame of the existing state. Some cities, such as Nairobi, Mexico City or Buenos Aires, dominate the economies and politics of their state. There are others, such as Montreal, Bilbao, Jerusalem, where, despite their size, wealth and prosperity, the citizens may feel marginalized within the state where they are placed for historical and cultural reasons as much as for political ones. Whilst, as a unit of analysis, the city needs to take account of those policies and patterns which are taking place at the level of the state, conformity to or approval of these policies cannot be assumed. Events in cities may run counter to the trends within their state and in so doing actually alter the very nature of the state within which they are embedded. The histories of Paris, St Petersburg, Istanbul or Teheran could certainly be written in these terms.

The uneasy oscillation of the unit of analysis between city and state is made more complex by the emergence of international organizations. Transnational corporations now shift investment across wide areas of the globe. The impact of these investment and disinvestment strategies on cities and states can be profound. The growth of, on the one hand, industrial zones and, on the other, 'rust belts' testifies to the rapidity of these changes.

International political coalitions also have a major impact on cities. The EC is certainly an emergent international political organization, perhaps even state, of considerable potential. It has already had an impact not only on the politics and economics of Europe but also on where cities and citizens place themselves in state terms. Do inhabitants of the city of Luxembourg see themselves more as citizens of the EC than of the state of Luxembourg? Similar doubtful patterns of allegiance, though for different reasons, may already be emergent in Antwerp and may be anticipated in Londonderry and Barcelona (though the position of the latter may now be clearer given the status of Catalonia within the federal Spanish state). The EC is not the only international political organization, of course, though it is currently backed by considerable economic force and political momentum. It may be that the Soviet Union is moving more towards the confederacy model of the EC at the same time that many in the EC wish to solidify it into a unitary state. For the purposes of this chapter it is necessary to note only the fragility of the units of analysis. In order to understand the social and educational issues and policies in many European cities it is increasingly necessary to shift the unit of analysis continually from the city to the state to the EC.

The issue of contrasts in the urban educational policy fields between Pittsburgh and Nairobi raises the further difficulty of the appropriate unit and level of generalization. What common language is there to talk about such differing cities? How can even their contrasts be expressed without lapsing into the discredited polarities of first and third world, or the patronizing and misleading vocabulary of developing or emergent nations? To speak of levels of urbanization implies a continuum or a historical process through which all cities must travel before arriving at the state of alleged perfection currently exemplified by the Western European or North American urban areas. Apart from the ethnocentricity of such classifications, they embody assumptions about economic growth within a world system still fractured by financial and military exploitations. If terms extrinsic to the city are chosen as social indicators or categories then the difficulties encountered with regard to the geographical unit of analysis are solidified. The differences between cities are then codified in terms drawn from the state, political and economic organization, cultural heritage, GNP per capita income, etc. Whilst, as indicated above, the oscillation between the various geographical units of analysis can be managed, it needs always to be sensitive to non-typical, non-conformist or openly dissident urban areas.

It is in terms of the differences *within* cities that there actually are common urban and urban educational themes between such apparently diverse cities as Pittsburgh and Nairobi. Cities are the geographical location of social and economic difference between groups. The extremes of wealth and poverty are present in both Nairobi and Pittsburgh. Certainly there is a relativity: the extremely poor are much poorer in Nairobi and there are many more of them as a percentage of the population of the city. In each case, however, the city concentrates and makes highly visible the contrasts between the rich and the poor. This concentration and visibility means that conflicts over scarce resources, not least education, between the rich and poor are more likely, more extreme and, in turn, more visible in urban areas. Financial wealth is not, of course, the only difference between groups within urban areas. In earlier writing (for example, Coulby and Jones, 1989) models have been offered of the various ways in which urban diversity can be categorized. One of the major reasons, then, that it is valuable to conduct comparative urban and urban educational studies is that large urban areas across the globe are sites of such highly visible differences and of conflicts between different groups.

The other major reason to justify the international study of urban issues is that the pattern of global urbanization is such as not to make it possible to separate developments in one city from financial, political and military events elsewhere. The international division of labour has speeded up not only investment and disinvestment decisions but also movements of people within and between nation states looking for work and wealth in those areas favoured by high investment or strong commodity prices. Neither the new international division of labour nor the pattern of urbanization that has accompanied it are fixed states. The international division of labour changes with increasing rapidity according to capital flows, market penetration and the consolidation of economic weight into political pressure (through the emergence of the EC as well as the military adventures of the USA). The resultant changes in urbanization, urban economic activity and urban form are as tangible in Strasbourg as in Seoul. Moreover, both the number of large cities and their actual size continues to grow, in China and the Soviet Union as well as in South Asia, Africa and Latin America. Yet such urban growth runs alongside events in the Middle East, the Soviet Union and Eastern Europe that have revealed the fragility of states despite their appearance of solidity and permanence. The international pattern of increasingly interactive and still expanding cities remains a key economic and political phenomenon. Despite wide variations in both the contexts and the levels of social provision within these cities, no single urban area can be understood in isolation from the rest of the developing system.

Thus apparently widely differentiated cities with apparently major differences in their educational policy issues can and must be studied within an international context for at least three major reasons. First, the nation state is an inadequate unit of analysis in urban educational studies. Second, highly visible differences in provision and conflict over these differences is a common theme in all cities. Third, the developing international division of labour, capital and decision-making means that the economic, political and, increasingly, educational development of cities in widely separated nation states are firmly interlinked.

The semiology of the city

The international interdependence and commonality of urban systems is not always reflected in the ways in which cities are portrayed and understood. This gap between the image of the city and people's day-to-day experience of it is manifested in the curricula of many urban schools. It is, then, necessary to begin to understand the semiology of the city as one of the broken links between the international political, economic, cultural and demographic influences which characterize all urban systems and the romantic, nationalist influences which inform so many of their school curricula.

For example, the rural–urban dichotomy/continuum still has power in the EC and North America but more at the level of symbol than of social experience. In other parts of the world widespread rural poverty continues to make urban living seem attractive. The continuing migration to large cities is the dramatic evidence of this. For some, the city is a sign of the possibility of economic prosperity and cultural freedom, for others the symbol of exploitation and alienation.

The importance of the semiology of the city is increasingly recognized in urban studies (Harvey, 1989; King, 1990a; 1990b). The West embodies its eschatology in the mean streets and high living of big cities. The city as heaven and hell is a potent image within Western urban literature and film. The examples are so many that any selection must be idiosyncratic: Chandler, Grass, Rushdie, Simenon; *Z Cars, Kojak, Casualty*; *Alphaville, La Dolce Vita, Bladerunner, The Third Man*. The eschatology is between the city as locale of (and sign for) violence and intolerance and the city on a hill dispensing political, moral and cultural certainties to the benighted lowlands. Whilst crime fiction provides the most striking and violent presentations of the diabolic aspect of this imagery, and Chandler's books provide the most vivid and symbolically rich example known to the authors, it can be detected in many other genres and forms as well as in the metaphors of politicians and press. The idealized city is a less frequent manifestation residing most frequently in mythology, fantasy or idealism –

Camelot, Minas Tirith, Utopia. Social experiment has favoured the garden city in England. The idealized city has only been assayed as part of the imperialist or post-imperialist dream – New Delhi, Casablanca, Brasilia (Rabinow, 1989).

Whilst the contrast between city and village has little power as an analytic tool within the current social demographic distribution of the EC countries, in many states, especially France, Germany and the UK, an idealized version of rural living is perceived as a retreat from the many hardships of urban life. The old Tönnies' dichotomies are revived within the strident signifiers of advertising, soap operas or the leisure industry. Whilst urban sociologists may see the urban–rural dichotomy or even continuum as a discredited notion, it retains power at the romantic and imaginative level for all those who look forward to escaping from the city at weekends, on holidays or at some point in the future, to a rural world of cottages, nature and *auberges*. However, a less superficial way of understanding the conflicts over culture, knowledge and value which is taking place within the cities of the EC might be in terms of two competing versions of European civic culture.

European civic culture

This chapter suggests that there are two conflicting versions of civic culture, the traditional and the international. Both are ways of seeing the history, society, technology and artistic activity of the continent. In both cases these are increasingly urban, though for different reasons. In order to exemplify these oppositional views of civic culture this chapter focuses on the cities of the EC. This narrowing of focus allows for some further exemplification of the educational issues, particularly in terms of curricula.

The terminology here may need clarification because of the level of generality. It is not being suggested that European culture is exclusively the product of cities and towns, nor that there are only two forms of this culture. Culture is the multitudinous product of different groups of people operating in collectivities as small as the family or as large as a prominent religious group or social class. It consists not only of products but also of rituals and practices. Child-rearing, the preparation, presentation and consumption of food and drink, sit uneasily alongside the diverse literary, artistic, religious, musical and constructive products in any attempt to make generalizations about culture (see, for example, Williams, 1981). Given the multitude of cultures across Europe it is obviously a crude simplification to polarize all this activity within two main headings or even to conceptualize European civic culture as an identifiable phenomenon at all. As ever, the purpose of attempting to establish categories at this level of generalization is to try to establish some conceptual purchase on diverse and shifting social phenomena.

It needs to be stressed that the establishment of a polarity between traditional and international European civic culture is in no way an attempt to offer a comprehensive classification of curricular systems. It is rather that this polarity is a helpful one in isolating one important aspect of curriculum definition. In European terms, this aspect is the extent to which a new European triumphalism is in danger of replacing state nationalisms as a limiting force within curricula.

Defining European civic culture is increasingly a political activity. If the full diversity of cultural achievement in European cities is to be recognized then the hegemonic traditional notion must be challenged. Traditional European civic culture has achieved hegemonic status not only through state and civil endorsement and subsidy of concert halls and art exhibitions; it is also achieved through national curriculum programmes and through the control of research agenda in higher education. The nature of the hegemony is in the increasingly close relationship between national and civic government, traditionalistic artistic activity, mass media and education systems. In order to begin to challenge this hegemony effectively, it is necessary to establish the broad frames within which such political activity can be recognized and challenged. The test for this typology is not as sociological abstractions but as terms which have real purchase on social, and especially educational, policy.

What this chapter terms 'traditional European civic culture' celebrates the civilisation its protagonists see to have been established on that continent and, effectively, nowhere else. They would point to the achievements of specific European cities as the unquestionable history not of one continent but of the whole of human civilisation (Gheverghese, 1991). Specific cities are seen as the physical embodiment and repository not only of European history but of human achievement. Examples of this include Athens, Rome, Florence, Paris, Amsterdam and London. This civilisation or culture will be conceptualized in terms of particular activities and particular outstanding proponents (almost all of them men). Philosophy begins with Plato and Aristotle. Architectural achievements are those of the Athenian acropolis, the Gothic cathedrals or Renaissance Florence and Rome. Literature is seen as an agreed canon of classic texts from Aeschylus to Yeats with, in the UK, an overwhelming stress on Shakespeare, and similar but not equal pre-eminence in other nation states given to Cervantes, Goethe, Dante and Racine. Music is seen to be largely the product of the German and Italian speaking states: current international fashion places Mozart in a position musically which, in terms of literature, Shakespeare only enjoys in English speaking states. Art and sculpture reach their triumphal period in the Italian Renaissance when Brunelleschi, Giotto and others rediscovered the perfections of Athenian form. Within this canon scientific and technological activities are less valued, but any questions would soon be answered with names like Galileo, Henry the Navigator, Descartes, Newton and Einstein.

Since this traditional version of European civic culture has been and remains so influential on both the form and content of educational systems, it may be worth spelling out some of the major questions that it raises. Why was civic culture created almost exclusively by men? Why did it occur on just one continent? Why is easel painting given so much importance as against road building or town planning? Why is composing concerti seen as distinct from and more important than draining swamps or designing factory systems? Why is this version of culture so monadic, triumphalistic, placid and conflict free? In fact the traditionalist is a sexist and imperialistic view of European civic culture. Even in the exclusive terms of culture which it seeks to establish, it draws only on a grotesquely impoverished canon. But the voices which are excluded from it are the only ones which offer it any possibility of greater depth. It is necessary to question it because it retains such power in both education systems and the way in which groups of people organize their political beliefs. For various groups, in various states, it can easily be interpreted as the triumph of Catholicism or the triumph of Protestantism, as the central role in global civilisation of a particular state be it as small and insignificant as Portugal, Holland or England. It is only non-contested because so many groups can contribute their own petty chauvinisms to the overall imperialism which perceives human history as 'The Triumph of the West' (Roberts, 1980).

What this chapter terms 'international European civic culture', on the other hand, sees the continent and its cities as part of a global system since before the rise of Knossos. It celebrates the great periods and achievements of the wider interactions of European cities and states: Alexander's openness to Persian culture, the influence of Eastern religions and moralities, the economic and cultural interchange between Venice and the East, the tolerance and economic vitality of the Cordoba Caliphate, the culturally enriching influences of the Raj not on India but on the UK. In the millennia of imperialism, internecine strife, religious persecution and racial genocide, it is admittedly hard to isolate the moments of celebration. But, if this is so, then it is all the more strange that they are almost entirely ignored within the traditional formulation. International European civic culture is an acknowledgement not only of the international contribution to European civilisation but also that European civil culture itself must be placed within an international context of which Europe is but a part.

International European civic culture acknowledges that the demographic pattern of the continent has been in ceaseless flux and that this flux can no more be stopped by the Treaty of Versailles than it could be by Offa's Dyke. The population and boundaries of Europe can never be finalized. It is necessary for the continent to find ways of adapting to this fact which go beyond fighting to the death to revise the last agreed boundary change but two. It acknowledges that the achievements of the continent are multi-faceted and go far beyond easel painting to scientific, economic, social and familial practices. It insists that all these achievements were and continue to be influenced by practices and people beyond the boundaries of Europe; that interchange with Africa and Asia has been a vital element in the economic and cultural growth of Europe. It recognizes that people from beyond Europe have, across many centuries, come to live in its cities and that their contributions have been an invigorating element in urban economic and artistic success. Similarly, demographic interchange between the states and cities of Europe has played a vital part in urban achievements. It would be wrong to provide an alternative list of famous protagonists, since this view of civic culture does not see it as the achievement of a small group of heroes; rather, it is the product of groups of women and men working together and in conflict over time. Nor is international European civic culture oblivious to the fact that the interchanges within and beyond Europe were most often the result in the first instance of exploitation and conflict. Demographic movement so often results from exploitation, imperialism and war. However, it insists that the real culture of European cities is the product of the heterogeneities produced by these movements and not some reified conflict-free art gallery or opera house.

Lest this be seen as a bland sequence of assertions of post-modernism, it can be emphasized that the outsider is a well-identified commonplace in the history of European civic culture. Traditional European civic culture might invoke El Greco or Conrad in this respect, whilst international European civic culture would appeal to Rushdie. The latter provides, especially in *The Satanic Verses*

(Rushdie, 1988), just such a celebration of and dirge for European urban heterogeneity as the above paragraphs advocate for international civic culture.

European civic culture and education

It is particularly in curricular terms that education systems in the EC and beyond must make decisions about which view of European civic culture a particular state chooses to advocate and reproduce.

Decisions must be made about languages. From the point of view of traditional European civic culture the questions are: will pupils be taught Latin and Greek, the languages of traditional greatness, or French, the language of civilisation, culture and eighteenth century diplomacy, or English, the language of imperialism and American economic domination? From the position of international civic culture pupils would be taught the languages of their own cities: Bengali in East London, Arabic in Paris, Turkish in Frankfurt. The languages curriculum of all the EC states also needs to acknowledge the regional linguistic diversity within states as well as the urban linguistic diversity resulting from ongoing demographic change.

The canon of literature to be studied is easy to determine within the values of traditional European culture. Similarly, traditional fine arts and philosophy, retaining a high prominence in the curriculum right up to higher education level, will reflect sexist and ethnocentric priorities. Whilst these areas of study would be much less important to an international European civic culture perspective, it would be necessary to undermine the whole notion of an accepted and orthodox canon and to ensure that pupils and students were exposed to a wide variety of material from across Europe and beyond and that an appropriate priority was placed on the cultural products and activities of the whole range of European urban groups. This is not merely to establish an alternative canon but to bring into the view of pupils and students the processes and criteria by which canons come to be established.

Perhaps most urgently the notion of historical studies as a celebration of 'The Triumph of the West' (Roberts, 1980) needs to be challenged across the cities of the EC. There is a danger that as individual state ethnocentric versions of history are gradually eroded they will be replaced by a European triumphalist version of world history and current events. Of course in the case of England and Wales, where a National Curriculum in history has just been established by statute, there is not even the danger of a shift from ethnocentrism to Eurocentrism (Coulby, 1991). Pupils and students in the EC need to understand the history that is gradually bringing them together as Europeans, but also the history that attempts to place Europe in a non-dominant interpretation of the events of world history. This need not just be a litany of guilt about imperialism, slavery and genocide – though it is hard to see how these topics can be avoided – it can include also a recognition of achievement quite outside Europe and the ways in which these achievements have or have not impacted on European development.

Such a debate about the curriculum has to include consideration of another major area where the notion of European civic culture needs to be developed, namely the education of teachers. Like the curriculum, this is an area where there is very little collaboration or communication between the member states of the EC. The initial and in-service education of teachers is an important process in the definition and reproduction of notions of European civic culture. There is scope for the examination of these processes within different states and for the consideration of ways in which they can be extracted from the traditionalist interpretation. There is a need to break down the barriers between national systems of teacher education. Whilst the processes of the single market will mean that industry, commerce and research, as well as politics, are increasingly conducted at a European level, there will be a danger that school systems will remain in national isolation. Ways need to be found to combat this in terms of the movement of pupils, students and teachers as well as in the explicit content of teacher education programmes.

To establish the polarity between traditional and international European civil culture still leaves many questions unanswered. These refer, in particular, to the ways in which traditional or international alternatives are determined and implemented in the educational policy of states and of the EC as a whole. If the polarity points to crucial differences in the way in which European curricular systems may be understood, then a whole range of political questions, beyond the scope of this chapter, arise, which refer to the people, groups and institutions in individual states whereby particular views of European civic culture are determined, challenged or reproduced.

The Treaty of Rome does not give the EC more than the most general salience with regard to education. The Commission and the European Parliament have been cautious about intervention in the educational affairs of member states. Some member states, in particular the UK, have been resistant to even the most general initiatives such as the Lingua programme or the Directive on language provision for 'the children of immigrant workers'. On the other hand, Portugal is now looking to the EC for substantial support for the expansion and restructuring of its entire education system. The Commission and the European Parliament will increasingly need to assert that education, not least the curriculum, is appropriately a European matter. In this respect the limitations which the Treaty of Rome places on the EC's involvement in educational matters will become a matter of urgent concern.

In terms of curriculum, then, European states need to choose between traditional or international European civic culture, between fanaticism or tolerance, between conformity or diversity, between nationalism or internationalism. In terms of the institutional and financial arrangements for education, parallel decisions must be addressed. Education systems must determine whether they are aiming to develop all their pupils and students or merely those representing particular social, cultural or linguistic groups. They need to determine what arrangements would allow educational institutions to prepare young people for the unpredictable European and international workplace of today instead of the secure nationalistic fictions of yesterday. It was asserted above that the definition of European civic culture was increasingly a political matter. The components of school curricula across the EC are probably the most important aspect of these political decisions. As states revise their curricular and assessment systems they will be taking decisions about which version of European civic culture will inform the future.

Conclusion

The European example shows how powerful particular conceptualizations of urban civic culture can be, and how pervasive their influence on school systems, particularly in terms of school and higher education curricula and the training of teachers. Analyses of other regions and other cities would have different starting points. The semiotics of cities in Japan and China are sharply different from those of the West. The cities which have been developed or redeveloped under periods of state communism would provide another contrast. There may be similar sharp contrasts with regard to the ways in which traditional and international civic cultures can be identified and on their effects on school systems. Certainly the influence of traditional European civic culture on the rest of the world is considerably less than its proponents would wish to belive.

What remains to be investigated is how far such a rigid polarity in terms of civic culture is helpful in understanding the systems of behaviour and belief which can be identified in cities outside Europe. Such a polarity may be less helpful in understanding school and higher education curricula in other regions. Moving towards a fuller understanding of the civic culture of cities in other regions is obviously an important task for the proponents of international civic culture.

References

Coulby, D (1991) 'The National Curriculum', in Coulby, D and Bash, L *Contradiction and Conflict: The 1988 Education Act in Action*, London: Cassell.

Coulby, D and Jones, C (1989) 'Urban education and comparative education: some possibilities', in McLean, M *Education in Cities: International Perspectives*, London: British Comparative and International Education Society.

Gheverghese, J G (1991) *The Crest of the Peacock: Non-European Roots of Mathematics*, London: I B Tauris.

Harvey, D (1989) *The Condition of Postmodernity: An Enquiry into the Origins of Cultural Change*, Oxford: Blackwell.

King, A D (1990a) *Urbanism, Colonialism and the World Economy: Cultural and Spatial Foundations of the World Urban System*, London: Routledge.

King, A D (1990b) *Global Cities: Post-Imperialism and the Internationalisation of London*, London: Routledge.

Rabinow, P (1989) *French Modern: Norms and Forms of the Social Environment*, Harvard: MIT Press.

Roberts, J M (1980) *The Pelican History of the World*, Harmondsworth: Penguin.

Rushdie, S (1988) *The Satanic Verses*, London: Viking.

Saunders, P (1981) *Social Theory and the Urban Question*, London: Hutchinson.

Williams, R (1981) *Culture*, London: Fontana.

Biographical notes on contributors

Asahiro Arai is a researcher at the Nippon Association for Education 2001 (NAFE) and Lecturer in psychology at the Institute for Vocational Training and Bunri College. He specialized in confluent education at graduate school at the University of California, Santa Barbara and has published many articles on comparative and primary education.

Leslie Bash is currently Principal Lecturer and Coordinator of Research and Staff Development in the Department of Education at Anglia Polytechnic. He previously taught in primary and secondary schools, the London Institute of Education, Rolle College, Mid-Kent College, and Bath College of Higher Education. He has specific interests in urban, multicultural and policy issues in education. He is the co-author of *Urban Schooling* (with David Coulby and Crispin Jones); *The Education Reform Act: Competition and Control* (with David Coulby); and *Conflict and Contradiction in Education* (also with David Coulby). He also edited *Comparative Urban Education.*

Miranda Bell was brought up in South Africa and her work at the University of the Witwatersrand in the late 1970s meant that she was a frequent visitor to schools in Soweto. The history of South African education and the operation of apartheid in education has provided the focus for much of her research work. She is currently Head of Communications at the Polytechnic of North London which has pioneered effective strategies in access to higher education for under-represented groups in the United Kingdom.

David Coulby is Head of the Faculty of Education at Bath College of Higher Education. Prior to this he taught in East London and lectured at the University of London Institute of Education. He has published widely in the areas of urban education and educational policy. His latest book, with Leslie Bash, is *Contradiction and Conflict: the 1988 Education Act in Action*. His current research interest involves curricula and teacher education in the cities of the EC.

Dong Jianhong is Programme Officer, Division of Cooperation in Education, Chinese National Commission for UNESCO. He is responsible for the educational cooperative activities with the UNESCO Principal Regional Office in Asia and the Pacific, involved in the execution of the Asian and Pacific Programme of Education Innovations for Development (APEID), the Asian and the Pacific Programme for Education for All, higher education programme, etc. He is currently working at the National Centre of Education Development Research, State Education Commission, for a six-month study programme.

Crispin Jones is a Senior Lecturer in Education at the University of London Institute of Education. He works in the Department of International and Comparative Education and the Centre for Multicultural Education. Prior to this he worked as a teacher and an adviser in London. His main research interest is the study of diversity in inner city schools. He has published widely in the areas of urban education and multicultural education.

Hiroshi Kimura is Head of the Research Division for Comparative Education at the National Institute for Educational Research (NIER). Kimura specialized in Educational Administration at graduate school at Tokyo University and has published many articles on comparative education.

Mikhail L Levitski graduated from Moscow Institute of Forestry in 1966 and received his PhD in education in 1988. He is now Dean of the Department for Continuing Education of University Teachers at Moscow Pedagogical University. He has a number of publications on the economics of education and educational management, including *Methodological and Practical Problems of Using Computers in Educational Management*, 1980, *Methods and Models of Measuring Effectiveness in Public Education*, 1984, and *Methods of Effective Planning in Public Education*, 1983.

Zhang Li was awarded a degree from Peking University (PU) in 1982, passed the advanced courses for postgraduates in the field of higher education and gave lectures to postgraduates as a part-time lecturer at the Institute of Higher Education of PU; since 1985, he has been the Deputy Division Chief of the Policy Research Office of the former Ministry of Education and the present National Center for Education Development Research of the State Education Commission. He has participated in several national research projects involving overall policy-making processes in China, and undertook research at the International Bureau of Education (UNESCO, Geneva) for three months as a visiting scholar; currently, he is one of the deputy directors of a project for cooperation between the Center and the United Nations Children's Fund during the period 1990–94.

Kevin Lillis worked in the Kenyan education service and the University of London Institute of Education. He has published widely in the area of Education and Development.

Tapas Majumdar is Professor of Economics at the Jawaharal Nehru University in New Delhi and Distinguished Professor in Economic Policy Management at the Development Institute in Gurgaon. He has published widely in the areas of economics and education. His latest book is *Nature, Man and the Indian Economy*.

Kevin J Moran received his masters degree in policy studies from the School of Education, University of Pittsburgh, where he is currently a doctoral student in the history and sociology of education. He has published in the *Journal of Social History*, *Journal of Urban History*, *Paedagogica Historica*, and *Journal of Education* and presented papers on dominant cultures and ethnic identities at the Freie University of Berlin. During the 1987–8 academic year, he conducted research in England on school knowledge transmission as part of a research collaborative sponsored by the Ford and Spencer Foundations.

Nikolai D Nikandrov graduated from Leningrad University in 1954 and received his PhD in education there in 1973. He is now a full member of the USSR Academy of Pedagogical Sciences and occupies the position of Chief Learned Secretary responsible for the overall planning of research in the 20 research institutes in the Academy. His main interests are in the fields of comparative education, methodology of educational research, and methods of teaching and learning. He is author of about 200 publications on these subjects, including *Programmed Learning and the Ideas of Cybernetics*, 1970, *Pedagogics of Higher Education*, 1974, *Higher Education Abroad*, 1978, and *Creativity in Teaching*, 1990.

Ton Peters was educated at Teachers College in the Hague and trained in educational sciences in Tilburg and the Hague. He has taught at primary level and in adult education. In 1976 he was appointed to the Project *Education and Social Environment* in Rotterdam, the most long-term experimental education project ever implemented in the Netherlands. In 1981 he was appointed Director of the Project. From 1985–90 he coordinated the educational priority policy in Rotterdam. Since 1990 he has been a policy-advisor on education, migration and employment-policy for the Rotterdam city council.

Meng Qingfen was born in 1953, graduated from the Langfang Teacher Institute of Hebei Province, worked at the Office of the Academic Degrees Committee of the State Council from 1981 to 1989, and has been one of the editors of the *Directory of Higher Educational and Research Institutions Authorized to Confer Higher Degrees in the P.R. China*. Now she is the Deputy Chief of the editing office of the journal *Research Trends* of the National Center for Education Development Research.

Haruo Sato is Adviser for Youth and Adult Education, Board of Education, Ohta Borough, Tokyo and Lecturer in Educational Administration at Takushoku University. Sato specialized in educational administration at graduate school at Tokyo Gakugei University and has published many articles on community education and educational administration.

Richard Teese is a Senior Lecturer in Education at the University of Melbourne. He is currently Project Director, Data, Information and Research Unit in the Ministry of Education in Victoria. The focus of his research is on unequal social selection in school. He has published papers on urban differences in school completion rates, curriculum placements, and examinations success. In 1984 and 1987 he was *maître assistant associé* and visiting scholar in the Centre de Sociologie Européenne in Paris. He has written on Catholic education in France and produced a comparative monograph on education and training in France and Australia.

Elwyn Thomas is Senior Lecturer, Chairperson and Head of the Department of International and Comparative Education, Institute of Education, University of London. He received his first degree in biological sciences at the University of Wales with subsequent higher degrees in education psychology and child psychology at the University of London. He has taught in primary and secondary schools in the UK, and held lecturing posts in polytechnics and teacher education colleges. His research interests include teacher and pupil stress, culture and schooling, cross-cultural aspects of teacher and pupil behaviour, moral education and parental influences on schooling. He was head of biological education at the University of Malawi for two years and spent a further five years as an educational psychologist working for the Government of the Republic of Singapore.

William B Thomas, a former Fulbright teaching fellow in Denmark and Belgium, received his doctorate from the State University of New York at Buffalo. He teaches history and sociology of education at the University of Pittsburgh. As an associate professor, he was a Visiting Fellow at the University of London Institute of Education, where he conducted research in British schools under the sponsorship of a Ford Foundation post-doctoral fellowship and the Spencer Foundation. He has published in journals such as the *American Sociologist*, *Journal of Social History*, *Paedagogica Historica*, *American Journal of Education*, *Journal of Urban History*, *Teachers College Record*, *Journal of Education*, *Journal of Negro Education*, *Urban Education*, *Phi Delta Kappan*, and *Phylon*. Other works have appeared in *Education and the Rise of the New South* (Ronald Goodenow and Arthur O White, eds), and *Black Communities and Urban Race Relations in American History* (Kenneth L Kusmer, ed).

Cheng Tiying, presently a lecturer in English at the Oriental Languages Department of Beijing University, first graduated from Beijing Normal University with a BA degree and then from the Nankai University with an MA. He has devoted much of his spare time to educational studies and has participated in the compilation or translation of several works on education including *Post-Secondary Education in China*, *The Development and Reform Tendencies of World Secondary Education*, and *Education Encyclopedia*.

Theo Veld is senior lecturer at the Department of Sociology and Social Policy at the Erasmus University in Rotterdam. His PhD thesis, 'Volksonderwijs en Leerplicht', is an analysis of the genesis of compulsory education in Dutch nineteenth century society. He has written articles on the history of nineteenth century education, the attitudes of different generations of an urban working class towards education, and on growing up as a bargees' child.

Geoff Whitty taught in comprehensive schools in London and Crawley New Town before becoming a Lecturer in Education at the University of Bath in 1973. He subsequently ran the Urban Education Programme at King's College, London for four years before becoming Head, Professor and Dean of Education at Bristol Polytechnic. Since 1990 he has been the Goldsmiths' Professor of Policy and Management in Education in the University of London. He has published widely on the sociology of education, curriculum studies and education policy studies.

Roger R Woock is currently Deputy Dean of the newly established Institute of Education of the University of Melbourne. From 1985 to 1988 he was Professor and Head of the Department of Educational Policy and Administrative Studies at the University of Calgary, Alberta, Canada. He has taught at Hunter College of the City University of New York and the State University of New York at Buffalo. He is on the editorial board of *Urban Education* and *Urban Review*. He is the author of many books and articles including *Power and Politics in Harlem* (with A Pinkney), *Social Foundation of Urban Education* (with H Miller) and *Confronting School and Work* (with P Dwyer and B Wilson).

Selected bibliography

The following selected bibliography complements the more detailed references to be found at the end of each chapter. It is confined to the important references, mainly in English, found elsewhere in the text. It contains books, papers, articles and journals that have general value for the study of urban education.

Readers wishing for more information on specific national or individual urban systems should therefore refer to the relevant individual chapter reference sections. It should be noted, however, that although most references are given in English, some of the individual chapter references contain titles that have been translated into English by the individual authors; the actual texts may be in another language.

This selected bibliography is organized in four separate sections: official papers and reports, books, articles and chapters in books, and selected relevant journals.

Official reports

Australian Schools Commission (1973) *Schools in Australia*, Canberra: AGPS.

Beijing Statistics Bureau (1990) *1989 Bulletin on Statistics of National Economic and Social Development in Beijing*, Beijing: China Statistics.

Carnegie Foundation for the Advancement of Teaching (1988) *An Imperiled Generation: Saving Urban Schools*, Princeton, NJ: Carnegie Foundation.

Cocoran, B *et al.* (1988) *Working in Urban Schools*, Washington DC: Institute of Educational Leadership.

Commission of the European Community (1977) *Directive of 25 July 1977 on the Education of the Children of Migrant Workers* (77/486/EEC), Brussels: CEC.

Commission for Racial Equality (1988) *Housing and Discrimination. Report of a Formal Investigation into the London Borough of Tower Hamlets*, London: CRE.

Council of Chief State School Officers (1987) *Statement on Assuring School Success for Students at Risk*, Washington, DC: CCSSO.

Council of the Great City Schools (1987) *Challenges to Urban Education: Results in the Making*, Washington, DC: CGCS.

Council of the Great City Schools (1991) *Return to Greatness: The Renaissance in America's Urban Schools*, Washington, DC: CGCS.

Department of Education and Science (1980) *Report by HM Inspectors on Educational Provision by the Inner London Education Authority*, London: HMSO.

Department of Education and Science (1984) *Education for All* (The Swann Report), London: HMSO.

Department of Education and Science (1986) *City Technology Colleges: A New Choice of School*, London: HMSO.

Department of Education and Training (1989) *Retention and Participation in Australian Schools*, Canberra: DEET.

Goh, K (1979) *Education Reform in Singapore*, Singapore: Ministry of Education.

Government of India, Ministry of Human Resource Development (1990) *Toward an Enlightened and Humane Society: Report of the Committee for the Review of National Policy on Education* (Achorya Ramumurti Committee), New Delhi: Government of India.
Government of India, National Sample Survey Organisation (1979) *National Sample Survey 32nd Round*, New Delhi: Government of India.
Government of India, National Sample Survey Organisation (1974) *National Sample Survey 27th Round*, New Delhi: Government of India.
Government of India, National Sample Survey Organisation (1988) *National Sample Survey 42nd Round*, New Delhi: Government of India.
Government of India, National Sample Survey (1988) *Sarvekshana*, New Delhi: Government of India.
Government of India, Registrar General's Office (1985) *Census of India 1981*, New Delhi: Government of India.
House of Commons Select Committee on Education, Science and Arts (1990) *Staffing for Pupils with Special Educational Needs*, London: HMSO.
House of Commons Home Affairs Committee (1987) *Bangladeshis in Britain*, London: HMSO.
Inner London Education Authority (1983) *Race, Sex and Class. 3. A Policy for Equality: Race*, London: ILEA.
London Borough of Tower Hamlets (1988) *Getting it Right: Draft Development Plan*, London: London Borough of Tower Hamlets.
Ministry of Education (1989) *Richness of the Uncompleted, Challenges Facing Dutch Education* (Report to OECD. Reviews of National policies for education, the Netherlands), The Hague: Ministry of Education.
Ministry of Trade and Industry (1986) *The Singapore Economy: New Directions*, Singapore: MTI.
Ministry of Education (1987) *Towards Excellence in Schools*, Singapore: Ministry of Education.
National Centre for Education Development Research (1989) *The Development and Reform of Education in China (1980–1988)*, Beijing: Peoples Education Press.
Research and Policy Committee of the Committee for Economic Development (1987) *Children in Need: Investment Strategies for the Educationally Disadvantaged*, New York: CED.
State Education Commission (1990) *1989 China Yearbook of Educational Statistics*, Beijing: People's Education Press.
State Statistical Bureau (1990) *Social Statistics Handbook of China, 1990*, Beijing: CSPH.
State Statistical Bureau (1990) *Statistics Yearbook of China, 1990*, Beijing: CSPH.
Tokyo Metropolis (1990) *School Basic Survey in 1989*, Tokyo: The Central Bureau of the Tokyo Metropolis.
Tokyo Metropolitan Board of Education (1990) *Public Education of Tokyo*, Tokyo: TMBE.
Tokyo Metropolitan Board of Education (1990) *Education in Tokyo*, Tokyo: TMBE.
US Department of Education (1987) *Schools that Work: Educating the Disadvantaged*, Washington, DC: US Government Printing Office.

Books

Adorno, T and Horkheimer, M (1973) *Dialectic of Enlightenment*, London: Allen.
Auerbach, F E (1971) *Measuring Educational Development in South Africa*, Johannesburg: South African Institute of Race Relations (SAIRR).
Ball, S (1990) *Politics and Policymaking in Education*, London: Routledge.
Bash, L *et al.* (1985) *Urban Schooling: Theory and Practice*, London: Holt, Rinehart and Winston.
Bash, L (ed) (1987) *Comparative Urban Education: Towards an Agenda*, London: DICE/UERG.
Bash, L and Coulby, D (1989) *The 1988 Education Act: Competition and Control*, London: Cassell.
Bater, J H (1980) *The Soviet City*, London: Edward Arnold.
Burnley, I (1980) *The Australian Urban System*, Melbourne: Longman Cheshire.
Burnley, I (ed) (1974) *Urbanisation in Australia*, Melbourne: CUP.
Carnoy, M and Levin, H M (1985) *Schooling and Work in the Democratic State*, Stanford: Stanford University Press.
Castells, M (1977) *The Urban Question*, London: Edward Arnold.
Castells, M (1978) *Cities, Class and Power*, London: Macmillan.
Castells, M (1983) *The City and the Grassroots*, Berkeley: University of California Press.
Castells, M (1985) *High Technology, Space and Society*, Beverley Hills: Sage.
Castells, M (1989) *The Information City*, Oxford: Blackwell.

Claydon, L (ed) (1975) *The Urban School*, Carlton: Pitman.
Coulby, D and Bash, L (1991) *Contradiction and Conflict: The 1988 Education Act in Action*, London: Cassell.
Creemers, B *et al.* (eds) (1989) *School Effectiveness and School Improvement*, Amsterdam: Swets & Zeitlinger.
Deben, L W *et al.* (1990) *Residential Differentiation*, Amsterdam: UvA.
Dickens, P (1990) *Urban Sociology*, London: Harvester.
Edwards, A *et al.* (1989) *The State and Private Education: An Evaluation of the Assisted Places Scheme*, London: Falmer Press.
Eldering, L and Kloprogge, J (1989) *Different Cultures, Same Schools, Ethnic Minority Children in Europe*, Amsterdam: Swets & Zeitlinger.
Engels, F (1969) *The Condition of the Working Class in England*, London: Granada.
Fishman, J (1975) *Language and Nationalism*, Roweley, MA: Newbury House.
Frank, A (1969) *Capitalism and Underdevelopment in Latin America*, New York: Monthly Review Press.
Franks, P and Morris, P (1986) *Urban Black Government and Policy*, Johannesburg: SAIRR.
Gellner, E (1985) *Nations and Nationalism*, Oxford: Blackwell.
Grace, G (1978) *Teachers, Ideology and Control*, London: RKP.
Grace, G (ed) (1984) *Education and the City, Theory, History and Contemporary Practice*, London: RKP.
Halsey, A (1972) *Educational Priority, Volume 1*, London: HMSO.
Harvey, D (1973) *Social Justice and the City*, London: Arnold.
Harvey, D (1989) *The Condition of Postmodernity: An Enquiry into the Origins of Cultural Change*, Oxford: Basil Blackwell.
Harvey, D (1989) *The Urban Experience*, Oxford: Blackwell.
Hill, T *et al.* (1989) *Education Progress: Cities Mobilized to Improve their Schools*, Santa Monica, CA: Rand Corporation.
Hillgate Group (1987) *The Reform of British Education*, London: Claridge Press.
Hirson, B (1979) *Year of Fire, Year of Ash, The Soweto Revolt: Roots of a Revolution?*, London: Zed Press.
Horrell, M (1978) *Laws Affecting Race Relations in South Africa*, Johannesburg, SAIRR.
Kane-Berman, J (1978) *Soweto: Black Revolt White Reaction*, Johannesburg: Ravan Press.
Katznelson, I and Weir, M (1988) *Schooling for All*, California: University of California Press.
King, A D (1990) *Urbanism, Colonialism and the World Economy: Cultural and Spatial Foundations of the World Urban System*, London: Routledge.
King, A D (1990) *Global Cities: Post-Imperialism and the Internationalisation of London*, London: Routledge.
Lloyd, P (1979) *Slums of Hope?*, Harmondsworth: Penguin.
Logan, J R and Molotch, H L (1987) *Urban Fortunes: The Political Economy of Place*, California: University of California Press.
Logan, M *et al.* (1975) *Urban & Regional Australia*, Melbourne: Sorrett.
McLaren, P (1989) *Life in Schools*, New York: Longmans.
Maher, C (1982) *Australian Cities in Transition*, Melbourne: Shillington House.
Marcuse, H (1972) *One Dimensional Man*, London: Abacus.
Massey, D (1984) *Spatial Divisions of Labour*, London: Macmillan.
Miller, H and Woock, R (1970) *Social Foundations of Education*, Hirsdale: Dryden Press.
Morton, H and Stuart, R (eds) (1985) *The Contemporary Soviet City*, London: Macmillan.
Narsing, Y P (1989) *Learning in Limbo. Experiences of Schooling in Soweto*, Johannesburg: Educational Policy Unit, University of Witwatersrand.
Neutze, M (1978) *Australian Urban Policy*, Sydney: Allen & Unwin.
Obudho, R *et al.* (1990) *Nairobi and its Environs*, Nairobi: University of Nairobi, Centre for Urban Research.
Pacione, M (ed) (1981) *Urban Problems and Planning in the Developed World*, London: Croom Helm.
Park, R (1952) *Human Communities: The City and Human Ecology*, New York: Free Press.
Park, R *et al.* (eds) (1925) *The City*, Chicago: University of Chicago Press.
Piao Shengyi (ed) (1990) *Development and Perspectives of Minority Education in China*, Beijing: People's Education Press.
Rabinow, P (1989) *French Modern: Norms and Forms of the Social Environment*, Harvard: MIT Press.
Rex, J and Moore, R (1967) *Race, Community and Conflict*, London: Oxford University Press.
Ringen, S (1989) *The Possibility of Politics. A Study in the Political Economy of the Welfare State*, Oxford: Clarendon Press.
Roberts, J M (1980) *The Pelican History of the World*, Harmondsworth: Penguin.
Ross, K *et al.* (1988) *Indicators of Socio-Economic Disadvantage for Australian Schools*, Geelong: Deakin University.

Said, E (1978) *Orientalism*, London: Routledge.
Saunders, P (1980) *Urban Politics*, Harmondsworth: Penguin.
Saunders, P (1981) *Social Theory and the Urban Question*, London: Hutchinson.
Scheerens, J (1987) *Enhancing Educational Opportunities for Disadvantaged Learners*, Amsterdam: North Holland Publishing Company.
Sharp, R and Green, A (1975) *Education and Social Control*, London: RKP.
Shor, I (1986) *Culture Wars: School and Society in the Conservative Restoration 1969–1984*, London: RKP.
Slavenburg, J *et al.* (eds) (1989) *The Dutch Education and Social Environment Project: Closing Report*, Rotterdam: OSM.
Street-Porter, R (1976) *Race, Children and Cities*, Milton Keynes: Open University Press.
Troup, F (1970) *Forbidden Pastures, Education under Apartheid*, London: International Defence and Aid Fund.
Walford, G and Miller, H (1991) *City Technology College*, Milton Keynes: Open University Press.
Williams, R (1973) *The Country and the City*, London: Chatto & Windus.
Williams, R (1981) *Culture*, London: Fontana.
Willis, P (1977) *Learning to Labour*, London: Saxon House.
Wilson, W J (1987) *The Truly Disadvantaged, the Inner City, the Underclass and Public Policy*, Chicago/London: University of Chicago Press.
Wong, A K and Yeh, S H K (eds) (1985) *Housing and Nation: 25 Years of Housing in Singapore*, Singapore: Maruzen.
Yeh, S H K (1975) *Public Housing in Singapore: A Multi-Disciplinary Study*, Singapore: Singapore University Press.
Yip, J S K and Sim, W K (1990) *Evolution of Educational Excellence*, Singapore: Longmans.
Zhu Tiezhen and Zhang Zailun (eds) (1987) *A Manual of Chinese Cities*, Beijing: Economics Publishing House.

Articles and chapters

Brimelow, P (1983) 'What to do about America's schools' *Fortune*, 19 September.
Bristol Polytechnic Education Study Group (1989) 'Restructuring the education system?', in Bash, L and Coulby, D *The Education Reform Act: Competition and Control*, London: Cassell.
Coulby, D (1991) 'The National Curriculum', in Coulby, D and Bash, L (eds) *Contradiction and Conflict: The 1988 Education Act in Action*, London: Cassell.
Coulby, D and Jones, C (1991) 'Urban education in Soviet cities', in Cowen, R and Jones, C (eds) *Essays in Honour of J J Tomiak*, London: DICE.
Cumper, P (1990) 'Muslim schools; the implications of the Education Reform Act 1988', *New Community*, 16, 3.
Giddens, A (1985) 'Time, space and regionalisation', in Gregory, D and Urry, J (eds) *Social Relationships and Spatial Structures*, London: Macmillan.
Guy, W and Menter, I (1990) 'Local Management of Schools: who benefits?', in Gill, D and Mayor, B (eds) *Racism and Education: Strategies for Change*, Milton Keynes: Open University Press.
Hartshorne, K (1990) 'Look back in anger: African matric results 1988–89', *Indicator SA*, 17, 2.
Jonson, R (1989) 'Thatcherism and English education: breaking the mould or confirming the pattern?', *History of Education*, 18, 2.
Jones, C (1987) 'Urban centres, space and education. A comparative perspective', in Bash, L (ed) *Comparative Urban Education: Towards an Agenda*, London: ULIE/DICE.
Lytle, J H (1990) 'Reforming urban education: a review of recent reports and legislation', *The Urban Review*, 22, 3.
Mao Guangru (1990) 'What is the content of the reform experiment of China's Urban Education?', *China's Education*, 2 August.
Muller, J (1987) 'People's education and the National Crisis Committee', *South African Review 4*, Johannesburg: Ravan Press.
Saunders, P (1985) 'Space, the city and urban sociology', in Gregory, D and Urry, J (eds) *Social Relations and Spatial Structures*, London: Macmillan.
Simon, D (1989) 'Crisis and Change in South Africa: Implications for the Apartheid City' (discussion paper), London: Institute of Commonwealth Studies.
Stillwell, F and Hardwick, J (1973) 'Social inequality in Australian cities', *Australian Quarterly*, 45, 4.
Teese, R (1987) 'Regional differences in high and technical school demand in Melbourne, 1951–1985', *Australian Geographical Studies*, 25.

Teese, R (1989) 'Australian private schools, specialisation and curriculum conservation', *British Journal of Educational Studies*, XXXVII.

Walker, S (1979) 'Educational service in Sydney: some spatial variations', *Australia Geographical Studies*, 17.

Whitty, G (1986) 'Education policy and the inner cities', in Lawless, P and Raban, C (eds) *The Contemporary British City*, London: Harper and Row.

Whitty, G (1989) 'The New Right and the National Curriculum - state control of market forces', *Journal of Education Policy*, 4, 4.

Whitty, G and Menter, I (1989) 'Lessons of Thatcherism: education policy in England and Wales, 1979–88', *Journal of Law and Society*, 16, 1.

Wilson, P A (1987) 'Lima and the new international division of labour', in Smith, M P and Fengin, J R (eds) *The Capitalist City*, Oxford: Blackwell.

Yingsheng, L (1990) 'Difference development: the best strategic choice for the development of cities and countrysides of our country', *Future and Developments*, 3.

Relevant journals

African Urban Studies
American Journal of Sociology
Economic Geography
Education in Urban Society
International Journal of Urban and Regional Research
Urban Education
Urban Review, The
Urban Studies

Index

For Product Safety Concerns and Information please contact our EU representative GPSR@taylorandfrancis.com
Taylor & Francis Verlag GmbH, Kaufingerstraße 24, 80331 München, Germany

www.ingramcontent.com/pod-product-compliance
Lightning Source LLC
LaVergne TN
LVHW012326100826
845148LV00017B/315

* 9 7 8 0 4 1 5 5 0 1 6 9 9 *